MW00818202

Integrating Body Self and Psychological Self

Integrating Body Self and Psychological Self

Creating a New Story
in Psychoanalysis and Psychotherapy

David W. Krueger, M.D.

Brunner-Routledge
New York • London

Published in 2002 by
Brunner-Routledge
29 West 35th Street
New York, NY 10001
www.brunner-routledge.com

Published in Great Britain by
Brunner-Routledge
27 Church Road
Hove, East Sussex
BN3 2FA
www.brunner-routledge.co.uk

Copyright © 2002 by David W. Krueger.

Brunner-Routledge is an imprint of the Taylor & Francis Group.
Printed in the United States of America on acid-free paper.

Cover design: Jennifer Crisp.

All rights reserved. No part of this book may reprinted or reproduced or
utilized in any form or by any electronic, mechanical, or other means, now
known or hereafter invented, including photocopying and recording, or in any
information storage or retrieval system, without permission in writing from
the publishers.

10 9 8 7 6 5 4 3 2 1

Library of Congress Cataloging-in-Publication Data
Krueger, David W.
    Integrating body self and psychological self : creating a new story in
psychoanalysis and psychotherapy / David W. Krueger.
        p. cm.
Includes bibilographical references and index.
ISBN 1-58391-054-9
1. Self psychology. 2. Self. 3. Body image. 4. Body image disturbance.
5. Psychotherapy. 6. Psychoanalysis. I. Title
RC489.S43 K78 2002
616.89'14—dc21   2002010553

OTHER BOOKS BY

DAVID W. KRUEGER, M.D.

Emotional Rehabilitation of Trauma and Disability

Rehabilitation Psychology:
A Comprehensive Textbook

Success and the Fear of Success in Women

The Last Taboo:
Money as Symbol and Reality in Psychotherapy and Psychoanalysis

Body Self and Psychological Self:
Developmental and Clinical Integration in Disorders of the Self

Destiny: An Uncommon Journey

Emotional Business:
The Meaning and Mastery of Work, Money and Success

What is a Feeling? (children's book)

What is Time? (with Lauren Krueger, in press; children's book)

Making Memories: Reflections of Parenting from the Head
of a Psychoanalyst and the Heart of a Father

Contents

Part III
Clinical Applications

Preface

My ideal doctor. . . . I can imagine *entering* my condition, looking around it from the inside like a kind landlord, with a ten-
ant, trying to see how he could make the premises more liv-
able. He would look around, holding me by the hand, and he
would figure out what it is like to be me. Then he would try to
find certain advantages in the situation. He can turn disad-
vantages into advantages. He would see the *genius* of my illness. He would mingle his daemon with mine. We would
wrestle with my fate together, like Rupert and Birkin in the
library in D. H. Lawrence's *Women in Love.* I would also like
a doctor who *enjoyed* me. I want to be a good story for him,
to give him some of my art in exchange for his.

> *Intoxicated by My Illness*
> Anatole Broyard

I was reflecting on the previous attempts I had made over the
last two decades to engage therapists and analysts. My initial
typical attempt at engagement would be some variation of
this exchange and internal dialogue: I am seated in the chair
across from this person I have never before met. I know I have
so much terrain to cover before there is any possibility of understanding. I am looked at blankly. This blankness is raising
questions in me: "Am I boring her?" "Am I shocking her?"
"Am I confusing her?" I am in need, and my need is making
me feel insecure, adding to what I already bring. I am in need
and sitting here, or else I would be at the beach. I wonder if
this person before me has gotten together with other persons
like her to decide which behaviors to be, which are accepted.

The blankness she has in her face raises questions on top of what drove me to arrive here: "What is this person across from me thinking?" "What is she feeling?" "How is she reacting to what I am saying?" "Am I too much?" "Am I too little?" I'm burdened by this person because of her blankness. It is upsetting my insecurity more. The experience of never knowing is in addition to this flurry of what she thinks, of the many, "Does she think I am (fill in the blank)?" And the (blanks) are mostly negative, such as stupid, ignorant, naïve. Her silence is unnerving. Too many of my experiences have been intolerable alone. I haven't known the questions to ask myself. It is very emotionally expensive to be in her presence. My feeling upon leaving was often as though I had been scolded by an unloving parent. Yet I kept going back. What would have been beneficial would have been to break through the glazed, hazy wall I erected unknowingly, and if she could have said, 'This is all really going to be okay.' It would have only taken something simple, but it was like she could never break character in the play being enacted, the role decided when the professionals got together and decided which ways to be with a patient. Those were the experiences I brought when I came to see you for the first time. Only now, after all this time, a time when we are almost done with our analytic work can I finally tell you.

A Patient

Introduction

When Freud (1923) called the ego first a body ego, psychoanalysis was based on the body, its drives and bodily events understood as fundamental to the organization of experience. The body self and somatic experience-representation have perhaps been left behind in the idealization of cognition, assuming the body as developmentally differentiated, Oedipal, and verbally accessible. Since Freud, psychoanalysis has consistently aligned the body with the unconscious, thereby relegating it to metaphor, not directly linked to sensory and affective experience of the moment.

Some patients, however, who are unattuned to their affective world, may not have the psychological register for some affect states, nor the representation of body self and psychological self for their integration. They make their bodies the narrator of what words cannot say; of sensation for which there is no lexicon; and of feelings they cannot bear in their conscious mind; of action language rather than verbalization. This difficulty of putting some emotional experience into useful language is subsequently shared by analysts. At times an artificial clarity or premature closure can be developed when the analyst tries to put unarticulated thoughts or feelings into interpretive generalizations or pattern matching of present and past.

The body appears in the narrative of dreams, metaphors, and symptoms, symbolic visions of inner landscapes, mysterious structures and configurations, and geographical terrain. An idea as well as a fact, the body is container and conduit of the emotional, a Rorschach onto which fantasies, meaning, and significance are projected. The body self is an idea, like the ego; the body is a fact. The body self and image is created by, and lives within, the imagination, the map within the actual territory of the body. We experience through our body, focus with it but not usually on it, as body is usually in the background. When the body cannot be naturally integrated, it remains in the foreground, accentuated by asceticism and alienation, such as fasting or self-mutilation, the instrument of action symptoms, the subject of narcissistic investment and excessive rumination, such as body dysmorphic disorder, or brought into focus by pain, physical illness, age, or weight.

The many configurations of optimum experiences of mother–infant interaction patterns such as nursing, cooing, bathing, holding, intermingling bodies in play, and physical aliveness are the very experiences activated as the analysand is held by the couch, stroked by the analyst's words, and matched in state of mind. For the patient, the analyst's body, as well as the analyst's undifferentiated body may be represented by the office, its contents, the couch. Sensations are first bodily experiences, and only later words. Body experiences are spoken at times in a language of state and state changes, desire, hungers, satisfactions, action symptoms, and other icons of developmental needs. It is difficult to conceptualize, translate, and talk about the preverbal and unformulated bodily experiences for which there may be no words, or even a language. Some experiences are of undifferentiated feelings not yet symbolized, or of ungendered and nonverbal body physiology not yet desomatized. Developmental disruptions may prevent a synthesis of mind and body, with resultant inability to recognize affect, to regulate ego state, or to formulate experience. Action symptoms convert any emotion into an action scenario involving the body with some substance or activity to serve defensive, self-regulatory, or perhaps attempt restitutive functions.

The embodiment in psychoanalysis of these preverbal, undifferentiated, or unsymbolized experiences may manifest in body-based transferences and countertransferences. Often unrecognized and unformulated, some procedural memories not paired with conscious awareness or verbal narrative are experiences in the bodies of both patient and analyst. Both these nonverbal transference–countertransference embodiments as well as their verbal counterparts can be addressed as fundamental, necessary experiences in the clinical exchange in forming a cohesive developmental foundation for the patients, and in psychodynamic as well as reconstructive understanding.

The body that is verbally mute and developmentally undifferentiated needs emotional access, description, understanding, and perhaps even construction in analysis. A patient may speak in action or somatic language when affect is either undifferentiated developmentally or when it has been traumatically fused with action. This process cannot be bypassed: a patient engaged in action and action symptoms may not be able to answer the question, "How do you feel?" They may not know the very experience they are defensively avoiding that is imbedded in action sequences. The subsequent awareness and differentiation of feelings is a stepwise process of how messages from the body's surface and interior are translated into shared verbal narrative.

I am attempting to mingle the language of the body and the language of the mind, to highlight in the analytic exchange the neglected end of the continuum of the mind–body experience of the simple and literal message and meaning, along with metaphor and symbol. We struggle daily with our patients to conceptualize unformulated experience, to give specificity to inchoate desires and experiences, and to make the complex and intangible as simple as possible. The clinical narrative that is cocreated by patient and analyst must achieve an ultimate simplicity, as experience-near as possible, and as specific developmentally and dynamically as two people can fashion a common ground to construct communication and develop a new story.

The unconscious is inscribed just as it is embodied. While the unconscious may be located in the medial limbic structures of the brain, it also originates from the skin, from the appearance of the body, and from the perceptions of notable others about one's body, including its attractiveness, functioning, and abilities. Body and body image are the intersubjective mutual creation of meaning and flesh, revealed and constructed intersubjectively, thus relationally. The body is inscripted by important others as well as subjectively articulated. Gestures, needs, somatic affects, and attachment patterns belong to the depths of time from when there were no visible islands, no shore as boundary, only shadows, yet is simultaneously living in the present moment. As with analytic narrative, also with one's own subjective experience of the body, the distinction between creation and discovery overlap.

All actions necessarily involve the body, and the body becomes an intrinsic component of self-organization brought to the foreground in actions, action symptoms, psychosomatic symptoms, somatic memories, and ultimately in self-representation. Every interaction with others is mediated by the body, and even when purely a verbal exchange, the senses, the gendered body, and the body self are all involved. We are always embodied, though aspects of that embodiment may be disavowed, disregarded, or ultimately disembodied by dissociation. The self that seeks embodiment, and the body that yearns for residence in the mind, integrate throughout development. The subtleties of mental states are interwoven with inchoate bodily states, and the two minds and bodies in the consultation room interact at multiple levels. For the entire compass of experiences occurring in the analytic space, words alone aren't important enough, as the "mind does not dwell entirely in the brain" (Ackerman, 1999).

In psychoanalysis, we often focus on scary fantasies, cold mothers, dead people, and bad dreams to perhaps lose happiness, creativity, hope, love, humor, inspiration, and other positive transformations, such as the challenge of staying with feeling good if you've got feeling bad down. Psychoanalysis has not found a celebration of nearly enough passions. There is often more energy expended in search of defenses and psychopathology, to get the patient to admit something by continuously illuminating it. The ultimate truth of the reason for misery is often mistaken as the ultimate truth for the experience of creating happiness. Theories are built around deprivation, deficit, and conflict, and hardly around any building blocks of contentment or joy.

We help our patients develop their own internal point of reference, to own their ambition and fashion their ideals, and to find their own voice in this new story. We become experts on the unknown, masters of scarcity, creators of new metaphors, all the while moving toward the fundamental, the simple. We speak of boundaries as limits but also as junctures, of reasons rather than of rules, of desires that seem inextricably linked with obstacle.

Meaningful interpretations not only make the unconscious conscious, but give recognition, shape, form, and a new model in the analytic context of that never before experienced by the patient. The longed-for early maternal soothing and intermingling of bodies can be as pressing and prescient a foreground transference configuration as the Oedipal can at a later point in the analysis, and the two, though they may share the bodies, all the senses, the urges and longings and desires, are quite distinct in meaning and analytic work as they are in developmental time and purpose.

Significant work has been done, especially since the early 1980s, to extend our understanding and shaping of verbal interpretations in ways that resonate with an emotional experience, ways and words that do not simply reveal what is there underneath the surface in prepackaged form, but that give definition and meaning to that which never was, and to that which is so vague and ethereal, yet so very real that there have not been the words to say it. The mind and body murmur, whisper, shout to each other, use many languages, speak many dialects. While we may be much clearer about specifying the nuances of our theories, we strive to find a meaningful exchange for the deepest primordial, as well as immediate sensory and psychic experience.

There are always three entities in a psychoanalytic encounter: the patient, the analyst, and the cocreated new story. There are no well-defined answers to be revealed or extracted, only meanings to be constructed. Psychoanalysis is the study of the ways in which we deceive ourselves, the subspecialty of how to know and change one's mind.

We are loyal to the central theme, the plot, of our life. We always return to it. Any departure from it creates trepidation and uncertainty, divergence from the known. That abiding narrative of one's life may be read as destiny, rather than created by personal authorship. A fantasy can be more real than the rest of one's life. Deviation from those central organizing themes, whether conscious or unconscious, or through the use of medication, will be only temporary unless one's mind and brain both change.

Psychoanalysis involves the art of seeing the contradictions and conflicts inherent in one's mind, the unconscious organizing assumptions ghostwriting a life narrative, the expectable but compromised developmental needs given distorted pleading voice, hoping to be heard.

Our patients will always tell us what is most important, what is therapeutic and what is not, and what their needs are. This may be spoken in simple, straightforward language, in somatic language, in enactments designed to demonstrate an internal experience, in the shadow traffic of transferences, or in the interchange in which there is activation of internal relationships for the patient in which the analyst plays a part, and the patient plays a part, and then later talk about it. Our patients are always teaching us what it is like to be them.

The enigma of psychoanalysis is that as both patient and analyst experience the more archaic layers of the psyche, each is in the present moment, more profoundly and simply, than ever before. The patient's earlier life experiences transferentially activated in the present move from vague, formless controlling procedural memory to juxtaposition with the new and different story. As the old story and the new story are both vividly alive and intermingled, the past can be interpretatively cleaved from the present, and a new developmental model mutually formulated as container and integrator of evolving meaning for current experiences. This dyadically evolving story, more than solely insight and understanding, is of developmental hope awakened and actualized in the mutually created narrative to integrate mind and body.

And how surprised our patients are to learn that their greatest fear is not in the shadows of the past, but in the light of this moment's change.

PART I

Body Self and Psychological Self Development

But first the notion that man has a body distinct from his soul is to be expunged.

William Blake, 1790

Emotions are no more and no less than the readout of internal body states.

William James, 1884

The ego is first a body ego.

Sigmund Freud, 1923

Primary emotions are always the result of body states.

Antonio Damasio, 1994

There is nothing that falls within the purview of psychoanalysis as a science of the human phenomenon that does not involve a bodily reference—explicitly or implicitly.

William Meissner, 1998

1

Body Self in Psychological Self Development

The body as represented in the brain may constitute an indispensable frame of reference for the neuroprocesses that we experience as the mind.

Our most refined thoughts and best actions, our greatest joys and deepest sorrows use the body as a yardstick.

The mind had to be first about the body or it could have not been.

Antonio Damasio
Descartes' Error

The infant searches swirling, formless surroundings for a knowing touch, a lock with parents' eyes, affirming a fortifying form and confirming a grounding presence, the quintessence of human attachment. This hope is relational, linked with soothing flesh and satisfied mouth, to become the building block of the psychological regulation of physiological needs and the foundation of trust; later, from this foundation of affiliation and effectiveness, excursions of exploration and assertive curiosity occur (Lichtenberg, 1989), allowing separation with affirming rapprochement.

The gentle whisperings and soft, murmuring echoes of sensation are outlined and contained as the infant's body is held in total suspension by the strong hands of another who knows that safety and passion are no paradox. To be wrapped in an encompassing cocoon of gentle vitality is simultaneously intense and calm. These felt sensory experiences, or their

3

unmet yearning, are reactivated throughout life; there is never a time that the desire evaporates.

Significant caretakers define the infant's body by interactive attachment, mirroring, outlining, and resonance with both interior and surface. This relational matrix organizes and gives meaning to body self. From before birth, there is an intersubjective dialogue, interaction, real (and later fantasied) relationship unfolding between the child and parents that fashions self development, including gender. The child and his or her body effects, shapes, and coauthors the relationship with parents, and vice versa.

Attachment Patterns

Attachment needs are, first and foremost, body-based needs. John Bowlby (1969, 1973) described a system of emotional and behavioral response patterns in the caretaker and infant that he termed the *attachment system*. Bowlby and Siegel (1999) described the attachment system as an inborn motivational system that organizes experiences, emotions, and memory processes of the infant in terms of attachment to, and innate communication with the mother.

The initial attachments are formed by the age of 7 months, are selective to only a very few persons, and lead to specific changes in an infant's brain function and behavior (Main, 1995). The attachment interactions and patterns with primary caretakers may be the initial and central foundation from which body self and psychological self develops and integrates.

Four categories of attachment have been defined by Main and Soloman (1991). Mothers secure in their attachments develop secure, consistent attachments in the infants; dismissive attachment styles create infants with avoidant patterns; mothers preoccupied with attachment demonstrate ambivalent styles of attachment. The fourth style of disorganized–disoriented attachment is a result of maladaptation from insecure attachment: The mothers diagnosed as chronically depressed or alcoholic are either unattuned to the infants or maltreat them, and children develop their own depressive patterns, difficulty in concentrating, and disorganized attachment behavior. Empathically unattuned parenting leads to one of two types of attachment: anxious–avoidant attachment, in which the individual curbs or buffers the overstimulating situation by avoidant or distancing behavior, or an anxious-resistant pattern in which the individual denies signals of overstimulation, and resists being comforted. Attachment disorganization pattern is exemplified by unresolved trauma in the parent resulting in parental fear in response to the child's distress. The child perceives that fear, reads it as an accurate mirror of danger, and the anxiety becomes manageable by external and internal detachment. These expectations and experiences grow into an entire representational system of attachment, of what it takes to maintain attachment, and the possibilities of attachment regarding regulation of affect, esteem, and tension states (Main, 1995).

These models based on procedural memory govern how other attachments/relationships will be approached in the future. The security of the child in the primary attachments determines how environmentally assertive and exploratory the child will be. The secure, avoidant, and resistant categories of infants evolve in these consistent ways: the secure stays secure, the avoidant becomes dismissive; the resistant, crying infant becomes preoccupied (Main, 1995). Infants and children must first develop a secure attachment to parents before they can venture into new territory. If this secure attachment is compromised or pathological, various adaptive efforts and accommodative maneuvers will be used to establish that attachment, or to reestablish it. These compensatory efforts to fill in what is missing developmentally, are perhaps used later in a more generalized defense against a variety of painful feelings.

While the attachment archetype with the primary caretaker forms the first template of interaction, the configuration is mutually determined: the way the infant behaves toward the mother exerts a powerful influence on the mother's behavior (Kandell, 1999). Similarly in treatment, the way in which the patient interacts powerfully shapes the analyst's response.

The regulation and alignment of states is dependent on accurate parental attunement to the child's signals and sensitivities well before words or verbal language are available. This attunement and engagement at a preverbal–nonverbal level is a foundation for internal connectedness of mind and body, and of human relatedness, with significant implications for what is most fundamental in an analytic relationship. The internalization of these attachment patterns creates the procedural (implicit) memory of self, self-states, and self-in-relation to another.

Secure attachments provide a sense of safety and containment in an environment that might otherwise evoke fear. Sensitive and empathically attuned caregiving create the experience and expectation that comfort and reduction of anxiety can take place through the attachment, later to be internalized as one's own. The child does not have to be possessive of the mother if he already truly possesses her. He only becomes possessive when he recognizes that he, indeed, does not possess her, and she does not respond as if he is entitled to her. Ownership, entitlement, and a sense of belonging cannot then be taken for granted and metabolized as internal security based on a secure attachment.

Attachment and attachment patterns are not synonymous with intimacy or dependency, but reference a particular, repetitive interactive style with corresponding internal organization. Attachment theories are explanations of how significant caregiver interactions affect the child's inner world, of the replication of parents' own attachment behavior when they were children, and of the continuity of attachment patterns and corresponding internal organization over time (Main, 1995; Fonagy & Target, 1995)

The attachment system of the physical and psychological tie to a primary caretaker and the exploratory motivation, pool curiosities to explore the environment; ideally, these two systems are complementary and not at odds with one another. It is up to the primary caregiver half of this attachment scenario, to make it acceptable to explore without losing the primary bond, to have emotional connection both ways (Stern, 1990). Attunement includes the matching of vocal responses with feeling, allowing the developing infant to translate from one sensory modality to another (Stern, 1990). Boundaries of the shared experience expand, the universe of feelings broadens, intensity deepens.

The compass of recognizable feelings assumes their developmental recognition and differentiation; later, for feelings undifferentiated and conflicted, the entire image of a feeling may have to be defined in outlining its shadow by obsession, or illuminating its reverse image by denial.

Fonagy (1999) demonstrated that there is a transgenerational transmission of these traits, and that the characteristics of the child could be predicted prior to birth based on studying the parents. The nature of the relationship that the mother and the father would develop with the child could be predicted essentially 80% of the time by knowing the attachment pattern history of each parent. There is a strong relationship between the particular patterns of attachment of a child by one year of age and their attachment patterns as an adult, as well as the pattern with the children that adult will parent (Levy & Blatt, 1999). Attachment theory offers an additional perspective from other views including unconscious motivation and unconscious fantasy. For example, the small child experiences terror in her panic state, wants to approach her mother for security, yet knows that her mother likely will not provide comfort, but a shaming response. This internal dilemma emphasizes lived experience rather than drive distortion.

Developmental Origins of the Body Self

Freud (1923/1961) said that "the ego is first and foremost a bodily ego" (p. 27). Since Freud used the term *ego* interchangeably with *self*, his indication was that one's sense of self, later evolving to a psychological self, first begins with a body self, established fundamentally through sensory input. The integration of this body self becomes a fundamental aspect of self representation, including body image.

The body self is a developmental hierarchy of experience and intellectual mechanisms progressing from images, to words, to organizing patterns, to superordinate abstractions and inferences that regulate the entire self-experience (Krueger, 1988a).

The close and careful attunement to all the sensory and motor contacts with the child forms an accurate and attuned body self in the child. These relational experiences, initially in development of bodily experiences, that form the initial experience of unity of mind and body, predicated on the initial establishment of the body self as container for the evolving psychological self. Both Winnicott (1965) and Stolorow and Atwood (1992) have emphasized how the caregivers' affect attunement is conveyed through initial, consistent, and accurate sensorimotor interaction with the infant's body. It is the accuracy and continuity of this sustained contact that allows the evolution of the psychological self: that we reside inside our bodies, that there is a unity of mind and body with evolving cohesion of body self and image, that psychological self evolves with the use of symbols and language to communicate internal experiences.

The earliest imprint of mother on the child is through the bodily sensations and feelings, the earliest body contact and reciprocity and attunement to body fluids, sensations, sensory matching, and secure holding emerges from a time before there were words or a language. In an elegant and innovative work, Wrye and Welles (1994) reconstruct this narration of desire from the powerful preverbal, inchoate yet very real, body experiences and memories emerging in transference and countertransference experiences in adult analytic patients. They suggest that these remnants of earliest body contacts may be expressed in the sensory, bodily experience mutually evoked that may link itself to the earliest care of the mother's attunement to body processes and body fluids of the child to form early maternal erotic transferences and countertransferences. Their focus on the preverbal origins of erotic transference, regarded at times by both patient and analyst as a psychotic core experience or an "erotic terror," can be understood and integrated, to provide the creation of the first true intimacy that some patients have ever experienced. Dramatic developments in infant research, newer understandings of early development, and expanding awareness of neurobiological and intersubjective experience all inform this appreciation.

The body and its evolving mental representation are the foundation of a sense of self. Since Freud's notion of the body ego, the consensus of most developmentalists is that the body self refers to the full range of kinesthetic experiences on the body's surface and in its interior, and the body's functions (Faber, 1985; Lichtenberg, 1978).

Lichtenberg (1978, 1985) describes the concept of the body self as a combination of the psychic experience of body sensation, body functioning, and body image. He hypothesizes that reality testing occurs in a definite developmental sequence of increasing awareness and integration of body self.

Stages of the Development of the Body Self

The development of a body self can be conceptualized as a continuum of three stages, the first of which is the early psychic experience of the body. The second stage is the early awareness of a body image, with an integration of inner and outer experience. This process forms body surface boundaries and internal state definition. The final stage is the integration of the body self as a container of the psychological self, the point at which the two merge to form a cohesive sense of identity (Krueger, 1989; Lichtenberg, 1978, 1985).

The Early Psychic Experience of the Body

Mahler and Furer (1968) have indicated that the earliest sense of "self" is experienced through sensations from within one's body, especially proprioception. These sensoriperceptive stimuli enable the infant to discriminate the body self-schema from its surroundings (Mahler & Furer, 1968); tactile sensations, the primary body experience during the first weeks and months of life, may be the first developmental experience of the body self (Kestenberg, 1975). Spitz (1965) observed the baby's inclination to concentrate on the mother's face, and particularly on the eyes during periods of feeding.

The mother's hands outline and define the original boundary of the body's surface; definition and delineation are provided to the infant's otherwise shapeless and boundless space. There is evidence that body experience during the first weeks and months of life is mostly tactile, and only somewhat auditory and visual (Shevrin & Toussieng, 1965). The awareness of the body based upon tactile sensations is the first developmental experience of the body self. The sense of body is the first sense of self, awakened by the mother's touch, the initial form of communication. The mother's hands establish the first body boundary; auditory and visual stimuli have an important role as early development proceeds.

The mother's empathic resonance with the infant's internal experience provides the infant with a mirroring and reciprocity that not only reinforces and affirms, but forms (Winnicott, 1971). If the mother is empathically aligned with the baby, this is the baby's first experience of effectiveness: Affect produces a reciprocal response in the mother. Mutually and reciprocally, the infant's internal state is also given form and definition by the accuracy of this empathic attunement. Kestenberg (1985) emphasizes the rhythmic movement between mother and child and the match in movement styles as a foundation in the bond between them and as a catalyst for the infant's development.

The accuracy of the empathic attunement is crucial, because it is the initial linking of mind and body experiences. If the mother is not accurately and consistently attuned to the infant, the basis for a mind–body division (nonintegration) is formed, inhibiting one's ability to develop emotional literacy. This awareness and language for feelings and internal experiences is initially established by accurate labeling by essential caretakers, developing road maps of internal and external experience through this interaction. This core sense of self-orbiting around body self and caretaker interaction defines this essential awareness and literacy.

This empathic attunement by primary caretakers is so essential that we see in some of our patients the absence of this awareness, with the reliance on external referents, the persistent search for mirroring responses, and for tangible representations of deficient internal affirmation. It is precisely when this development does not occur, or gets derailed, that psychosomatic symptoms or other body stimulations or self-harm are created to bridge between mind and body.

There is an inevitable skewing of acceptability and judgment of parents around certain experiences, varying individual to individual. Certain body parts, fluids, functions, or actions become infused with particular feelings, connotations, and values. It is out of these experiences that passions, prohibitions, and perversions emanate. In the extreme absence of these empathic responses, the emotional vacuum of "black hole" experiences is created (Grotstein, 1990). More difficult than the absence of the experience of mirroring and affirmation is the response of shaming, in which the child is taught to be ashamed of feelings, functions, affects, or aspects of body or self. The affect state of shame and resultant hiding have obvious implications in the clinical exchange.

The infant's first awareness of self from parental mirroring and interaction has been widely investigated (Emde, 1983; Mahler & Furer, 1968; Papousek & Papousek, 1975; Stern, 1985; Winnicott, 1965). A number of early developmental experiments demonstrate a motivation for mastery—to actively and effectively determine an outcome and experience effectiveness (Demos, 1985; Kestenberg, 1975; Papousek &

Papousek, 1975). The desire for competence becomes a factor in psychic development as early as 4 months of age with the development of imaging capacity (Demos, 1985). The first demonstrable desire for mastery occurs at 3 to 4 months; Papousek and Papousek (1975) have demonstrated that beginning as early as 4 months, the infant's basic motivation is to function effectively. With particular patterns of head movement, 4-month-old infants could activate a light display. The results demonstrated that infants experience pleasure in actively determining the visual stimulation. As the infants eagerly repeated their movements to trigger the lights, they watched the visual display less and less: The pleasure and impetus to repeat the movement appeared to be associated with the effectiveness of their action rather than with the actual outcome. The clinical importance of this principle—the motivation to be effective even if the result is detrimental—will be expanded in chapter 8. White (1959) terms this "effectance pleasure"—the pleasure in being a cause[1] which is the infant's first chance to determine parental behavior. This motivation for effectiveness continues, changing in expression, form, and content throughout development. The efficacy pleasure is the subjective experience of competence (Fosshage, 1995).

Lichtenberg (1989) suggests that the earliest developmental need/motivational system is based on the psychic regulation of physiological requirements. This psychological regulation, occurring within the infant–caregiver unit (Sander, 1980), when optimum, becomes internalized as relational patterns for self-regulation. The child's early experiences of accurate attunement and reciprocity create the internal experience of effectiveness. When empathic failures occur at this early developmental level, and there is ineffectiveness at self-regulation and symbolic representation, symptoms later emerge as attempts to unconsciously regulate affect and tension states in a physiological way. Plassman (1998) demonstrates this reciprocity of prenatal and postnatal "body psychology" as a "dialogue with the body" that has its origin within "the dialogue with the primary objects."

Somatic qualities and sensory experiences of each of the five senses all are distinctive somatic languages with their own developmental history, and are unique to each individual. While we have come to be more interested in fantasy and the mind, the native language of the mind is of somatic experience. The senses are the lexicon of the body, as the most fundamental experiences are perceived, processed, and recorded through

---

1. I am assuming, but not discussing, the necessary neurophysiological components to the formation of the body self. First, of course, is an intact sensory system, with an innate ability to distinguish one's own body from the body of another, and the full ability to develop imaging capacity.

the senses rather than through fantasy and psychic representation. The first contact with the mother is that of touch, a skin contact of being bound, held, and affirmed through somatic experience, the skin envelope (Anzieu, 1990). Even Freud suggested that all feelings are in some way memories of the senses that repeat and reiterate early even preverbal experiences (Freud, 1926/1959, p. 290).

Somatic experiences as well as affects may also be psychically experienced and registered, even though it may not be fully symbolized, or even symbolized at all (Sweetman, 1999). Some of the dimensions of sensory, sensual, conceptual experiences help to define a gendered self; similarly, when the sense of self is not cohesive or when it undergoes a disruption, these similar experiences may be used in an attempt to integrate the self around any specific sensory experience. In the most extreme of instances, this effort can become repetitive, in which the individual repetitively attempts to organize self as well as regulate affect and tension through body stimulation.

Definition of Body Surface Boundaries and Distinction of the Body's Internal State

This stage of development begins at a few months extending into the second year of life, and is characterized by a sense of reality based on an integrated body self emerging from newly discovered body *boundaries* and body *internal states*. Outer boundaries of the body become more specific and delimited.

Anzieu (1990) and Kuchenhoff (1998) describe the body images or ego-boundary representation, and specifically that the skin serves the psychological function of defining and differentiating self and object as well as in evolving an intrapsychic space. Awareness of body self allows one to contain and organize the intrapsychic space of evolving psychological self. The "skin-ego" (Kuchenhoff, 1998) serves as stimulus barrier to preserve this evolving development.

Empathic parental mirroring and reciprocal interactions with the child's experience as point of reference molds both internal as well as body surface sensations into distinct and coherent functions of the child's self. Inner and outer become distinguished. The boundaries of the body provide a limiting membrane between what is "me" and what is "not me." The child's experience becomes that of a unit rather than a collection of parts (Winnicott, 1971). The individual develops criteria for identifying the limits of the body self, where the body ends and the rest of the world begins, corresponding with the development and differentiation of psychic representation and functioning (psychological self) within the container of body self development. Brief absences from the need-satisfying object can begin to occur, as can temporary suspensions of empathic contact. This sense of body self-unity is essential to subsequent ego integration, physical coordination and grace, and the ability to experience pleasure in bodily activity.

Prolonged physical or empathic absence of the caregiver, characterized by inconsistencies of response with failure in the mirroring function, may lead to disavowal, splitting, or defensive fusion, with resultant distortions of body self and subsequent ego development. Concurrently, body boundaries may not be distinguished, resulting in a failure to develop cohesive recognition and distinction of internal states.

Symptoms may emerge as active attempts to define the *body surface*. These may include such activities as the wearing of heavy, loose clothing to stimulate the skin, preoccupation with textures, yearning for and fearing the touch of another, compulsive weight lifting to distinctly outline the body muscle mass, or body mutilation.

Skin, frequently the location of self-inflicted injuries such as cutting, burning, biting, wounding, or etching, is an inscription on the physical boundary, the largest organ of the body, the one that demarcates "me" from "not-me." The skin encompasses so much sensory detail, having cavities or pockets of taste, smell, hearing, vision, and touch, with a language that includes blushing shame and the gooseflesh of fear (Cohen & Mills, 1999).

The receipt of pain establishes (or regressively reestablishes) a boundary—an experience of existing as a bounded, contained entity. The following vignette illustrates pathology at this stage of development. (The vignettes presented are not designed to illustrate psychoanalytic process, rather to illustrate a specific aspect of development, its pathology, and attempted reinstitution).

Vignette 1

Cindy, age 15, presented with a severe depression, chronic emptiness, and compulsive self-mutilation. She had no evocative body image, and had little awareness of any feeling other than emptiness alternating at times with severe tension. With Cindy's birth, her mother became extremely depressed and withdrew from her emotionally, only to manage a succession of baby-sitters. Her father was an international airline pilot, available only episodically, but when home reportedly attended primarily to his depressed wife.

When Cindy could not evoke or provoke responses from her parents, she felt as if she didn't exist. She would then repeatedly rub the skin on her arms with a pencil eraser until she bled. When she saw blood from her self-mutilation, she felt more real, and tried to establish real sensations through pain (and, unconsciously, the boundaries of her skin), validated by blood, confirmed later by scarring (a hypertrophied boundary). She was reassured temporarily when she found that she could not erase herself; she was indelible, permanent. The pain, as well as her primitive sense of permanence, relieved her tension for a brief time. The reality of her most basic self, her body, buttressed feeling real, of existing. She created a temporary organization of her chaotic state by establishing the boundary via her skin, outlined by pain and accentuated by scars.

The Definition and Cohesion of the Body Self as a Foundation for Self-Awareness

A new level of organized self-awareness begins at about 15 months. This is confirmed by observational studies of the infant discovering himself in the mirror at 15 to 18 months (Spitz, 1957), and by the acquisition of the semantic "No." The capacity for and function of "No" is defined by Spitz (1957) as evidence of the emerging distinctness of the "I" and "Non-I", moving toward autonomy and self-awareness. "No" developmentally states, "I am not an extension of you and your body or your desire; this is where you end and I begin—my body is mine and mine alone."[2]

In normal development the experiences and images of the inner body and the body surface organize and integrate into an experiential and conceptual whole. Consolidating a stable, integrated, cohesive mental representation of one's body is a key developmental task during this period, with an evolving sense of distinctness and effectiveness. The body self experience, body images, and self-concept cohere to form the sense of self, and is a prerequisite to an internalized sense of psychological self. This synthesis of body and psychological selves provides a unity and continuity over time, space, and state (Demos, 1985).

For some time, analytic literature has not addressed a clear or consistent conceptualization of the evolution of body self and image (Burton, Fransella, & Slade, 1977; Rizzuto, Peterson, & Reed, 1981). Body image is assumed to be something that one either has or does not have; as

---

2. Beginning at 16 to 18 months, infants discover that they are what creates the image in the mirror. They reach for the label on their own forehead (Modaressi & Kinney, 1977) and reach to touch a smudge placed on their own nose rather than the image in the mirror (Lewis & Brooks-Gunn, 1979). Mahler and Furer (1968) and Piaget (1945) agree (from different theoretical vantage points) that in normal development a cognitive sense of separate existence and of body self can exist by age 18 months. Exploration and familiarity with body parts have already begun by this age.

if it is fixed and either accurate or distorted (Bauman, 1981; Van der Velde, 1985). With the beginning of concrete operations at approximately age 6, a true separation of self and object, and a more distinctly complete body image become possible as abstract ability crystallizes.

The first awareness is of the body. The first symbol is also of the body—a part of the oneness of mother and infant and a bridge to something external: food, a blanket, a thumb. The imaging capacity of the infant matures, and symbols are used more flexibly and reliably, undergoing refinement into various internalizations, including the formation of a body image.

Development research (Spitz, 1965) and clinical observation (Blatt, 1974) emphasize the significance of developing boundaries between inner and outer experience as well as between self and others. It is necessary for these basic boundary distinctions to be established before the mental representations of self and other can undergo more complex differentiation, articulation, coherence, and integration in the developmental process. What becomes internalized is not the object or its functions but one's experience of and with the object. One uses this experience to form images and fantasies of internal objects (Grotstein, 1987).

The developmental experiences of the body self that become represented as body image begin in the first awareness through the mirroring self-object, evolving in healthy development into a cohesive, distinct, accurate, and consistently evocative image of one's body and its relationship to its physical surroundings. The body image must evolve accurately as one's physical body matures, and be integrated in the development of the psychological self.

The development of self-empathy begins with empathy to one's own bodily experience (body self). By maintaining distinctions between the inner and outer body self experiences, the individual establishes the distinctness of self and other.

This model of body image development (and study of pathological nondevelopment) is integrated with other developmental functions—especially, as Freud suggested, of ego and self development. The principles of therapeutic intervention in disorders with body self pathology are predicated on knowledge of normal development and potential disruptions, and their symptomatic manifestations.

Images are concrete and easily accessible ways to code, store, and retrieve information. The transformation of information into an image is a standard mnemonic device. Visual images are probably the first means of thinking and information processing. Piaget (1945) demonstrated that infants have the cognitive capacity to retain mental images of objects seen and then removed from their view. There appears to be a hierarchy of intellectual mechanisms ranging from images to words, to organizing patterns, to superordinate abstractions and inferences that regulate the entire experience of the self.

Schilder (1956) characterizes the evolution of thinking as an advancement from images to symbols and concepts with less sensory quality. This evolution in cognitive capacity parallels the changing image of the body and the growing ability to abstract the concepts of body self and emotional self.

Self-boundaries are presaged by body boundaries; the intactness of both are related. The developmental nonformation or regressive indistinctness of both body and self boundaries in pathological psychic states are elements of this same process in its dysfunctional state.

A body image projective drawing or internal image at any point in time is an arbitrary slice from the ongoing process of maturation, as one's body image slowly evolves from birth to death. The body self seems to consist of a group of images that are dynamically and preconsciously centered on body experiences. A body image is a conceptual composite deriving from all sensory modalities; the individual's sense of cohesion is also a conceptualization, because the entire body cannot be simultaneously retrieved from memory. In addition to the mental representations, later developmental influences include the reactions of others to one's appearance. Usually preconscious and uncritically internalized, they are not as static as the term *image* might imply. One's body self and body image are developmental processes undergoing gradual maturational change with a cohesive core, analogous to an intact psychological self. It is only when pathology is introduced in this process that change becomes abrupt, symptomatic, and prominent.

When a body image has been insufficiently formed to sustain the stresses of developmental maturation, it regresses in response to emotional events, and the self-state will display rapid oscillations. When such individuals are in regressed states such as narcissistic rage or depletion depression, their body images oscillate as well. Comparisons with body images drawn at other times show remarkable parallels to emotional states (Krueger, 1989a); that is, at a time of particular emotional turmoil, the body image becomes more distorted, vague, or less cohesive. In the course of successful therapy, patient and therapist will see a process of maturation, cohesiveness, and distinctness of body image, which parallels developmental maturation.

Body self and its derivative representation, body image, are fluid processes interconnected with and mutually complementary to the psychological self and its derivative representation, self-image. The accurate empathic mirroring of the entire depth and range of the infant's responses establishes the basis for the subjective experience and integration of the body and self. The imaging capacity is crucial to establishment of the objective experience of the body self, and the associated distinctness between self and object.

The emerging capacities to subjectively and objectively experience one's body and one's self as object and as origin of contemplation parallel the increasing ability to use symbols. The enhanced subjective and objective experiences of the body and psychological self support Lichtenberg's (1985) concept of the "self-as-a-whole," being an initiator and a director of intentional actions.

Meissner (1997a) elaborates on the body image as the cumulative set of images, fantasies, and meanings about the body and its parts and functions; body images are representational while the body self is structural. The body image is an integral component of self-image and the internal representation of the self. Sandler (1994) described body image as the basis of self-representation. Body image may be an essential bridge between mind and body (Yorke, 1985). Since the early 1980s, neurophysiological research has produced significant and salient data on the development of the body image from the initial movements in utero to the differentiation of the mental self in the third year of life (Lenche, 1998).

By 18 to 24 months of age, the process of brain maturation and emerging body experience and awareness has developed to include bowel and bladder mastery. The focus on internal body experiences and on the regulation of these boundaries (bowel and bladder sphincter control) further defines internal and external, and the control of passage between the two, and helps to consolidate body image.

Genital awareness, sensation, and exploration also begin at about this time, and further broaden body awareness. Galenson and Roiphe (1974) have found an increase in genital perineal awareness in boys and girls between 18 and 24 months of age. This awareness follows increased capacity for sphincter control and increased urethral sensation. The associated exploratory activity is less related to excitement than to proud exhibitionism.

The physiological consolidation of these sensations promotes a desire to explore, to exhibit one's self, and to be looked at, admired, and affirmed. A painfully negative self-consciousness may result from parents' disapproving regard at this time. The caregiver's response to exhibitionistic behavior is crucial in determining whether affirmation-integration or shame-segmentation will predominate in the infant's self-image.

Early developmental milestones are characterized by greater separation from the mother, increasing clarity of self and body boundaries, greater integration of body and psychological self, and initial experiences of one's self as the origin of action and intention. The individual grows from undifferentiated to symbiotic to a differentiated state, all in the context of maturing, ever-changing self-object relationships.

Intersubjectivity and State Change of the Body Self

What may be the most central activity in the entire process of analysis is that which is also the most central joint activity of a caregiver with a child: the mutual regulation of state changes (Stern et al., 1998). *State* refers to ego states, a psychophysiological state of consciousness incorporating an entire spectrum of perception, processing, and inscription of meaning. The infant's fundamental states are regulated by a primary caretaker, and include hunger/satiety, sleep/wakefulness, activity/rest, arousal/calmness, and degrees of social contact. With evolving maturity, more complex states are added to these regulations of physiological and psychological needs: affiliation, attachment, exploratory/expressive, adversarial, and sensual/sexual (Lichtenberg, 1989). The state specific experiences, the meanings attached, and the movement (regulation) between states blend seamlessly into one another in normal development. When a state becomes distinct and extreme, such as terror in response to trauma, the particular state may be dissociated, that is, experienced and recorded in a different tract of the brain; state specific memory and state dependent learning within that state may not be remembered in a different, more relaxed state.

Attunement, recognition, and matching of these different states arouse the infant to perceive and record relational knowledge, accurately identify and arrange self-experiences, ultimately to internalize the process of state changes for internal regulation. Mutual regulation occurs between mother and child, as well as between analyst and patient. Emotion and subjectively experienced affect (feeling) are accompanied by bodily changes, especially autonomic. Additionally, affects have an intersubjective function of seeking a connection and communication with another.

What is emotion? Neuroscientists tell us that emotion consists of three components: an *appraisal* of the situation or stimulus regarding its relevance to the perceiver; an *activation* of biophysiological changes based on that appraisal that involve the body and effect the brain itself; and *subjective feelings*, the result of the appraisal, feedback, and bodily activation connected with meaning and affective significance (Eckman, 1999). Feeling is thus the conscious, subjective experience, while emotion is the entire response involving mind and body and biological and psychological interconnections between the two.

Stimuli perceived in emotional processing is fundamentally *sensory*, as experienced by one or more of the sensory modalities. This fundamental emotional processing based on sensory perception is not initially the higher order, symbolic, metaphorical significance we often think of in formulating an analytic interpretation. This fundamental bedrock of emotion is perception of basic parameters of safety/danger, familiarity/ unfamiliarity, rewarding/unrewarding. The brain center for appraisal in the limbic system processes this information from the sensory organs to determine fundamental emotional significance, not relevance in terms of higher symbolic meaning but in fundamental survival and balance of the individual. On the basis of this fundamental perception, the limbic system then activates other relevant parts of the brain for full emotional processing.

When emotion is activated, the bodily changes that are involved are of three types: endocrine and hormonal changes, the viscera or internal reactions of the autonomic nervous system; and the musculoskeletal system of muscle movement as part of an emotion.

Bodily experience is a fundamental aspect of emotion, because emotion links mind and body. Emotion also links the minds and bodies of patient and analyst. Neuroscientists indicate that emotion does not cause bodily changes, but that emotion *is* bodily changes (Damasio, 1994; Edelman, 1992). Emotion organizes not only our thoughts and behavior, but also our perception and memory (Eckman, 1999).

Affect regulation is a central mechanism of self-development as well as self-pathology, and is developed by emotionally charged important relationships the create a neurobiological impact and the organization of brain systems that process affect. The emotional communication of parent to child directly regulates the infant's psychobiological state. The attachment interactions facilitate the maturation of the infant's limbic system and right brain, and secure attachments lay the foundation for the effective regulation of emotional motivational states (Schore, 1998).

Fonagy and Target (1996, 1998) have described in a series of studies how the development of the sense of self is an interpersonal process interacting with important others, emphasizing that the caretaker unconsciously ascribes a mental state to the child, which is internalized by the child, laying the foundation of a core sense of mental state and self. They found that the capacity for reflective self-awareness, the ability to reflect on one's own experience, is even more significant in determining health or pathology than the particular attachment experiences that are remembered.

An essential aspect of development is the primary caretaker's sorting and screening the stimuli that impinge on an infant in order to regulate tension and affect, as well as to create a model to sort out relevant stimuli externally as well as internally. This unity of parent and child develops a bodily coherence that evolves to a developing self with a limiting membrane of inside and outside (Flax, 1990). It is in establishing this process, this continuity of experience with mother and cohesiveness of internal point of reference of self-differentiation that allows a separation to gradually occur, to have physical and mental coherence, in a body self with an inside and an outside, and a distinction between one's own and another's body.

When the hardwired, biologically defined internal experiences correspond with accurate affect attunement and regulation by the caretaking adult, an affective sense of core body self results (Stern, 1985; Totton, 1999). Stern (1985) elaborates on the affective attunement as being the frequently repeated interactions of the baby with the adult corresponding with a similar rhythm or activation profile that matches the child. For example, when the baby makes a noise by banging, the parent makes a similar noise, or when the older child accomplishes a motor task and feels exuberant, the mother mirrors that exuberance. Stern (1985) has found that most attunements occur with the vitality affects: those captured in somatic and dynamic terms such as "surging," "rush," "explosive," "bursting," "fading away," "crescendo," or "fleeting." These vitality affects are distinguished from usual "category affects" of rage, grief, fear, or joy, etc.

This intersubjective relatedness can develop by means of imitation, usually of somatic gesture, movement, or sound. Imitation, however, only indicates what it is like to do what the child did, not what it was like to be the child and to experience it as he or she did. Rather than this exact robotic imitation, a parent takes a central aspect of the behavior and selectively plays it back to the baby to indicate participation and sharing of inner experiences (Stern, 1985). This communicates the shareable world of internal affective states, of how we can best let someone know that we know what it is like to be that person.

Stern (1990) distinguishes imitation and mirroring (both being the display of matching experience), from attunement, the specifically selected and elaborated attention to take parts of a behavior, expression, or verbalization, and to reflect an inner experience that is an analogue rather than a copy or imitation of that experience. This "analogic matching" is a specific manifestation of empathy, perhaps done intuitively by a parent with a child, and more specifically applied by an analyst to a patient.

The caregiver, by close attunement to the mental state of child, helps to create a mental representation in the child of their own sense of body self and later of psychological self. The close followings and attunement of affective states create a sense of effectiveness in the child, of mutual modulation of state changes. The caretaker's awareness of mental state creates the child's capacity to regulate mental state. The close attunement and reciprocity of mental state creates a secure attachment, and the capacity of the child develops optimally to have a representation of body self and later a representation of psychological self. By this reflective functioning, the caregiver creates a developing representation of the mental state of the child (Fonagy, 1998). Fonagy (1998) believes the child becomes aware of the caregiver's representation of it as an intentional being, and this becomes part of the core of the child's psychological self. The child discovers himself as an intentional being in the behavior of the caregiver. The accuracy, completeness, and continuity of attunement to mental states and the mastery of state changes is necessary to result in a stable and coherent self-representation by the child.

Fonagy and Target (1995) demonstrate self-development in which the concept of a psychological self evolves through the perception of one's self in the mind of a significant other. This mirroring function includes not only empathic resonance with feeling, physical, and psychological states, but also of the uniqueness of the mind and thoughts of the child.

When fundamental defining experiences of body self and psychological self do not occur, there is a desperate quest for attuning, validating external responses, and corresponding arrest in symbolic representation of one's body and self (Fonagy & Target, 1997; Krueger, 1997). A self-experience or self-representation may then have to be achieved through somatic stimulation or through self-harm, the latter being a particular attachment disorder (Farber, 2000).

Effectiveness is an essential aspect of presymbolic experience in the first days and weeks of life as infants discover and attempt to master the sources of pleasure and avoid unpleasure, such as learning very quickly which gestures and movements bring a mother closer, and more attuned, and those which are ineffective in eliciting a response, or even induce rejection (McDougall, 1989). This earliest nonverbal, or at least presymbolic somatic language becomes the communication, and the foundation of effectiveness and of body self experience.

In the hoped-for unity of mother and infant, a seamless blending meets desires before they become full frustrations. Later, with frustrations that are optimal, a separateness and distinctness evolve. When developmental disruption occurs, various attempts to recreate this immersion (or to create it for the first time) give rise to a gallery of compensatory mechanisms as symptomatology. Of equal valence is the desire for autonomy, self-functioning, and individuation motivated by the quest for effectiveness/mastery. Mastery and effectiveness endeavors evolve from awareness and differentiation of internal somatic experiences to their representation intersubjectively and reciprocally, ultimately to symbolic representations via gestures, sounds, and language. This desomatization is actually a gradual integration of mind and body, specifically of body self and psychological self as a unity. The merger with the mother in order to differentiate is the original paradox. It allows other paradoxes to develop, such as having something on the outside represented on the inside, to be transformed on the inside representationally so that it is no longer the same thing as what is still there on the outside. A mother may exist as a soothing and caretaking nurturer internally, and be far from that in reality; this fantasy of self-object functioning rather than an actuality, forms the basis for what may later be the idealized memory of nostalgia (Krueger, 1998).

Language supplants some of bodily communication, but never replaces it altogether. With symbolic representation and later object constancy, mental representations continue to gain more power than physical expressions.

The central theme of our life, an organizing center around which we perceive and process, may seem to have infinite possibilities. With adequate development, higher order themes such as achievement, intimacy, or personal growth may be more central. Yet in developmental arrest or disruption, the themes narrow and harden to center around fundamental developmental needs, continually expressed and pursued in quest of developmental advancement. A partial listing of such themes may include bonding with another, validation, mirroring, nurturing, idealization, self-regulation psychologically or physiologically, affiliation, exploration, and assertion. When any of these basic developmental needs are not met, the pursuit establishes the theme, and the individual's quest for the self-object/developmental need becomes an identity. The persistence of these needs is determined by the initial success and integration, or the failure and the subsequent seamless integration when the needs are met, versus the ways in which we try to conceal and subsequently attempt to meet and conceal the needs (and by that attempt, to paradoxically reveal the needs). The central organizing themes may exist around each of the fundamental development needs of body self development and its integration with the psychological self.

Those individuals who use their bodies perversely do so for developmental missions that have gone awry, derailed from initial need satisfaction, to an alternate pathway that simultaneously is proxy for the developmental hunger.

The early body self experiences of skin contact, sensory experiences, touch, and movement stimulations all occur in contact with significant caretakers. Symptoms as well as some perversions, compulsive activity (eating, exercising, self-stimulation), and addiction to stimulating substances create a bridge to a discernible threshold of body experience as a basic foundation of the sense of self. One tries to fill in or compensate for what was missing, with defensiveness built in because each of these are substitutes or component parts of contact with others. In perversions, experiences are delimited to a very circumscribed fantasy/act in which complete control and subjugation is central, focusing on an aspect of a person, such as a body part, rather than the whole, with fearful intimacy avoided.

Bodily states, experiences, sensations, and metaphors become the pathway to of the patient's internal experiences, to engagement of more authentic awareness and experience, and to a greater degree and depth of intimacy in both internal and intersubjective terms. These bodily expressions and experiences have been the psychological deadlock of internal experience, and their perception currently becomes the pathway back to this beginning, to the simplicity of emotionality. This mutual focus on the surface rather than the depth of experience paradoxically allows a more complete and authentic experience of the self. These bodily experiences are also at the surface rather than at the depths of particular states of mind. The sound bytes become the signal of how experiences are perceived and processed in a fundamental, physical way.

Fundamental to psychoanalytic theories, traversing even those theories that differ from psychoanalysis regarding the motivation behind human behavior, is the theory of mind–body integration. In addition to certain kinds of empathic failures, certain activities and toxic experiences for the child can create a misalignment, even an opposition between mind and body. The mental function and intellectual process may need to compensate for a neglected as well as an abused body self-development, becoming an entity into itself, split off from the body, segmented from the nurturing of parental caretaking and development. The self becomes disembodied, rather than embodied, when not bounded by important caretakers in the environment (Winnicott, 1957). The mind and body do not develop to an intimate association.

Just as a patient may regard and speak of body and feelings in a detached way, the body may be emotionally reacting to internal experience, and the language of the body's expression is thus of central importance. There can often be dramatic body expression, such as migraines headaches, gut spasms, or other bodily expressions of emotional experience without feeling the emotion other than through the body. The use of the body as vehicle and container of emotional expression takes a tremendous physical toll, and often physiological pathology can then manifest when the body is persistently used in this way, leading further away from feeling, as the physical pathology is concretized by a physician and a diagnosis.

John Updike described a boy's shapeless and formless fear. The small boy had no idea what his fear was about, but occasionally he would go to the cellar, for there he knew to be afraid of spiders. There, his fear of spiders seemed a tangible entity on which to focus his fears. Spiders were the remedy, not the cause of his fears: the spiders made his fear visible and finite, creating a mastery, a determination of cause and effect with an inherent remedy. His fear had become understandable, even trivial.

We have to name our world in order to live in it, to identify, experience, and name our feelings to reside inside them. The recognition of body self, the subjective experience, and the objectification of it are all necessary to be an inhabitant of one's body.

Body Self to Psychological Self

The body is the primary instrument through which we perceive and organize the world. We regularly return to the body as a frame of reference throughout development. Subsequent learning and experiences are referred to what has already been sensorily experienced for confirmation and authentication (Rose, 1980). The first symbols and metaphors refer simultaneously to the body and to the outside (nonbody) world.

The special emotional significance with which each individual infuses elements of external reality is often associated with an object's or event's representation of a body part or function. The mother is first experienced as an extension of the infant's body, function, and needs, all of which are perceived as the same at this stage of development. The mother exists as a holding environment to meet the infant's needs in a way so unobtrusive that the infant does not experience his needs as needs (Ogden, 1985). When the mother is empathic and regularly present there is neither need nor capacity as yet to form symbolic representations of her.

The entire caregiving system, including parents, must continuously adapt to permit the infant's increasing regulatory capacity. The system must grant entrance to the newcomer as his own agent. When the caregivers recognize and accept the infant's need and ability to independently effect events, they provide the conditions that establish the infant's capacity for self-awareness, and ensure that an awareness of self will be the basic referent of behavior organization. The child will be able to appreciate what behaviors lead to what states. This self-initiated goal realization will be experienced as the infant's own.

The role of the caregiver in nurturing the developing child's internal regulatory capacities must be ever-changing in content while consistently empathic in process. It is systems training, teaching competence in organizing and regulating one's own behavior in order to achieve goals. The experience of effectiveness is central. The caregiver facilitates goal realization and provides conditions that are conducive to the child's initiation of goal-organized behavior throughout the developmental spectrum.

These behaviors become more complex and sophisticated during the process of development, and the caregiving system must be prepared to permit as well as to promote the persistent broadening of the child's organizing capacity.

The Bridge Between "Self and Other": Potential Space and the Transitional Object

At about 4 months of age, and with the attainment of a capacity for mastery and satisfaction with one's own effectiveness, comes an early awareness of frustration and consequent separateness (Winnicott, 1971). When the mother is empathic, the infant begins to experience her response to the affects and action he originates. He simultaneously experiences feelings of frustration, because the mother is not an absolute extension of his body, his needs, his wishes. The frustration of some of his desires is inevitable, and, when well-timed and carefully titrated by the caregiver, it encourages development of frustration tolerance and facilitates symbol formation.

The transitional object can be used initially to effect this separation, by being a simultaneous symbol of the mother and a symbol of separateness. The transitional object is a symbol for "separateness in unity, unity in separateness." The transitional object is at the same time the infant (the omnipotently created extension of himself) and not the infant (an object he has discovered that is outside of this omnipotent control) (Ogden, 1985).

Food can be recognized as the first transitional object. Food is the extension of the mother's body (breast), conveyed as nurturance, emotionally and physically, to become part of the infant's body. Other transitional objects are a part of the infant's body (his thumb), or represent the mother's body (a blanket caressed as the mother's skin).

The dialectical process (i.e., of a "me" and "not me") involves two opposing concepts that create, inform, preserve, and negate each other: Each stands in fluid relation to the other (Hegel, 1807/1927). Although this dialectical process moves toward integration, each integration creates a new dialectical opposition, a new dynamic tension, and finally the sense of subjectivity from which self-awareness emerges.

Self-awareness begins in the child's discovery of himself through what he sees reflected in his mother's responses. Self-awareness thus begins with an awareness of body experience, sensations, and physical presence. The evolution of self-awareness progresses from reflexive reactivity to the experience of "thinking one's thoughts and feeling one's feelings," and ultimately to intentional self-reflection.

This process facilitates self-awareness (subjectivity), the connection of meaning to experience and then to understanding (objectivity). The (pathological) opposite is an equation of experience with action—the object reflexively acted upon when urge and action are fused without intermediating evaluation. This is another level of potential space: a distance between urge and action. Contemplation and judgment reside in this potential space; without it, one is reflexively active, "impulsive."

What is first and most clearly observed is also what was first experienced: the body and bodily sensations. This leads to the more developmentally advanced experience of self, then to more abstract conceptualizations and representations of the self, including body image and self- image. This unity of body and self (body and mind) may suffer developmental interruption or arrest at any point, creating a deficit (nonintegration as opposed to split) in the progression and integration of body self and psychological self.

Fonagy (1998) describes the capacity to symbolize conscious and unconscious mental states both in oneself and in others as their capacity to "mentalize," a way of giving "wholeness" to others through an understanding of mental processes that create an understanding of the actions of others in the world. Prior to this conceptualization of mental representation of the object, without a mental representation of a significant other and without the conceptualization mental states, recognition is partial and tied to specific situations since the overview of mental functioning is absent.

The symbolic function of mentalization is crucial in understanding development of an integrated body self and psychological self and the ability of children to develop the capacity to reflect on their own experience and behavior as well as to conceive of others' feelings, intents, desires, knowledge, beliefs, and thinking. As the child is able to reflect on the meaning of the behaviors of others, he is also able to find meaning in his own thinking and experience. This ability, evolving by ages 6 to 8, contributes significantly to affect and tension regulation, impulse control, self-monitoring, and the experience of oneself as a cause, of self-agency (Fonagy & Target, 1997). The connection of this self-reflective function is intimately linked with attachment, and the parents' mirroring of the mind, thinking, and mental states of the child in the attachment process.

The capacity of the caregiver to understand and reflect on the independent and unique experiences of a child's body and mind not only encourages secure attachment, but the accurate reading of the child's physical as well as mental state creates the fundamental experience of effectiveness for the child. This resonance and symbolization of the internal state leads to a more effective affect regulation (Gerely and Watson,

1996) as well as secure attachment, providing a firm basis for the understanding of mind and mentalization (Fonagy, 1999).

Fonagy's (1998) developmental research on self reflective functioning in children illuminates a process allowing both a distinctness and an integration of body and mind. Prior to the age of 6, the child's subjective reality is characterized by two ways of processing external situations: a *physic equivalence* mode, in which the child expects his internal world to correspond to what is on the outside, that everyone thinks and perceives exactly as he does; and a *pretend* mode, in which the child believes that what is inside has no relationship whatsoever to outside events. At around age 6, children develop a theory of the mind, the capacity to develop the idea that people have beliefs and ideas, and that these may be true or false. They also recognize that their own belief may not be the same as another person's, that their mind is unique.

These two modes of understanding, kept separate until about age 6, are integrated by the child in a way that Fonagy calls *mentalization*. This reflective mode of mentalization is a transformation that allows a theory of mind in which the child comes to see that his mental states and ideas can be reflected upon. This theory of mind requires a special form of empathy from caretakers, now including teachers, in which the child's mind, as distinct from parents or anyone else, can be reflected upon to enhance the child's point of view. The child then develops the awareness of having a mind of one's own rather than being an extension of parents' ideas and desires. The mirroring and validation of the child's unique mind, and autonomous thinking allows the child to be able to further distinguish internally between thoughts and feelings, as well as interrelationally between how she thinks and others think and experience.

Failure of this self-reflective capacity creates a difficulty in distinguishing and developing one's own ideas and internal points of reference distinct from those of one's parents, but also the distinctions of feeling and action, internal fantasy and external reality. (Fast-forward to adulthood: The nonintegration of the pretend mode may disallow experiencing success and affirmative response as authentic, as a component of one's true self; rather, accomplishments, perhaps even ambition and boldness, remain as "pretend," cordoned off internally, while accomplishments are regarded as fake, and oneself as an imposter.)

In presymbolic organization, there is knowing, but there is not a self that knows. By age 5, there is recognition that another individual has a differently organized mind. By ages 5 and 6, one can imagine that another's mind is differently organized from one's own. By the middle of the second year one can say, "I know." But it is not until the fifth year that can one say, "I know that you know" (Beebe, 1999).

A Preliminary Note on Potential Space, Impulsivity, and the Analytic Process

The ability to transcend one's immediate situation is reflected in the capacity for symbolism and reason—the process of standing apart from an object or experience in order to objectify it. Objects of observation may include one's own thoughts, body, or behavior, as well as the actions or appearance of other people.

Bodily awareness and self-awareness both depend upon some capacity to transcend one's body and self in order to observe. Body awareness requires only some potential space for observation; self-awareness requires a capacity for abstraction, since "self" is an intellectual concept rather than a physical construct, like the body and its sensations.

The development of self-awareness provides one with the capacity to objectify one's self and the world, and with the capacity to have and use symbols. To see one's body (and, later in development, one's self) as both subject and object requires a third position: the observer. This capacity to transcend one's situation is inseparable from the capacity for self-awareness. The awareness of one's body and self requires the capacity to stand somewhat apart from that which is being observed, and to view one's body and self in a particular situation or context. From that distance, one becomes able to evaluate subjectively and objectively, to abstract, to reason, and to choose among many possibilities for action.

Judgment resides intrapsychically in this (potential) space between urge and action. The most notable manifestations of developmental arrests are impulse disorders (the fusion of urge and action without a contemplative potential space) and addictive disorders (urge and action directed solely toward supplying the self with affect regulators, largely somatic yet also symbolic of a soothing self-object such as food, drugs, alcohol, money, sex).

The space that potentiates the intrapsychic dialectic is replicated in the relationship between patient and analyst, a collaborative observational effort from opposite ends of a line of sight. Developmentally analogous to the first caregiver's holding environment and symbiotic union, the union between analyst and patient must be established before the patient can progress to separation and individuation. The analyst must contact the patient empathically as the analyst–patient dyad becomes subject and object for mutual observation, experience, and scrutiny prior to the patient being able to establish himself as the observer and subject of his own motivations. This first step in conveying an understanding of the patient's experience is to be, in essence, inside it together and listening from the allied vantage point of the patient's internal experience.

This need was put most succinctly by one analytic patient, who felt that I had missed the mark by not first resonating with her experience before I made an interpretation. She said, "I want you to be where I am. I need to know you can be with me first before I can go someplace new with you." From this basic foundation of empathic immersion together will emanate subsequent developmental, conflictual, object-related aspects of the transferential–countertransferential as well as real, human to human blends of old story and new story.

The failed development of a capacity for physical and psychological self-awareness in an individual results in rigid confinement to one particular emotional and ideational context, which might be clinically referred to as "concrete" or "not insightful." When the freedom to create and to design one's world is perceived as absent, the individual typically allows the desires or directives, real or imagined, of others to determine the conduct, and responses are limited to pleasing conformity or antagonistic rebellion. Passive, pleasing conformity and active opposition both reflect a diversion of individual freedom, in that both behaviors respond to an external rather than an internal point of reference.

2

Body Self Developmental Disruptions

A subterranean passage between mind and body underlies all analogy.

> Ella Sharp
> *Dream Analysis*

The latest findings in physiology suggest that the mind doesn't really dwell in the brain but travels the whole body on caravans of hormone and enzyme, visibly making sense of the compound wonders we catalogue as touch, taste, smell, hearing, vision.

> Diane Ackerman
> *A Natural History of the Senses*

The development of body self and psychological self-awareness occurs as an interpersonal process interacting with, and defined initially, by important others (Fenster, 2000; Tustin, 1986). Children who are securely attached to at least one parent develop accurate subjective awareness, and later self-reflective awareness and a defined self-experience earlier and more completely than children insecurely attached (Fonagy & Target, 1998; Seligman, 1998).

Those individuals who have significant disruption of this essential development of body self and psychological self manifest less internal regulation of affective states and a more tenuous cohesion of both body self and psychological self (Krueger, 1989). These individuals more prone to disruption or disintegration must then enhance their own subjective awareness of fundamental body self in various ways if they are to achieve

that representation. In extreme instances, to register a subjective awareness of body self, they may attempt somatically and especially through
sensory channels to create a vivid and more explicit representation. Activities such as excessive running, cutting, eating, or sexual activities may
serve the function of stimulating awareness of body self experiences in
order to anchor, to organize, and to focus specifically on tangible, somatic feedback. Various symptoms of self-harm use the lexicon of the
body in action language to articulate experiences inchoate and unformulated (Farber, 2000).

The foundation of early body self is formed by sensory contacts with
the mother's body, including her skin, voice, and even eyes (Winnicott,
1960; Geddini, 1992). The shaping and containing via the surface of the
mother's body creates the initial experience of embodiment, the fabric
and form of body self. The embodied self evolves in psychic representation to a psychological self integrating mind and body (Lichtenberg, 1978).

The experience of an embodied self is of having the shape or containment of the self within the body. Disembodiment, in which the patient may feel uncontained, boundaryless, without shape or substance, a
"blob," or a "nothing," invisible, or dissolved results from failed representation of psychic embodiment. Empathic nonattunement to the internal experience in the child's early development fails to establish an internal point of reference for self-reflection and self-attunement.

With failure of this initial embodiment, one of several maneuvers
may then be created by the child to augment or supplement this needed
developmental experience. Psychosomatic symptoms may create the affirming validation by way of pain or feedback of the reality of the body
(Fenster, 2000). The child may turn to his or her own body to create such
satisfaction and various ways to self stimulate, even to self-harm. Tustin
(1986) notes that autistic children callus themselves in order to create an
artificial, inert barrier instead of simply skin, containing on the nameless
dread "that they could liquefy and spill away." This containment and
encapsulation may be present in individuals who have not had the consistently attuned experience of containing and defining human contact,
and subsequently need to create a concrete experience of embodiment
with specific boundaries.

The tangible experience of the body, its stimulation by activity or
through the senses, allows a focus that is specific and concrete when
there is no consistent, cohesive representation of body self or image. These
concrete, often action oriented body stimulations are necessary when a
sense of self is disorganized or elusive through more abstract means of
thoughts, feelings, and fantasies. That bridge, usually built through stimulation of one or more of the senses, creates a symptom, such as self-harm
in inflicting pain, an eating disorder, an addiction, or a psychosomatic

symptom to internally bridge mind and body. The intent is to change the way one feels by creating some union of mind and body in order to experience a representation of the body within the mind, even if only temporarily. It is a partially satisfying counter to emptiness, an isolation of mind without body, body without mind, or to reverse dissociation. When mind and body are not developmentally integrated, a bridge between the two is continually necessary.

The effect of trauma can be similar to that of nonattunement or inaccurate empathic recognition of the child's emotional states, in that the resultant dissociation as defense against trauma significantly reduces self-reflective functions, as well as leaving emotion at a somatic level. The protective defenses utilized in trauma of altering consciousness, of disconnecting mind and body, significantly disrupt awareness both of the self and of feelings, and in so doing impact continuity of memory, awareness of the self, and cohesiveness of the self. The psychic numbing of blocking or distracting from overwhelming affect has been demonstrated in a number of studies, from the actual impact of trauma (Ulman & Brothers, 1988), to include the impact of the dissociation of Holocaust survivors on their children (Laub & Auerhahn, 1993; Fonagy, 1998).

Various somatic experiences and their expression may contribute to the compensatory securing of otherwise insecure attachments. Although the physical symptom internally unites emotion and bodily experience, it also serves as proxy for an authentic attachment and accurate mirroring, a compensatory bridge. If the dependence on parents needed in childhood is predicated on somatic expression of symptom or malfunction, it is then engrained in the pattern of behavior if its effectiveness is positively reinforced. It then becomes conditioned automatically and autonomically as prerequisite for a response.

The original experiences of the infant's body in juxtaposition to that of the caretaker combines an intermingling connectedness as well as a sense of space and distinctness of each. This developmental analogue of intrapsychic and interpersonal space evolves to an autonomy and mastery of integration of mind and body. Individuals not accustomed to experiencing their bodies, sensations from their bodies, or attunement to different nuances and subtleties of sensory experiences, do not live in or throughout their bodies, do not have physical intensity or intimacy with their bodies, or with the bodies of others. Symptoms simultaneously attempt a reconnection with their bodies and symbolically meet developmental needs. Any substance or activity may serve as substitute self-object function (e.g., eating disorders, addictions to mood-altering substances, to the intense preoccupation and focus on qualities and textures of collected items; Krueger, 1997; Farber, 2000).

With this failure of synthesis of body self and psychological self, the two remain somewhat distinct and parallel. Distress in one finds expression in the other, such as the use of drugs, alcohol, or food to regulate emotional distress. Another illustration is the "black hole" or deadness experienced and internalized from a caretaker with later attempts to fill the empty space and its despair by everything from psychosomatic events, addictive reliance on others, to activities or substances that create a sense of "something" to fill the "nothing."

Derailment of early body self experiences of knowing and integrating the fundamental sensory and experiential building blocks, results in individuals being inarticulate about their own body and sensory awareness. When these fundamental experiences have not been seen, heard, resonated with, and responded to by essential others in the caretaking environment, regions of experience become undefined, awareness muted, and the body self and sensations remain unsymbolized. These missed developmental experiences, unmet needs, and muted awarenesses become an abiding quest, an identification fashioned into a core organizing yet unconscious assumption of defectiveness, or of bodies within an affective orbit of shame.

Throughout development, consistent attempts to affirm value and worth, to create mirroring and validating experiences of the core self, especially of the core body self and fundamental sensory experiences, fashion and affirm a core belief of inadequacy and of defectiveness. If the pursuit is to have others validate and affirm, despite remarkable and consistent success, the core organizing assumption is not eradicated, thus leading to a deeper etching of the seeming validity of defectiveness. When positive, affirming responses result from successes, the vertical nonintegration remains, as the internal disavowal becomes, "If they only knew who I really am," or "They just don't know the real me" (Krueger, 1983).

If fundamental interactive experiences that define body self and psychological self are either missing or inaccurate, the mind and body do not get integrated. The most extreme of undefined internal perception would be alexithymia, the "not knowing" of internal body sensation awareness, to the point of removing oneself from one's body, in essence to observe it as if it were not happening, analogous to a traumatic event resulting in dissociation.

Patients attempting temporary self-object experiences from an amalgamation of a fragmented self-cohesion may seek various sources. Repeated traumatic or abusive experiences may have a strong organizing effect because of the intensity and familiarity of the recreated affect, with physical pain a recurrent experience. Confusion, failure, pain, or trauma may all become more familiar and thus a more organizing and cohesive experience than the occasionally more unfamiliar burst of feeling good or of success. Pain manifested in the body becomes tangible, a reminder of the control that one has lost and attempts to capture in a body that is not experienced as one's own. Pain can become an identity crystallized, and though a symptom of an illness, nonetheless an identity becomes visible.

A second source of self-object experience may come from those substances or activities that provide a comfort from psychic pain. Substances, activities, and objects have both defensive and regulatory effect because of their physiological soothing and triggering of affect due to emotional significance. Risk taking, self-harm, smoking, drugs, alcohol, and food may all be used in habitual and addictive activity in that they provide relief not for one specific need but for a range of distresses and discomforts. Regardless of the source of distress, the activity, substance, or object may be used to create relief.

A third area of self-object experiences may be derived from fantasies that can be organizing and cohesive. These fantasies may command disproportionate energy when they are used as a means to create an affect state of invigoration or cohesion that might otherwise be elusive. The main pathological consequence arises if the individual persistently resorts to the fantasy and attendant behavior as a means to relieve unrecognized distress from a variety of sources from problems in any motivational system (Lichtenberg, Luchmann, & Fosshage, 1992). As long as the dominant motivation is to preserve the fantasy and absolve doubt, little attention can be given to the sources of distress. Threats to dislodge the belief or illusion that has become the source or revitalizing experience, relied on to cope with stress from a variety of sources, can be quite anxiety provoking. Illusory but consistently re-creatable self-object experiences can take on a life of their own.

Pathological Sequences in Body Self Development

Research on deficiency states in infancy has demonstrated that failure to develop a normal psychic representation of the body may result from insufficient intensity of stimulation as well as from cognitive and emotional overstimulation (Dowling, 1977; Shevrin & Toussieng, 1963; Wolff, 1960). The following proposal is an evolving attempt at further specificity in the developmental origin of what Battegay (1991) has referred to as "hunger diseases" from the inadequate meeting of the psychological regulation of physiological needs or the overgratification of these fundamental needs to produce such clinical syndromes of eating disorders, substance abuse, compulsive shopping, or compulsive sexuality, to name a few. More contemporary addictions include exercise, self-mutilation, online computing (Farber, 1997), and compulsive shopping and spending (Krueger, 1988b; 2000). These action symptoms are addressed more specifically in Chapter 7.

Certain developmental disruptions in body self-formation and evolution may be linked to the resulting restorative efforts manifest as psychopathology. Early developmental arrests in the process of establishing a stable, integrated, cohesive body image seem to result from one or several maladaptive interactions (Krueger, 1989a, 1997). These early developmental pathological sequences cluster into three groups, with associated body self-image pathology and consistent symptomatic configurations. Although not mutually exclusive, the types of psychopathogenic interactions can be described as a predominance of interactive patterns: Overinstrusiveness/overstimulation, empathic unavailability, and inconsistency or selectivity of response.

Each of these three types of pathological sequences/interactions seem to result in specific developmental arrests, associated types of pathological manifestations (Krueger, 1989a) each impacting the sense of self at a basic body self level, with absence of a coherent, accurate, cohesive, organized body image and blurred body boundaries (Garner & Garfinkle, 1981; Krueger, 1989a; Rizzuto, et al., 1981). Lacking internal evocative images of a body self or a psychological self, they rely on external feedback and referents, such as the reactions of others to their appearance and actions, or to mirrors. There is a distinct lack of object and internal image constancy, with the arrest in body self development paralleling the arrest in development of psychological self.

Disturbances in differentiating self and other effect the ability to create symbols, to distinguish the symbol from the object symbolized, and in turn promotes a particular kind of developmental arrest: self-referential thinking that is concrete without the capacity for abstraction or representation of the body and its contents, including affect differentiation. Though perhaps quite articulate and accomplished, these individuals may feel lost when focusing internally and not have a language for feelings (Krystal, 1988).

Lacking an ability to distinguish symbols from objects symbolized in regard to their self-state awareness, they elicit self-representation and regulate affect via the felt experiences of their own bodies. Their representation of self must emerge from the body self experience, not from a symbolic representation of the self, because, for these individuals, a viable representational image of the self has never developed. The psychological distance required for developmental progress beyond a transitional object is unavailable at this concrete non-symbolic operational level. *Symbolic equations* rather than *true symbols* predominate (Segal, 1978). Symbolic equations differ from true symbols because they are experienced as the actual object rather than as emblem, such as the use of food in the bulimic patient. With a symbolic equation, there is no "as if" quality, only an all-or-nothing concrete experience. At these times of insult or perceived empathic disruption, they engage in action sequences (action symptoms) that in some way stimulate the body such as pain, gorging, starvation, overexertion, risk-taking, sex, wrist-cutting, body mutilation, drug, or alcohol abuse to *create* a sensorimotor experience of the body self.

The creation of somatic symptoms or a somatic bridge to facilitate development may focus on a transitional symbolizing function/object (e.g., food) as a way-station to integration of mind and body, prerequisite to the true formation of symbols with "potential space" for fantasy. The somatic symptom or action symptom, such as ingesting or restricting food, may be viewed as meaningful, attempted adaptations designed to address developmental needs. This attuned focus to the scenario in which the symptom is embedded allows understanding of the developmental quest of the patient.

These patients are not primarily denying body awareness and feelings, for they have not developmentally attained, desomatized, and differentiated affect and bodily sensation; they have not as yet integrated mind and body enough to defensively split them. At the time of a current emotional insult, their organizing function is to direct focus on the first and most basic organizer of ego experience and structure: the body self.

Higher order, more structured pathology involves regressive retreats to more intact body self representations and regulation at a time of threatened self-representation. "Concreteness" in certain patients may be a defense against ongoing differentiating processes (Bass, 1997), as opposed to those developmentally arrested patients who have not yet fully distinguished and differentiated body self and psychological self cohesion, and are, as a result, concrete, especially in reference to themselves and their internal states.

In more developmentally advanced psychopathology, there is an integrated body schema, with more highly organized and dynamically/symbolically significant loss fantasies, such as castration anxiety or immobilization. Unconscious fantasies of losing vital body parts or functions occur in conjunction with emotionally charged relational interactions and Oedipal issues. In those individuals with more structurally intact psychopathology (e.g., psychoneurosis), the fantasies of loss occur without severe threat to a sense of self-cohesion. Body self cohesion and representation are basically intact and play an important role in these instances, but these symptoms occur at the level of fantasy rather than in action symptoms.

Treatment Implications

Although the clinical considerations are addressed more fully here in the treatment section, there are certain specific implications deserving introduction. The restitutive attempts described here compensate for a vague or indefinite body self and noncohesive psychological self, and are a central issue in treatment. They can be understood initially as attempts to meet arrested developmental needs as well as to defend against painful affects. The entire psychodynamic scenario within which the action symptom is embedded must be empathically understood and interpretatively addressed, because it is much more than simply defense through action.

Deadness and Black Holes

How do you fill the empty space left by a parent who is not there, who is unavailable, the development need unmet, the feelings not resonated with? All these experiences comprise the unformulated experience of being unable to occupy that space with a full sense of self and even of fundamental experiences of physical sensation and bodily presence. The parent not there, the developmental experience unmet, and the physical or emotional experience not resonated with cannot then occupy that space. The resulting conclusion of defectiveness can be concretized in body image representation, such as a patient who was not hugged or touched lovingly by her mother, and developed the belief that she was like the troll under the bridge with scaly, bumpy skin that must be disgusting to touch.

A "black hole" experience is the magnetic pull into the intense interpersonal and intersubjective space of the internal deadness of the mother (Eshel, 1998). The astrophysical term *black hole* is described by Hawking (1993) as a set of events caused by the collapse of a massive star in which the dying, shrinking star's gravitational pull is so strong that light can no longer escape. If light cannot escape, neither can anything else, and everything is sucked inside by powerful gravitational forces. Eshel (1998) has described individuals whose "interpersonal and intersubjective psychic space is dominated by a central object that is experienced essentially as a 'black hole' . . . "

The black hole, the interpersonal phenomenon of being sucked into the compelling pull of a mother is such a powerful primordial experience as to cast a shadow over every subsequent relationship, fearing the magnetic pull toward deadness and loss of self-definition. The resultant protective detachment creates emptiness and loneliness, but always within imminent threat in being close to and drawn back again into the black hole and its powerful gravitational pull.

The child's intersubjective emotional space then becomes focused on the mother and her deadness, blankness, and emptiness, as the child desperately and intensely tries to revive, repair, or cure the mother so that she can then respond to the child. The black hole experience describes the compelling, gripping, seductive yet annihilating experience of being pulled into this parent. It is not at all a static space, and certainly more than an empty space. These experiences and the imprinting with this parent have psychic and somatic components. The deadness can be experienced physically, being paralyzed at the edge of the black hole, being afraid of being sucked into it. For other individuals, this becomes the art of brinkmanship, of going to the edge repeatedly, but always pulling back and never allowing engagement or attachment in a relationship, fearing the original annihilation.

An important aspect of parental function throughout childhood is for the parent to be able to receive and accept, contain and regulate, modulate and detoxify the child's feelings, especially angry or bad feelings. The mutuality of interaction requires this regulation in order for the child to accept feelings as her own, to own, explore, and further discover internal experience.

If the child looks to the mother's face and sees a "foggy mirror or a frightening window, the child must dissociate in order to cope with that reflection" (Looker, 1998). When the parent is disconnected from her own internal experience, the child is also emotionally unconnected and mystified with her interior. When this inaccurate and unavailable mirroring does not occur, the child may then respond in a dissociative manner in which all aggressive, exploratory, assertive, and expressive strivings have to be forfeited. Some, or much of the child's own vitality is then restrained, disallowing a mind and body connection and continuity. Without this freedom of expansion and exploration, the child is unable to move into and inhabit her own mother's mind and body as a necessary way-station in claiming her own "personal dominion" of mind and body space (Raphel-Leff, 1994).

The child locates herself in her mother's eyes, movements, gestures, touches, words, expressions. She may not be able to find herself in the vacant dissociative stare; she may lose herself working to evoke response from the inattentive, nonresponsive rigid body of the parent, absent of hugs and words.

3

The Gendered Body Self

But the minute I start breaking this strange body down into
its constituents, it is dead. It does not know me. Carbon does
not speak, calcium does not remember, iron does not weep.

Loren Eiseley
The Night Country

I think rather than dividing into men and women, the world
actually divides into people who are calm and people who are
restless.

Steve Martin
Border Crossings

The earliest sense of self, including body self, is located in a male or in a
female body, while the characteristics of gender are being defined and
formed. The earliest imprints of gender identification are fashioned by
the representations of anatomy and physiology, identification with the
gender of primary caregivers, and the intersubjective shaping of gender
and sexual identification characteristics and traits are taught and modeled.

A sense of one's gender is a fundamental organizer of body self and
psychological self, both of subjectivity as well as a component of selfobject
experience (Pangrel, 1996). The first recognition and registration that we
make of another person is according to gender. We do this by viewing the
geography of body. Everything else follows.

Gender is a complex matter, having both genetic, physical, and psychological components. Genotypic gender is genetically determined, while
phenotypic gender is determined by the development of internal and ex-

ternal genitalia (Ibid). Gender identification is the subjective perception of one's gender, of maleness or femaleness, while sexual orientation is comprised of sexual identity and preference for sexual partners. Behavior of males and females differs from just after birth, enhanced by the differing treatment by parents. Gender is used by the child as a way of organizing self-cohesion and the regulation of self-esteem (Kiersky, 1998).

Originally, the baby creates the parent, and each mutually influences the other. On my weekend farm I recently saw the change created by motherhood. A Bantam chicken, skittish and indistinguishable from many others except by her particular color markings, was suddenly transformed as she sat on her eggs around the clock, calmly looking up at me, eye to eye. When her three chicks hatched, she instantly became their protector, constantly aware of where each was, of keeping them close to her, of tucking them under her body each night. The chicks, from embryonic egg, had created a mother, entirely transforming her personality.

Gender is an important aspect of the experience and internal representation of both body self and psychological self, an aspect of self-experience that is formed in the matrix of intersubjective interaction with primary caregivers. Gender is a fundamental organizer of subjectivity as well as objectivity (Pangrel, 1996), a given in all interactions with others, significant or not.

Growing up is pervasively gendered. There are constant reminders within the culture and the family of the exclusion and inclusion criteria of each gender, especially emphasized around sexual role stereotypes, of what is feminine and unfeminine, masculine and unmasculine. Psychological self becomes shaped by gender and sexual role stereotypes and perceptions of the body. Gender is one of the conventional and unspoken ways in which we order and organize our universe.

In the hippocampus, the seat of the unconscious, couplings, associations, and assigned meanings are organized around gendered body self experiences and perceptions. The child's experience of his or her body is organized and given meaning in a relational matrix, just as gender is used by the child for cohesion and self-esteem organization. In the early mutually regulated experiences and exchanges, the child locates himself in the parents' responses, eyes, face, and reciprocity of bodily experience. The mirroring back of everything that is experienced in face, body, gesture, and action allows the child to find himself in these responses, or, in their absence, to lose himself (Kiersky, 1998). Each of these bodies is innately gendered.

Our embodied selves are inherently gendered, as we may not be able to experience ourselves except in the context of gender. We may not be able to imagine experiencing the self as ungendered, in a way that is not colored by gender. Our embodied and gendered selves of male or female may be as inseparable as mind and body, as body self and psychological self, except in those nonintegrations of developmental arrest expressed as dichotomies, as unjoined mind and body, as incoherently articulated gender with hypertrophied boundaries lacking true distinctness and definition.

The inherent experiences that are gendered become the unspoken, invisible gendered self. When there is uncertainty, deficit, or conflict about what is within a boundary, the boundaries themselves become rigidly defended, belying their permeability. Boundary crossings abound as well as boundaries being a juncture between. Various contents become specifically assigned to gender. Others remain universal. There are ineluctable differences of gender, such that women nurse babies, as anatomical differences become certain given assignments of gender.

Gender includes both conscious and unconscious fantasies of the gendered and sexual body from all internal and intersubjective experiences. From the earliest moments of life, differential treatment shapes self-experience by informing both boys and girls which of their qualities and behaviors will be most rewarded with self-object response and affirmation, and which will not (Lang, 1984). Core gender identity is established in the first 12 to 18 months of life and is elaborated thereafter with identifications and roles, and is positioned in conjunction with separation–individuation issues. Gender identity is more complicated than a single line of development, and contains a plurality of developmental intersections of experience, identity, and positions. It is, however, one of the Oedipal phase recognitions that though one may have multiple identifications, one may be only one gender, and have only one same-gendered alliance with a parent. It is here that rejection of the opposite sex has an initial foray. It is only later, during the adolescent replay, that there can be a renewal of cross-sexed identifications and access to both the repudiation and the romance of the opposite sex. Nonrigid inclusiveness, complementarity, sexual role identities of masculinity and femininity, all get revived again during adolescence to be redefined and reintegrated.

We do not feel in gender defined terms, though gender is always present. We will never know what it is like to both feel "like a girl" and "like a boy," because we will never know of the experience of the other: An animal raised in captivity does not know the meaning of "freedom." We may intersubjectively have self and gendered self defined by certain characteristics, but the concept, seemingly crisp and distinct, is quite blurred, porous, and overlapping. How will we ever know what an opposite gender-related experience is, as compared to experiences of feeling childlike versus adult?

While being the most fundamental organizer of body self experience and representation internally and externally, gender is also one of the significant organizers of the psyche. For most individuals, it is one of the unquestioned certainties of self-experience and regard, a given. Often many experiences that would otherwise be marginal, equivocal, and uncertain can become gendered to feel integrated and ego-syntonic. Gender differentiation and gender identity are so fundamental that the differentness and the overlapping aspects are so often taken for granted. While basic developmental needs are not gender-specific, gender perception shapes both the needs and their expression. Consider, for example, the gender-specific assumptions of exploratory, assertive, adversarial, and aggressive motivations. The earliest sense of the female body and the male body get represented both emotionally and mentally, and are experienced vividly from physical awareness and sensations. The body is fundamentally involved in psychic development, and the girl's body is central to her development as the boy's body is to his, and the bodies are different (Bernstein, 1993).

Each developmental juncture combines a unique combination of bodily and psychological interplay for both male and female. The specific aspects of each gender at developmental points of pubescence, adolescence, marriage, pregnancy, menopause, and aging offer yet another opportunity to amalgamate and articulate body self and psychological self. The foundations of the self and the basis for the distinction between self and object are shaped by assimilating bodily experience and mental representation. The child's separation-individuation as well as hope of achieving an enjoyment of one's body and of oneself is based partly on the experience of seeing, modeling, and internalizing the parent of the same gender, the enjoyment and comfort with all aspects of that parent's body.

Gender includes the subset of sexual role prescriptions of what we do as a boy or girl, man or woman, the shape and texture of the expressions of developmental needs, of behavior aligned with male or female, and of how we think about being male or female. It is all this, yet more, for it is how we internally perceive, organize, and direct what we are doing; it is who we identify with, and what we internalize from significant others and significant aspects of society. We infer identity by gender.

Could we ever imagine experiencing ourselves other than through our gender, informed and organized by it, from within our embodied (and therefore gendered) selves? The world is gendered, and to encourage someone not to recognize or acknowledge that would be to ignore reality. Kiersky (1998) states that mind and body, as well as "doing" and "being" a gender are inseparable.

We can never transcend our gender, but we do not have to be bound by it, by its stereotypic constraints. Gender is both an idea and a reality. While gender is pervasive and assumed, gender crossings presuppose a gender boundary. That assumption of gender being a "given," whether it is doing or being gender, or both and more, has only recently begun to be questioned. Gender may be so fundamental to our concept of self and others that to take it away, or attempt to transform it, until only the recent few decades was considered a signal of psychosis. Much of how gender gets defined and even transmitted is constructed culturally. Each of us consciously and unconsciously incorporate prescriptions for gender behavior, acceptability, and meanings. There is a great deal of internalization of the body of culture into the gendered body and its representation in an individual.

The filter through which gender experiences pass is determined by other belated developmental needs and experiences, family context and shaping, as well as the subjective experience of the forming self in which gender assumes meaning and shape. When caregivers condemn behaviors or qualities as gender-incongruent, shame and self-doubt may result. Aspects of self-experience may have to be suppressed or even dissociated developmentally in order to maintain ties with needed self-objects. The child may then develop gender-incongruent behaviors as adaptations to failed empathic responses or acceptance by caretakers.

What is constitutional bedrock and what is constructed and transformed through experience with others is being reexamined. Gender as well as the body self are signified and shaped through interaction with significant others.

Dimen (1991) speaks of the core of gender being the contrast between male and female and that we each developmentally absorb such as masculinity and femininity and the cultural, interpersonal, and intrapyschic divergences. The body as gender and as sexed and sexual in a masculine or feminine way develops contingently with the mind as gendered and as sexed: the allowable and the constructed experiences of each gender/sex shape the mental representation of all components and of their synthesis.

There has been considerable challenge to the traditional psychoanalytic view of gender as singular, formed through unitary identifications. Gender is considered more as an organizing core identity challenging polarized concepts of male-female, masculine-feminine, heterosexual-homosexual, father-mother (Aron, 1995).

Primary Femininity and Masculinity

Elise (1997) proposes that we replace the term and concept of *primary femininity* with *primary sense of femaleness* to refer to the earliest sense of self derived from the girl's mental representation of her body. While unstated, the corresponding replacement term would be *primary sense of maleness* that would refer to the boy's sense of self deriving from his mental representation of his body. How many traits, experiences, and self-definitions are linked to being in a female body or in a male body? Do these characteristics stem from the body itself, or become attributed to and organized by the gender of the body? In transsexualism, the core gender identity of maleness or femaleness seemingly rooted in the biology of the body, is not primarily about the body, but about the incongruity of psychological and biological gender.

There are many aspects and levels of representation, and those about the body and anatomical sex are the most fundamental assumptions and expectations of behavior and regard by self and others. Masculinity and femininity are about the attributes that correspond to gender, but not about gender itself. A homosexual can be feminine, or its caricature, effeminate, thus reversing the usual gender alignment with masculinity.

Mayer (1995) has reviewed research to conclude that from about 20 months of age girls are both aware of and pleased with their genitals and are "happily female." From this she distinguishes primary femininity as a separate developmental line and different from the ideas postulated by Freud of girls struggling with what they are lacking, the phallic castration complex, and thus being unhappily female. These findings suggest that one's initial representation of the body is what it is, not what it isn't, and that sex and gender become a fundamental aspect of the foundation of development of both body self and psychological self. This fundamental identity is both intrinsic to the body and amalgamated with it in normal development.

Butler (1995) has suggested that during a transition from latency to adolescence boys dislike and disdain girls and their femininity (thereby their own femininity, projected). This disavowal of their own femininity is a ritual passage in establishing a male identity. This repudiation is generalized to all girls, and peer group identification is sought. An arrest in development at this phase can lead to a prolongation of the search for the masculine, the continued repudiation of the feminine, including latent homoerotic aspects that may manifest as homophobic. Boys, perhaps more than girls, must renounce any gender-inconsistent qualities or traits because boys have to go through separation-individuation with an opposite sexed parent, the mother. Little boys, using the preoperational all-or-nothing thinking, view masculine and feminine traits as mutually exclusive, and become more focused on establishing an unequivocal gender identity (Hansell, 1998). The need for this thorough cleansing of disidentification of all gender-related qualities is testament itself to how overlapping and interwoven experiences and behaviors are that are categorically assigned to one gender or the other.

Likewise, girls in adolescence have a nodal developmental integration of female gender identity in being, largely uninvited, a container for the projective identification of males for their devalued, unwanted, and discarded femininity; at the same time, the boys are as curiously attracted to both these qualities, as well as the young women who are their projective containers. Hansell (1998) elaborates that masculine logic as well as female desirability are based on embodying in the female the femininity split off from boys, wherein she becomes the container for sensitivity, passivity, and vulnerability, the traits repudiated by boys as feminine. Girls also at this developmental juncture need to renounce what they see as gender inconsistent traits, those aspects of masculinity mutually viewed by both boys and girls as strength, competence, and dominance.

Stoller's (1976) work on primary femininity, in which he studied girls who are born without vaginas or who had masculinization of external genitalia, and those who were biologically neuter though normal in appearance, emphasizes that the assignment of sex and rearing of the child outweighs anatomy. Experiences from the body, including sensing and sensations then become organized within the concept of gender of psychological assignment; thus, both sex and gender in this way are the ideas about the body and the organization of those ideas and experiences. In these instances, it is evident that the body does play an important part, but the organization of meaning and the attribution of significance can be powerfully determined in psychological terms.

With gender imprecision or conflict, a hypermasculinity or hyperfemininity is constructed for both defensive and reconstitutive purposes, sheltering against any ambivalence.

Gender differences in emotional awareness, expression, and interaction have been noted in observational studies of normal children: In boys ages 2 to 3, the main focus of activity is excitement and exuberance, while the girls had subdued affect and less excitement-exuberance (de Groot, 1994). While gender differences in aggression may be linked more to hormonal effects, the gender differences in activity are more linked to infant–caregiver interaction (de Groot, 1994), and may have implications regarding active, mastery experiences.

Sexual Identity

The earliest interactions and identifications are generally with parents of both sexes, and a core of bisexuality may evolve for the girl to a primary sense of femaleness (Elise, 1997) or primary femininity (Mayer, 1995), and primary maleness for the boy (Stoller, 1975).

Body self representations include gender identifications with both primary caretakers. Gender consistency of body and psyche with each other and with overt sexual orientation becomes a congruent mental representation of body self and psychological self. Cogender identity and designated sex becomes one of the assumed, unquestioned alignments that we all have and accept. It is when there is an incongruity that the painful disorder of gender identity puts into bold relief the stereotypic, rigid, all-or-nothing gender prototype. The concept of bisexuality illuminates the wish to have the self-representation from both sexes predominantly manifesting in the gendered sex of one's body, and to have the object choice of both sexes (Elise, 1998). Sweetnam (1996) added that the concept of bisexuality must include recognizing a desire to be loved and erotically acknowledged by both sexes.

The multitude of sensations coalescing in an experience of what it is like to be a man or a woman may be evoked and affirmed in various ways, some of which are pivotal on sexual experience. There are certain gender sensations and gender related bodily experiences that become organized in various ways. The body self is never an ungendered position, though much of the time it is an ungendered experience. Sensory-based gender experiences are almost always taken for granted, yet are inescapably defining. Each of the gender-based sensations comprise some component of what it is like to be uniquely a male or a female, a man or a woman.

Sexual identity within gender is the fundamental context from which we experience only the sexual and erotic. Masculine and feminine identification, evolving out of gender, is so contexualized that it may be impossible to define what is and is not gender-related or even gender-determined. Sensations, body self experience, and similar subjective experiences not innately contained to gender, may be invisibly shaped by gender designations.

The gender repertoire of an individual may be quite rigid, impenetrable, and this gendered self-concept may affect one's participation in sexual activity, in certain roles and stereotypic pursuits and restraints in life. Elise (1998) emphasizes that the experiences of gender may contain a multiplicity of varied expressions of self without a threat to one's sense of self or to one's core gender identity.

There may be no universal developmental narrative of gender or sexual identity, but consensual narratives that are generalizations, a common ground formed from the arrival from different directions, places, and reasons. The gendered sense of being a man or being a woman is a final consolidation of gender identity and sexual identity that seems to conform roughly with the gender of the body. Gender as a component of core identity is so fundamental, so much a given, that we do not question it until there is developmental derailment. Since it is formed so early, usually within the first two years of life, it is often conflict-free but conflictual only if psychological gender and body gender are different (Stoller, 1975).

Transsexualism

The body is a site for recording gender, as well as registering other disparate notations such as trauma. Experiences otherwise unsymbolized, such as inchoate experiences of anxiety, or of nothingness, also become recorded and organized within the body. Incoherences, inexpressible meaning, and unsymbolized feeling may also become crystallized as somatic experiences. Sensations as well as pains of the body may become an organizing narrative.

The interplay of defensive and compensatory structures can be viewed most readily in transsexualism. The transsexual syndrome illustrates self-object disturbances leading to this solution as an attempt to deny the impact of trauma and repair a self-defect, meeting self-needs through self-object functions of merger, mirroring, idealizing, and the search for an alter ego experience. Transsexualism concretizes and brings to the preoccupying foreground a disorder of the nuclear, gendered self. How much gender plays a role in the sense of self is brought into focus by transsexualism. This developmental arrest occurs at an early stage in life before the solidification of the internal representational self and at a prestage of defense, and transgendered people's relationships are often oriented toward archaic self-object needs.

Using the biological male transsexual as illustration for discussion, as well as in the following case example, the failure of a biological male to synthesize a cohesive sense of self results in a compensatory, vulnerable structure with desire to merge with a woman and be acknowledged as a woman, as well as a disavowal of what is male/masculine.

The transsexual's demand for external validation and transformation is an attempt to concretize in gender an otherwise elusive self-cohesion and identity. This compensatory structure consolidated into gender identity is designated to repair a defect in the self. A defensive structure covers over a defect in self and is activated at particular times, especially when the patient feels misunderstood or disconnected from an important selfobject, and converts passivity into activity in an active attempt at mastery of preserving self-functions or integrity. Transsexualism incorporates both compensatory and defensive structures, including a defense of turning passive into active, but also represents a permanent way of life. Psychic elaboration may be precluded as the obsessive preoccupation becomes externalized, and resolution is attempted via bodily transformation and transsexualism rather than by psychological work. The narcissistic pursuit for perfection and invulnerability are designed to counter painful experiences of vulnerability and even fragmentation.

Treatment Considerations

While we are always teaching others how to respond to us, there are, however, aspects of the teacher which have to be recognized, of which gender is one. Gender is a kind of transference, as part of what is perceived and organized based on one's internal model. Our own experiences from preverbal to present, are determined by gender-related interactions and mutual constructions. While gender is never absent, there are many aspects that make it far from the foreground.

Jan Morris (1991), the writer, has spoken of perceived gender differences, including that it matters whether a writer is male or female. She knows both, being a biological male from childhood into adulthood and having sex change surgery to then live as a woman. She speaks of many aspects of writing and traveling, of how the female is perceived as not threatening, more vulnerable, more conspicuous, finds fewer doors closed against her, even to the observation that women are kinder to women than men are to men. Having experienced both relationships, she speaks from her controlled study of one.

Feeling resides in detail. Detail of any of the sensory or bodily based experiences that a patient references is as equally important as emotional detail. For example, as a patient is describing a sensual feeling, the detail of exactly what the experience is, from each of the senses, and the feeling and action from each of the sensory tracts is important in understanding a total experience and associated meaning. To live in and own one's own body, a gendered and sexual body, involves sensory detail. Annie Sweetman's (1999) article on sexual sensations and gender experience gives careful and important attention to sensory detail, filtered through gender-specific senses. So much of psychoanalytic literature is written in metapsychological construct rather than the intricate detail of how we talk with patients, of how we experience being with them, and get them to talk about the exquisite and specific detail of their experience of being, of thinking, and of feeling.

The mutual creation of an analytic experience is a movement from experience of the other as a creation of one's own internal perception and development, to that of experiencing the other's distinct and separate subjectivity, external to oneself (Ogden, 1994). When patient and analyst come together they collaboratively and simultaneously affect and alter the joint experience of the newly created relationship. The relationship, the work, is about subjectivity as well as intersubjectivity. We use this subjectivity to provide access to many aspects of a patient, including those of gender, sexuality, and related identifications. We also use it to tease out those experiences and assumptions that are attributed to gender but do not necessarily belong there. This intersubjectivity becomes a new "body of work" for analyst and patient.

Many experiences, especially sensory, have become automatically associated with assigned gender meanings and assumptions, or, alternatively, developmentally divorced from gender and sexual significance, and may need to be reexplored in analytic work. This process of exploration that forms and transforms is one in which we work, at times of body self sensations, with a range of experiences from unformulated, preverbal to symbolized Oedipal and beyond. We create a unique understanding, the story that has its own rhythm, intensity, and shared meaning.

It is the hope of every psychoanalytic patient to be understood by the analyst at both a conscious and unconscious level. This would include an innate understanding and appreciation of the inclusions and exclusions of a gendered and sexual body self. We must not assume that we know, from our own model and our own development, exactly what each patient's experience is; instead, we must stay curious, inquisitive, alert to and searching for detail and especially the detail of each patient's subjectivity. To know what it is like to be inside their gendered, sexual body and psychological self, their experience at any given moment. The meaning of gender as well as a masculinity/femininity lies both in what is contained and imparted with meaning, as well as what has been excluded. So much of meaning lies in the differences between things, in coexisting dualities.

One may not need to be a certain gender or a certain sexual orientation, or have had certain experiences, to analyze a person well, so long as all experiences are welcomed in the treatment room, and nothing has to be exiled (Kiersky, 1998). That is, if certain desires and feelings are not welcomed or not registered in the analysis, not resonated with in order to be understood in the coconstruction of the new experience intermingled with the old, then something will be missing in the analytic story and the analytic experience. The joint exploration must be truly mutual. It cannot be one-sided; a one-person psychology is not enough, because there may be too many experiences that are unknown, unexperienced, unfathomable, as well as intolerable alone.

Gender and sexual identity have a multiplicity of meanings, a range of associated experiences, and a uniqueness for each individual. Gender identity is a component of self-esteem regulation and self-cohesion, and any departure from gender conformity may create threat of embarrassment or shame.

Gender and sexuality are not the same thing, yet each is inter-subjectively fashioned and undergoes evolution and change throughout life. Each is formed through attachment with significant others; each has powerful regulatory and self-defining capacities throughout life. Gender is intimately linked and determined by the patterns and qualities of attachment (Kiersky, 1998).

In the clinical situation, we often see how ambiguous gender is, how easily it can be transcended when, as analysts, we become a father, and then a mother, at times a brother or a sister, or at other times a nongendered voice of soothing to our patients, a function that they cannot as yet do or be. Transference can create us to be gender-irrelevant and gender-free. We enter into this transitional cocreated space with our patients to become gender-assigned, at other times to be rendered gender-neutral. It is in these times that we may have a whisper of the experience of the trans-sexual, where the internal experience may be in contradistinction to one's body. We must remain open to accepting this temporary assignment, to wear it for a while, and not prematurely foreclose the transferential need by forcing it into a container with which we are more familiar or comfortable.

A deep appreciation of gender allows us to disregard as well as to accept its total reassignment in order not to miss the experience of our patients. Boris (1986) exemplified Bion's approach in saying, "If the 10 o'clock a.m. patient is one we know to be a married man in his 30's, we know too much, for how are we to attend to the 4 year old girl who has just walked in?" (p. 162).

Benjamin (1995) comments that as human beings we use an important other as an internal representation, and at the same time respect that person as an external subject with his or her needs. Our relationship matures as we develop the capacity to be "in the middle," rather than entirely separating or individuating. Mature development is not being like an island, but of interactive reciprocal relationships, having some select and essential others with whom varying degrees of intimacy are experienced. The various aspects of being human are not categorically restricted to specific gender. This development continues throughout multiple phases of childhood, adolescence, and adulthood, and includes the simultaneous growth of a plurality of self-experience interacting, of interacting states within oneself, and with the states of important others on the outside.

4

Mindbrain

Our senses define the edge of consciousness and because we
are born explorers and questers after the unknown, we spent
a lot of our lives pacing that windswept perimeter.

Our senses connect us intimately to the past, connect us in
ways that most of our cherished ideas never could.

The brain is a good stagehand, it gets on with its work while
we are busy acting out our scenes.
Diane Ackerman
A Natural History of the Senses

The brain is a dark, silent world filled with life saving illusions.
Diane Ackerman
Deep Play

Every thought and feeling has a chemical consequence; mind is one of the
job descriptions of the brain. With every new experience, and thus every
memory, the brain responds by modifying its connections. Interactions
between mind and brain, psyche and body influence each other (Kolan,
1999). We may not be aware of the implicit duality that we render in
speaking of a "mind" and "body," overlying the assumption that there is
a "self" or "mind" as distinct from a body. Closely related in this assumption is the separation of conscious from the unconscious mind.

Mind and brain are more than partners in a dance, more analogous
to Siamese twins, yet an attempt at any analogy falls far short in depict-

ing the complex relationship and interaction. The nervous system develops its own pathways. When a usual pathway is blocked, an alternate pathway is created. Nature's imagination is rich, for alternative compensatory programming and adaptations occur spontaneously. The mind, as well as the brain, are minutely differentiated in form and function, actively constructing a sense of self out of the myriad experiences of any moment. The ability of the mind to create an organization and an order out of even the most extreme of circumstances and experiences demonstrates the adaptivity and the plasticity of the human psyche.

Conscious and Unconscious Emotion

For emotional stimuli, input comes via the senses to the *thalamus*, which crudely filters it and passes it to the *amygdala*. The amygdala is the structure of the limbic brain that gauges the emotional meaning of something, assigning significance to incoming sensory input.

As the storehouse of emotional memory of personally attached meaning, the amygdala initiates of unconscious process: The assigned *meaning* of sensory input is coupled with basic patterns of response. Automatic and autonomic responses occur on the basis of these couplings, such as fight–flight. The amygdala is designed to detect danger and respond to it automatically, which is typical of any mammal in a fight for survival.

After this automatic and largely unconscious screening process by the amygdala, messages are processed through the *hippocampus* to filter basic experience through higher levels of *meaning* and *memory* to ascribe significance within a context. The hippocampus creates and retains the factual memories and patterns about an emotional experience, while the amygdala retains the emotion that goes with those memories (Kolan, 1999). Unconscious associations are laid down in the hippocampus. This processing through the hippocampus of the context of events allows sorting of meaning: a snake behind a glass container in a zoo is differentiated from a snake on the ground, coiled to attack; a hand of friendship on the shoulder is differentiated from a hand placed to initiate an attack. A traumatic event may create a new coupling, for example, a hand on the shoulder as the beginning of a rape experience and generalized subsequently to any hand on the shoulder resulting in a feared response. The *associations* of "free association" emanate from the emotional *linkages* in the amygdala and the *meanings* assigned by the hippocampus.

From the hippocampus, where an experience is put into the memory system indexed as to the meaning assigned, information is then processed through the *left* and *right hemispheres* of the *frontal cortex*, which are the conscious mind. Here in the conscious mind, emotions, emotional memory, associations, and structuring is ordered, and recontexualized in complex representations. Working memory, conscious associations, reason, and logic all reside in the frontal cortex. The amygdala receives sensory input and initiates a variety of bodily and emotional responses even before this input has been processed by the cerebral cortex, the logical and conscious brain. The amygdala activates readiness, including increasing blood glucose, heart rate, muscle tenseness, and alertness. At the same time, the message goes to the cortex to process the information and fit the responsiveness with what is known, and the representation to fit with other known information. This pathway through the amygdala initiates a response prior to involving the logical systematic thinking brain, and allows us to respond instantly and think later, to have emotional responsiveness and even emotional learning without consciously knowing what we are responding to, even as we begin responding to it.

This process is the unconscious processing of emotion. This neurological pathway describes explicitly some of what Freud was speaking of as unconscious emotions. In this way, we have responses without knowing exactly what it is we may be responding to: the unconscious processing of fundamental emotions. That concept has received considerable criticism, for how can one have an unconscious feeling or an unconscious fantasy? The answer refers to neural pathways of automatic autonomic responses not immediately processed in a cognitive way to have understanding of meaning and significance. This template is operative in the many experiences we have throughout the day of having a "feeling that just happens" without being aware of what it is that stimulates sadness, anxiety, or some other basic feeling. These "gut feelings" and "intuitions" about a person, an object, or other stimuli can be processed often to an understanding, by traversing the neural networks of cortical associations to infer what happened at a subcortical level to reconstruct meanings and significance. Originally intended to protect from danger, evolving in evolution to couplings of various complex patterns of experiences and meaning, these may be useful, or may interfere significantly with emotional learning. An example of such an interference would be a persistence of a pattern of fight-flight, without understanding why, resulting in a generalized phobic avoidance of whatever has been originally coupled with this stimulus.

Memory and Desire

The most fundamental and powerful feelings generated in the amygdala and processed in the hippocampus become the blueprint of attachment experiences and emotional meaning. The circuitry between the limbic system and frontal cortex fashions the conflicts and treaties between mind and body, feeling and reason. When emotion and logic are in full partnership, mind and body developmentally unfold in synthesis.

Although much is known about memory and desire, they both remain in many ways a deep mystery. The medial temporal lobe and the hippocampus mediate declarative (explicit) memory storage: conscious memory for people, places, and things. Procedural and associative (implicit) memory is unconscious and is evidenced in re-creating a process or a performance, such as remembering how to ride a bicycle after many years of not being on one. Procedural memory involves primarily the amygdala, and its foundation of the biological expression of unconscious mental life. Transferences are procedural and associative memories activated in the treatment setting. The left frontal cortex receives, processes, and organizes information in a logical, orderly fashion, and sequentially sorts in problem solving. In its analytical functioning, it is the time-keeper of the brain. The left cortex both categorizes and creates novel images and representations, and manipulates words and symbols to fashion personal and unique meaning for the individual. This is where the ego is located in the brain, where stimuli are sorted into representational elements, categories, structure, and unique, individual meaning.

The right cortex is involved with global, nonverbal, emotional communication and experience. Sensitivity and attunement to emotionality is in the right frontal cortex, but this area has no capacity for analytical thinking.

The brain is symmetrical. The right cortex, the emotional, creatively responsive part of the brain is bilaterally activated along with the left cortex that organizes information in logical, orderly fashion. This bilateral symmetry of activation and synthesis of function of left and right brain is what we refer to as being "present," attuned to internal affective experiences, and objectifying and processing information with an observing ego.

Stress and Trauma

The chemical messenger released by the thalamus-hypothalamus to the amygdala as the first step in the brain's response to stress is corticotropin releasing hormone (CRH). In the chemical response that follows, corticosteroids are released, readying the body's reactivity to danger or stress, including raising blood levels of cortisol. This response influences the amygdala to work to control stress or fear-related responses such as arousal, vigilance, and avoidance (Sternberg, 1999). This feedback loop is intricately linked with the body's immune response as well as a brain-regulated stress response. Too little corticosteroid results in a hyperactive immune system with resultant susceptibility to inflammatory diseases including arthritis, chronic fatigue syndrome, and mood disorders including depression; overstimulation of this axis, such as from chronic stress, will cause excess cortisol, shutting down the immune system prematurely with increased susceptibility to infection (Sternberg, 1999). Fundamentally, stress dulls the body's immune responses, creating greater susceptibilities and infection. The reverse is also true that with enhanced immune response by diminished stress, resistance to such diseases such as cancer is enhanced (Sternberg, 1999).

These released hormones excite the amygdala but inhibit the hippocampus. The amygdala, then, will have imprinted emotional and unconscious memories of the stressful event, even more vividly etched because of the excess stress hormones. These same corticosteroids inhibit the hippocampus and prevent or retard the formation of a conscious, explicit memory of the stressful event. The amygdala, fully functional from infancy, can record stress and trauma in unconscious memory, and the hippocampus, not fully formed until around age 3, cannot record earlier traumatic stress as a specific conscious memory at all. Even later with inhibition, the hippocampus is much less likely to record it with conscious access.

The filing system of the brain records memories in two ways. The amygdala registers emotional intensity while the hippocampus processes time and place. When an experience is highly traumatic, the amygdala overrides the hippocampal function by recording emotional intensity without regard to time and place. When replayed, in an affectively charged "flashback," the traumatic memory is often as terrifying as the original, still timeless and without context. Being able to locate the experience in time and place allows a more accurate perspective, and the detail, perhaps bolstered by photographs, reports, or diaries may help to set the experience in perspective and refocus the memory.

With terror, the particular annihilation anxiety of trauma, sensory information comes to the thalamus, is passed to the limbic system, and the amygdala sends messages to the rest of the brain to activate the noradrenergic system to be alert to the environment. This screening process by the amygdala is done automatically and largely unconsciously. In trauma, certain signals, especially of sensory input such as specific sights, sounds, or sensations will trigger the trauma-sensitized amygdala to send signals that danger exists, causing a fight–flight response. The hippocampus then serves to sort meaning and serve a screening function to ascertain significance. The fight–flight patterns, especially when coupled with trauma, reach deeply into the old brain, the limbic system.

When sensory input occurs that is a trigger of previous trauma, the amygdala reads this as current trauma, sending messages to the neuro-hormonal system to trigger a fight–flight response, so that a physiological response to trauma occurs, even though consciously and logically someone may see the event accurately as nontraumatic in the present moment. The hyperactivity due to trauma is the way that the body remembers: Via the hippocampi memory processing, these traumatic memories are remembered as isolated sensory experiences that are not integrated into a large conceptual and balanced meaning (van der Kolk, 1998). Often these memories exist as isolated sensory sensations with very little narrative or meaning attached, analogous to when a patient wakes up in the middle of a surgery and feels traumatized by being paralyzed.

Trauma and Brain Lateralization

Traumatic memory is lateralized. The lateralization that occurs in early trauma has significant implications in terms of processing subsequent emotionally charged material as well as for treatment. If people get traumatized early in life they deal subsequently with highly charged emotional stimuli primarily by lateralizing to the right cortex, the emotional, nonlogical part of the brain, and lose connection (dissociate) from the left cortex, the rational and logical ego functions (van der Kolk, 1998). This lateralization of processing in trauma patients has been demonstrated on PET scanning and EEG activation (van der Kolk, 1998). Additionally, people with no traumatic background process material bilaterally, no matter how emotionally provocative the stimulus (van der Kolk, 1998). Someone with a traumatic background with a neutral positive stimulus, preferentially processes this on the left side of the brain (tending toward intellectualized responses without emotional connection); painful stimuli get preferentially processed on the right side (tending toward emotional responses without balance of reason, logic, or context). This means that individuals with prior trauma are processing this information with the part of their brain that has the least ability to analyze it and sort it rationally. When this medial–temporal region housing the limbic system gets activated by emotionally charged stimulation, there is little activity (electrical activity and blood perfusion) in the left frontal lobe of the traumatized individual, which is where the ego, the conceptualized self, resides. The left brain is not able to anchor the individual in the present moment to say, "This is a memory; this is the present time." The earlier experience comes alive, not as an earlier experience, but as an enveloping present experience.

Van der Kolk (1998) has found that the specific part of the left brain that gets inactivated when someone experiences trauma is the left anterior frontal cortex (Broca's area), the part of the brain that translates personal experience into communicable language. When a person experiences a trauma, the capacity to talk about it shuts down. That is, as we get close to the essence of patients' traumatic experience, the part of the brain processing experience into words and a language is no longer able to talk. Free association, the notion that talking will set you free, is the very process that is inactivated at stressful times in trauma patients. To urge discussion, to interpret resistance when a patient is unable to process emotionally, may be further shaming and frustrating.

Clinical Implications

We are always reminded that the brain is the organ of mental activity, the house of the mind. We also cannot forget that the mind and the body are not separated in a dualism, as the processes and products of the mind have a great deal to do with the processes and products of the body.

There is increasing scientific evidence that changing one's mind and changing one's emotional experience in intensive psychotherapy and psychoanalysis changes the brain: neuronal connections are rewired, resulting in changes in the way of experiencing, processing, integrating, and understanding emotional information (Vaughan, 1997). Schore (1994) has found that right brain communication of pleasurable affect between parent and child builds neurological structure, a structural change visible by PET scan. Intensive psychotherapy and psychoanalysis bring about substantive changes in behavior as well as structural changes to the brain; the same may be true of psychopharmacological treatment, in that both produce functional and structural change in the brain (Kandell, 1999).

Kandell (1999) cites evidence that changes brought about in the function and structure of the brain by intensive treatment also produce an alteration in gene expression, and these alterations in gene expression subsequently produce structural changes in the brain. Experimental work indicates that changes in long-term memory leads to alterations in gene expression and, subsequently, to anatomical brain changes. Kandell (1999) further notes that in the sensory and motor areas of the cerebral cortex, the representation of body components depends on their use as well as on the particular individual's experience. Structural changes are more readily achieved in the early years of life, as evidenced by the fact that musicians who learn to play their instruments by age twelve have a larger brain representation of their fingers on their important playing hand than did those who started later in life (Ebert, et. al., 1995). These long-lasting changes in mental functions also involve alteration in gene expression (Ebert et al., 1995; Kandell, 1999).

Kandell (1998) states:

> When a therapist speaks to a patient and the patient listens, the therapist is not only making eye contact and voice contact, but the action of neuronal machinery in the therapist's brain is having an indirect and, one hopes, long-lasting effect on the neuronal machinery in the patient's brain; and quite likely, vice versa. Insofar as our words produce changes in our patients' mind, it is likely that these psychotherapeutic interventions produce changes in the patient's brain. From this perspective, the biological and sociopsychological approaches are joined. (p. 466)

In a traumatic experience, the stress hormones excite the amygdala, forming unconscious emotional memories of the event, inhibiting the hippocampus to preclude formation of a conscious memory of the traumatic event. This is a source of amnesia for a traumatic event, at least of conscious, recalled memory of that event. Additionally, the lateralization to right cortex processing is a disconnection from bilateral processing, meaning that where one gets into a changed brain functioning (altered state) to become lost in a feeling state: the disconnection from left (logical, ego) brain means the person is marooned in the right brain, lost in his or her feeling. This is the brain functioning of the clinical expression of state changes, including extreme changes of state in dissociation.

What effect, then, does psychotherapy or psychoanalysis have on trauma? A fear pathway laid down from the amygdala to the cortex influences the entire functioning of the cortex; the cortex, however, by insight and understanding, is relatively less effective going in the other direction to change the amygdala. The function of therapy is to understand coupling of original experience, the automatic assigned meaning, and to create new couplings, interrupting the automatic trigger, while forming new procedural memories in the context of treatment, and to release the charge behind the original experience. This is fundamentally the rewiring of the brain by the mind via relearning. This relearning is initially about having learned emotional association come to life in the process of interaction, especially with the form of transference, in order to create a new set of experiences and coupling, to be laid down as memories in this new story, the therapeutic relationship. Both new and old experiences are vividly alive in the process of treatment. As well, emotional memory experiences, previously inaccessible to conscious awareness, become activated. What happens in treatment is that new emotional experiences are created in the empathic immersion in the therapeutic relationship with its foundation of trust: A new story is created that exists side by side with the old story of procedural memories manifesting as transference, expectations, and emotional and cognitive couplings. The old model and experiences are interpretatively cleaved from the new model and therapeutic relationship: The here and now is distinguished from there and then. In this way, a new emotional experience and context allows information to go in the other direction, from the cortex to the amygdala to rewire the connection of emotional memories, and to create new coupling of emotion, stimuli (triggers), and meaning. New emotional associations are learned, and previous associations are not activated.

Gradually, as this process comes more and more into focus, and the trauma patient becomes more practiced at becoming present, at regulating state changes rather than passively experiencing shifts, the patient begins to know, and then to know *what* he or she knows. Subjective awareness of self and state adds concurrently to the experience of being able to become self-reflective. This is the process of bilateralization, of using both the right and left hemisphere concurrently, as is the case with individuals who have had no trauma and consistently process bilaterally. Bilateral processing allows continuity of all emotional experience (right brain) over time, state, and context (left brain).

That we create our own individual and unique life stories in a day-by-day, moment-by-moment way has been demonstrated with research findings about the consistency of an individual's central organizing themes regardless of the type of stories they create. Fantasy stories, memories from the past, recall of favorite childhood stories, and the stories of dreams are thematically consistent across all genres for their unique central organizing concepts of themselves (Vaughan, 1997). For example, someone who has been abused and neglected early in childhood will fashion scenarios and repetitions of victimhood, perceive and fantasize about it, actively seek validation of the abuse, and emphasize the perpetual quest for freedom. However, their reality orbits around their central organizing assumption of victimhood and suffering, an assumption that is both conscious and unconscious.

Allowing a different experience, an immersion in understanding and creating a different lived experience, and change of patterns in the psychoanalytic relationship permanently alters the brain (Vaughan, 1997). Neuronal interconnections change and new neural networks are created in response to intense, sustained emotional immersion in the clinical experience. A new lived experience and current story are synthesized, while understanding and having activated, side by side, the central organizing concepts of the self and of important others from infancy onward.

This procedural, associative memory, especially in the context of the lived experience of the interaction with the psychoanalyst, is classically referred to as *transference*. The development of the new experiences in the interactions between the patient and analyst creates new sets of both implicit and explicit memory. The transference, the old story of procedural memories, becomes activated within the new story and "relational knowing" of the therapeutic relationship. That is, while the new procedural memory is being created, the old procedural memory is also being activated, so that there is the juxtaposition of the new and old stories, side by side, both alive and vivid.

Both Sander (1997) and Stern et al. (1998) have developed the idea of moments of meaning in the interaction between patient and therapist that represent the creation of new implicit memories that allow the therapeutic process to move to a new level without necessarily having conscious insights, but rather changes in experience and behavior that rearrange the patient's procedural strategies for being, relating, and experiencing in a different way.

5

Body–Mind Memory in Development and in the Clinical Exchange

You can always rely on your body for memory instead of your mind. Your body will tell you the right thing. That's the way I've learned theater—by being told to trust my stories, that they're valuable, but also to trust my body, that when it moves and I make a sound, whatever comes out is the truth, or the first thing that comes out is the most creative thing even if it sounds wrong or stupid or not politically correct or boring.

Peggy Shaw
Bomb

What is remembered is what becomes reality.

Patricia Hampl
Memory and Imagination

Of all the body's 11 systems, only two, the immune system and the central nervous system, store memories. Both have a central role in distinguishing self from nonself. Just as the immune system remembers some of what the body has forgotten, the mind stores memories unknown even to itself. Immunological memory, as specific as for one tiny virus, lasts a lifetime; lymph nodes, the hard drive storage site of the immune system, have a large megabyte capacity as a repository of infectious–immune memory. If the immune system fails to distinguish self from nonself, autoimmune disease results as the body rejects this perceived alien component. The immune system can only store memories of previous events; the mind can create memories of events that have never occurred (Krueger,

1998). Many things can distract the memory storage of both the immune and nervous system, including drugs, malnutrition, stress, infection, and age. The fundamental mission of the memory of both systems is the same: to protect and to inform. Each of two body systems that have memory, has a central role of distinguishing self from nonself. If the immune system fails to distinguish, by not recognizing nonself, the result may be a cancer; the body misperceiving an aspect as nonself and rejecting this alien component may result in autoimmune disease.

Memory Systems

There are four distinct memory systems: working memory, explicit (episodic) memory, semantic memory, and implicit (procedural and associative) memory (Baddelly & Hitch, 1974). Working memory, or recall, is distinguished from the three longer term memory systems.

Working memory involves the storage and use of information for short periods of time of less than ½ minute. An example is holding items, such as telephone numbers, in mind. Working memory is assessed by the digit span test on mental status examination, and referred to as *short-term memory* or *recall*. Damage to the prefrontal cortex produces working memory impairments (Shimanura, Janowski, & Squire, 1991), as does disruption of physiology of the central nervous system. Working memory integrates perceptions of the moment and combines them with prior information stored about past experience and knowledge (Fuster, 1997).

Explicit or *episodic memory* is the recollection of specific instances from our past, of factual information within a particular spatial or temporal context (Tulving, 1983). This conscious memory of facts and ideas is the snapshot recalled at a particular time or place, such as an event last year or what was served at dinner last evening. Explicit memory requires conscious encoding and conscious recall, and involves the frontal brain and hippocampus. This is the "screen memory" or incident that may represent an entire process otherwise inchoate, wordless, or formless.

Semantic memory, the associations and concepts underlying our general knowledge of the world, is a fund of knowledge not dependent on contextual cues for retrieval (Tulving, 1983). Recalling content from a general fund of information, such as how many months in a year, or who was the president during the Civil War is the retrieval of semantic memory that is not dependent on recalling the context or the particular episode of learning situation in which the information was acquired. Semantic memory seems to be distributed in its storage throughout a number of neocortical areas, and even to be mediated by a neurobiological system distinct from other memory systems (Heindel & Salloway, 1999).

Implicit memory is a combination of procedural memory, the working knowledge of skills and procedures/processes, and associative memory, the connection linking schemas when neural networks are activated (Weston & Gabbard, in press, a). Implicit memory is an essentially unconscious form of memory expressed through specific operations comprising a task or the repetition of a process. An illustration of procedural memory is the acquisition and retention of motor–cognitive skills such as riding a bicycle, a task that can be remembered many years later without any subsequent cues or relearning. Another illustration is recreating complex behavioral patterns, such as the type of attachment pattern experienced as an infant re-created precisely both with one's own child two or three decades later as well as in significant adult relationships, including transferential.

"Transference" is one recognition pattern we have for procedural memory, in which perceptions, regard, associations, and relational patterns from earlier development with significant caregivers becomes activated in the clinical exchange. Procedural memory can exist despite significant deficits in other memory systems (Heindel & Salloway, 1999). Procedural memory is present from birth, and requires no conscious process of recall or awareness of remembering while one is engaged in a process. Procedural memory is a combination of emotional memory (amygdala and hippocampus with frontal cortex) and motor memory (from the basal ganglia). These emotional (associative) memories are the interactional sequences and patterns of the process of experiences and relationships.

Memory is not a particular entity or "thing" stored in a particular place in the brain, nor is there any particular neuron that stores a memory (e.g., of mother). Memory is a "process of neuronal firings along units of a particular memory system" (Beebe, 1999). There are many memory systems, and more than one system may be involved with each memory. While memory is a process, the retrieval cue can be a "thing," and may trigger a memory in any of the systems of memory.

In the analytic situation, the analyst can be the retrieval cue, some specific aspect of the analyst, what is talked about, or something that is sensed by the patient about the analyst, an unconscious perception. Old experience activated intermingles with the new analytic experience. Memory is coconstructed, meanings retranscribed, and memory and its uses are transformed.

Loren Eiseley (1971) writes in his essay, "The Brown Wasps" of the 60 years a particular tree had taken root in his mind as an image of home, discovering later that the sapling cottonwood had for 60 years been growing in his mind, though not in reality.

> I have spent a large portion of my life in the shade of a non-existent
> tree. It was without meaning, though my feet took a remembered path.
> In 60 years the house and street had rotted out of my mind. But the
> tree, the tree that no longer was, that had perished in its first season,
> bloomed on in my individual mind, unblemished as my father's words.
> 'We'll plant a tree here, son and we're not going to move anymore.
> And when you are an old, old man you can sit under it and think how
> we planted it here, you and me, together" (pp. 235–236)

His memory of the tree "was part of my orientation in the universe and I
could not survive without it." His memory was nostalgically revised, as
nostalgia airbrushes memory to set it on an idealized stage, remembering
the past as better than it was (Krueger, 1998). This memory of the ideal
rather than the real may be defensive as well as serving important selfobject
functions, as a formative component of internal ideals.

Although we spend much time on explicit, symbolic memory, it is
the procedural and associative memory amalgamated with the cocreation
of new procedural experiences and associative links that may offer most
promise of incremental change in the analytic situation.

Making Memories

The amygdala plays a vital role in emotionally charged memory, mediat-
ing emotional responses by coordinating incoming information between
the thalamus and the cerebral cortex to match sensory cues with expressions of feelings. The hypothalamus governs the autonomic, automatic
response to such feelings as fear, and the conscious processing of emotion
takes place in the frontal cortex (LeDoux, 1996).

Memories have to be encoded in ways that they can be retrieved.
Engrams, the stored fragments of an incident in memory, contribute to
our subjective experience of memory's experience and meaning. Engrams
are not the only source of the subjective experience of remembering. Various patterns of connections, words, images, and concepts are activated
by a specific request or stimulus to remember. Without the query to stimulate, the engrams remain dormant until certain cues awaken them from
their quiescent state to enter awareness. Each of the senses can be a tripwire
for the emotions and can carry us to past experience. Proust smelled a
cookie and 1000 pages later was still remembering; a picture calls up an
entire era; a sound brings powerful experiences to center stage. Each of
the senses has memory, as does the body collectively as a whole, and our
mind is a composite of memories of conscious and unconscious, of physical and feeling, and of multiple states of mind.

We perceive and encode experiences and perceptual images, and organize these by affect (Reiser, 1999). Neurobiology furthers this notion that perceptual images and associative connections are mediated by the corticolmbic system that binds the images to the affect originally accompanying the experience (LeDoux, 1996). That every experience encoded in the brain is filed, always and inexplicably, with the affect connected with that experience, means that affect organizes memory, a fact that is crucial and fundamental in the clinical situation. Core memories organized around experiences, especially early experiences, become more powerfully linked with greater intensity of affect. This affective organization of memory heightens the meaning of the use of free association in the analytic process, as affective connections to important conscious and unconscious experiences are accessible in this way of following the thread of detail for the theme of affect.

Retrieving a memory is an act of reconstruction, such as conceptualizing a dinosaur from bone fragments. The reconstruction of the dinosaur and the real dinosaur are not the same thing, but may bear a resemblance to one another. One who remembers the memory and the subjective experience of recalling the past event are related, but are distinct. The stored fragments of memory contribute to the conscious experience of remembering, but the active remembering is more comprehensive. An experience in the present resonates with a past experience, and the two form a stereoscopic view to construct a memory. The memory constructed is different from the past in that remembering is a present experience. The subjective experience of the rememberer is the combination of the retrieval key activating the engram, set on a current stage of here-and-now experience. Remembered feeling is present feeling. This stereoscopic view of feeling changes experiences of both the past and present, continuously evolving. Feeling that is remembered today incorporates the view and subjectivity of feeling that is remembered of the past. Memory is a continuously constructed experience and evolves with its own storyline. Memory is also cocreated in the intersubjective arena of psychoanalysis. One vivid demonstration of the mutual influence of cocreation was a statement by a patient, "My mother of this analysis is different from the mother of my first analysis."

Memory, rather than a picture of the past as exact replica, is more about connecting neural networks of engrams stored in the brain with current patterns of experience that activate this engram. If the pattern of current experience is similar enough to a previously encoded pattern, remembering will occur (Schacter, 1996).

Some of what we do in sharing a memory with someone else is to go to the common, shared engrams that will elicit the experience; we keep going until the friend's memory is jogged or we find a common ground.

We scroll through various signifiers of experience, as a search engine does in a computer, to retrieve material until we hit on a cue for a mutually recognized experience. Two subjectivities come together in shared experiences finding common engrams, usually an objective aspect of the experience, such as a specific event. In the process of analysis, new experiences and new engrams are created as the narrative of the new, lived experience of analysis develops. All memory is in some way a re-creation of previous experiences of self or self with others. Although sharing a meaningful experience together, at times two individuals may not be able to find corresponding or shared cues to elicit the memory due to the two very different subjective experiences.

Lived experiences encode implicit and explicit memory. The patterns of needs and caregiver activity are experienced and organized, as well as categorized, generalized, and even abstracted primarily into procedural memory, with icons of episodic memory. Memory is an attempt to impose order on the environment. We are always engaged in the ongoing activity of categorizing and recategorizing both our experiences and events as we perceive them in the world.

What may be the most central activity in the entire process of analysis is that which is also the most central joint activity of a caregiver with a child: the mutual regulation of state changes (Stern et al., 1998; Lichtenberg, 1998). State refers to ego states, the states of consciousness and awareness incorporating an entire spectrum of feeling experience. Initially, an infant's fundamental states regulated by a mother, include hunger–satiety, sleep–wakefulness, activity–rest, arousal–calmness, degrees of social contact. With evolving maturity, more complex states are added to these regulations of physiological and psychological needs: affiliation, attachment, exploratory-expressive, adversarial, and sensual-sexual (Lichtenberg, 1989). The state specific experiences, the meanings attached, and the movement (regulation) between states blend seamlessly into one another in normal development. When a state becomes distinct and extreme, such as terror in response to trauma, the particular state may be dissociated, to be experienced and recorded in a different tract of the brain; state specific memory and state dependent learning within that state may not be remembered in a different, more relaxed state.

Accurate attunement, recognition, and matching of these different states arouse the infant to perceive and record relational knowledge, accurately identify and arrange self experiences, ultimately to internalize the process of state changes for internal regulation. Mutual regulation occurs between mother and child, as well as between analyst and patient, and this regulation has significant impact on the making of memories within each state of mind.

Traumatic Memory

In the course of normal development, the amygdala becomes functional before the hippocampus (Eckman, 1999), so that traumatic memories early in life may not be explicit memories, only emotional, procedural memories. Unlike early psychoanalytic beliefs of infantile amnesia, brain development rather than conflict is largely responsible for the failure of explicit memory prior to age 3 or 4. Contemporary neurobiology has demonstrated that repeated or ongoing psychogenic trauma actually impacts and injures the hippocampus to disrupt its function (Brenner, 1996).

With experiences of trauma, memory imposes itself with certain unpredictable and unforeseen triggers. At times the triggers are not always apparent, but may be subtle and symbolically related rather than explicitly linked. Some part of the memory may be evoked by a visual or other sensory cue only peripherally related. Certain "flashbulb memories," such as remembering where we were at the time of hearing about Kennedy's assassination, or when the Challenger exploded, are etched in memory in the freeze-frame fashion of a shocking event. These deeply etched memories, especially ones of personal trauma, demonstrate the persistence of personal memory, especially when coupled with highly emotional experience. Emotionally charged events are commonly recalled as a repetitive, intrusive replay.

Inescapable traumatic memories, though vivid and detailed, are also subject to distortions, errors of perception due to high emotional charge, and may be prone to change over time (Schacter, 1996). An example of memory distortion involving the body can be seen in a psychoanalytic case reported by Good (1998). An adult woman had a recurring traumatic memory of having her clitoris removed when she was 5 years old. Due to recurrent and repetitive dreams involving the removal, Good recommended that she have a gynecological examination to further explore this matter. The examination showed that she was anatomically normal, that her clitoris had not been removed. In exploring this early childhood fear so vivid as to become a memory, the patient recalled that between the ages of 3 and 5 her highly religious mother made her wear a device to make it physically impossible for her to masturbate. The highly charged emotional context of this event created a source amnesia, a difficulty in distinguishing between an actual and imagined event.

Schacter's (1996) comprehensive work, *Searching for Memory: The Brain and the Past,* concludes that actual emotionally traumatic events, generally persistent, often quite accurate and detailed, are also at times prone to decay and distortion, especially with the passage of considerable time. The theme of these extensive studies is that memory is not simply an activated picture, moment, or impression in the mind, but is a complex construction crafted from multiply determined sources, internal and external.

Memories of the past are often encoded within the state of mind of the individual at that moment in time, which may determine many aspects of the perception. For example, Williams (1992) reported on overgeneralizing autobiographical memories of severely depressed patients. Memories encoded by quite depressed patients are biased toward negativity, general negative themes, and current incidents that fit with prior negative experiences. Their tendency to encode and retrieve through a negative filter creates a repetitive bias of perception. The PET scans of these depressed patients also show reduced activity in the left frontal lobe fitting with the disproportionately larger amount of right frontal lobe (emotional) processing.

Mood-congruent retrieval, a term used by some research psychologists, is roughly analogous to the term used by trauma researchers of *state dependent memory*. The mood-congruent retrieval is somewhat broader, and has grown from numerous experiments that demonstrate that when one is in a sad mood, there is broader access and persistence of remembering negative experiences. The research from mood-congruent retrieval has important clinical applications, as these biases, due to prevailing mood, may distort the accurate memory and perception of childhood as well as current experiences, skewing toward negative perception and processing (Schacter, 1996). Thus, the regulation of affect and state in the treatment context is essential, as the state of mind determines what is perceived, processed, remembered, and integrated. Likewise, patients with chronic pain recalled the degree of pain they experienced in the past directly as related to the degree of their current pain level (Eich, Reeves, Jaeger, & Craff-Radford, 1985)

Psychogenic amnesia is the temporary loss of memory usually caused by a psychological trauma. This loss of explicit memory of particular episodes or even of personal information from the past is usually motivated to temporarily escape or to sequester an overwhelming or intolerable experience. Psychogenic amnesia, characteristic of dissociative states, can be quite delimited and specific, such as when emotional stress is associated with a specific event or a specific theme, and memory may be lost for that experience only. When new information is encoded in a particular state of mind, whether a depressed state, or from a drug or alcohol altered state, it is remembered more accurately and fully when that particular state is re-created. In its more vivid extreme, state dependent retrieval for a dissociative patient aligns specifically with state dependent learning/encoding.

In dissociation, an emotional state being induced, for example, by terror, creates an altered state of consciousness in a different tract of the mind with a split-off stream of experience, memory, consciousness, and thought that is state dependent in its learning/encoding and state specific in its retrieval. Though information and experience often overlap, or have crossover between tracts, in extreme situations there may be full detachment from conscious awareness. Dissociation is such an important and often unappreciated issue in psychoanalytic treatment that it will be explored separately in chapter 9.

Contemporary neurobiology has eliminated some specific areas of clinical and interpretative application for psychoanalysis. A model recognizing both conflict and deficit must also consider the effects of stress on memory formation by patients with a history of trauma, to consider the timing of therapeutic interventions to "strike while the iron is cold" (Yovell, 2000). Patients with a history of trauma have a hypersensitive amygdala and exaggerated cortisol response to emotional stress overwhelming their hippocampi, rendering them unable to process some of the best interpretations at a time of stress or dissociation (Yovell, 2000). We must continue to monitor and modulate the level of affect for each patient to take into account this interplay of amygdala and hippocampus. Conflict driven repression of emotionally painful memories from a psychological perspective is a different vantage point from the neurobiological view of a compromised hippocampus and hypersensitive amygdala (Yovell, 2000).

Changing Memories

Two kinds of knowledge and memory are both experienced and constructed/reorganized in psychoanalysis. One is an explicit or episodic memory of specific events and instances; the other is implicit, a memory of procedures, associations, and processes. Explicit memory is conscious, represented symbolically and verbally, and often in analysis is focused in terms of content and meaning.

Implicit, procedural knowledge is about processes, about lived experiences of interpersonal relationships, such as what it is like to be with and interact with another person. This implicit process, this relational knowing can also be represented by certain symbols and representations. A theory of interaction focuses understanding on the entire system. The coconstruction of a new story within the analytic experience of two individual subjectivities begs an understanding of how new stories are constructed by two quite different people. Interactions at the overt, verbal, symbolic level have been given significant attention, while interaction at the implicit procedural level has received much less attention. The implicit, procedural interaction is less quantifiable, objectifiable, and may be both nonverbal and invisible.

Implicit procedural memories suffused with emotion organize transference expectations (Simon, 1991) and organize emotional themes and continuity from childhood into adulthood. It is at the implicit procedural, often nonverbal level that powerful emotional themes sometimes expressed by face, action, gaze, vocalization, and body create nonverbal organizing principles (Beebe, 1999). The breadth and range of explicit memory offer icons of conscious continuity with the past, while procedural memory provides the present moment with continuity of informed experience, perception, sensory, and cognitive input.

Each activation of the memory system of the patient is a coconstruction based on verbal or nonverbal, internal or external cues from both the patient and the analyst. As a coconstruction, each activation of the memory network is a new construction, an amalgam of the network and the cue, an interactive event (Eckman, 1999). This interactive mutual reconstruction of memory allows for new experience, the interweaving of old and new stories to create new experiences and incremental change. This new construction is a combination of the old experience and the new experience side by side, offering the possibility of change by cleavage of the two to be more purely inside the new experience. By memory being interactive and coconstructed, it is altered and transformed each time it is retrieved in the analytic process.

In the early phase of analytic work, the analyst needs to understand how (and if) an image of the analyst and the collaborative work can be evoked and sustained (the degree of object permanence and corresponding evocative imagery). For patients with significant developmental arrest, we may discuss how long a state of calmness after a session lasts, how long and in what ways can the patient sustain the continuity of the mental representation of working and being together. For example, for certain patients, when there is a disruption of a long weekend or vacation early in treatment before there is this self-sustaining capacity becomes permanent, I have discussed whether taking something from my office, such as a book or object, may be a tangible way to represent the continuity of our work together: a kind of "transitional object" to remind and to sustain. Some tangible object may be the sensory anchor for continuity when evocative memory of a consolidating self structure is not yet permanently formed developmentally, or is vulnerable to emotional disruptions. Analogous to the toddler's blanket to preserve a symbolic connection with the mother in order to make excursions away, the concrete object becomes an icon of the attachment bond to sustain continuity until it becomes more permanently internalized.

We remember that which fits our expectations, that which is part of the theme, the plot of our lives. An entire population may look at a portion of the earth and see dirt; an archaeologist may look at the same dust, see a significant pattern, and uncover meanings from another civilization. When certain themes, familiar patterns, and central organizing concepts change, then the past as well as the present changes. This is not an "ah-ha" experience, but a process of looking back, and looking forward, and both look different. To reintegrate in the present, patients often find that their past also changes, that they no longer view the past in the same way. The entire mosaic, rather than selected tiles, is in full focus. A patient who had organized her childhood memories around trauma and neglect reflected at a point in the termination of our analytic work: "My childhood looks more normal now, not always centered around problems or what wasn't happening. I realize I was only looking at the painful, the negative. I see the whole picture better now." Conversely, other patients may be able to know, finally, how very painful and traumatic aspects of their childhood actually were, now that it does not have to be disavowed or dissociated, and they no longer are alone in dealing with it.

Memories are not all that we possess of our childhood and earlier life; we retain these lived experiences and their transmuting influence by how they have shaped our lives and influenced our own development and destiny. These conscious and unconscious expectations form the magnetic poles around which innumerable bits of present experience form patterns of a life story. Psychoanalysis, the coming together of two people to make a new life story for one of them, becomes the substance and outline for a current text of meaning, and informs future anticipation. Ways of remembering are multiplied as an autobiography is constructed and reconstructed. Collage is assembled into coherent composition, transforming interior landscape.

Ferenczi (1932/1988) indicated, "The patient is not cured by free-associating, he is cured when he can free-associate." Lacan (1977) added, "The patient is not cured because he remembers; he remembers because he is cured."

Stories and their themes keep us from feeling lost, they are handles to grasp when the passage of time is associated with decreasing memories. The stories of our lives become our lives. Memories are always constructions. Some patients search hungrily, longingly for memories; others are trampled by memories. The illusion that photographs will remedy creeping uncertainties speaks to the predictable unreliability of our memories. Our autobiographical memories are complex constructions of forgetting, remembering, and creative organization. We continue an internal dance with those truly important in our past, memories with their own echoes, and how possible or impossible to fully come to the end of our past remains in the balance.

As psychoanalysts we are constantly reminded of memory's fallibility, that we will never actually know in fact what happened during our patients' childhoods; yet we can reconstruct the past from the lived experience, the procedural memory blossoming within the analytic process. Rather than being retrieved, as in an archaeological dig, the past is continuously reconstructed in the analytic process. Procedural memories are activated and reconstructed within the subjective experience of present remembering in the context of a relationship with the particular analyst. Certain memories may be sustaining and organizing, incorporated into self-concept, with significant disruptive consequences associated with change. Interpretations, classically the comment by the psychoanalyst to make the unconscious conscious, are designed to change and to rearrange conscious knowledge in the patient. The process of the intersubjective interchange, the relationship, rearranges implicit understanding and knowing. This "new story," the implicit "relational knowing" reorganizes both present and past. In this application, psychoanalysis must embrace general systems theory, and incorporate the concept that applying a new context rearranges the system (an individual mind, or more broadly, an individual self as well as the external systems in which the individual is a part). A new pattern is established for a new experience, which also affects already established patterns by altering them in a unique way. Every element in the system then undergoes a change. What is considered interpretation broadens from highlighting unconscious manifestations to a broader range of illuminations and distinctions. "Interpretation" includes distinguishing past from present, formulating a developmental step/process/model as distinct from earlier experiences; empathic, interpretative focus may also be on aspects of a patient unseen or disavowed, to crystallize in words and concept a pattern of relating, enacting, or experiencing in the transference–countertransference. A procedural memory transcribed and activated into the present process in these and many other ways is a broad definition of transference.

Transference being procedural and associative memory that is activated in the analytic relationship is simultaneously simple and complex. Some aspects of this new shared implicit knowing and relational experience will remain implicit, some explicit. It changes both patient and analyst as well as the shared intersubjective creation.

The moment in which past, present, and transference experience within the analysis come together for interpretative recognition, an "ah-ha" moment, is rare, often illusory, and mythical in actual experience, paling, in comparison to the many, continuous "present moments" with shared experiences, back-and-forth discussion, collaborative knowledge, and exchange that is both complementary and mutative. These moments of change appear as another step in an evolving process, another line in an ongoing story, collaboratively coauthored with the patient as point of reference/protagonist. Present moments center around affective experiences of integrating knowledge and insight by an empathic bridge of analyst to patient, the internal prototype of the bridge.

This implicit knowledge, this relational knowing, is not only making conscious that which is unconscious, but is creating a relationship that omits nothing of the patient's experience. The analytic exchange is, in part, a combined process of painting in Day-Glo orange that which is camouflaged in habit, and creating new meaning, new experiences, and perhaps even new contexts of experience. This change of internal system for the patient is concurrent with a new intersubjective system being created mutually by patient and analyst. It is participatory, two real people focusing on the experiences (at least out loud) of one person and of the patient's internal system and the cocreated analytic system. The analyst is always working, always looking internally, always aware of internal experiences, contributions, biases, and values to attempt to inform yet to keep in the background in order for the patient's meaning and experience to be in the foreground. Change occurs in this intersubjective context of creating a different experience, an implicit experience/knowing/memory built into the course of analysis and ultimately into the process of this new story.

In a psychoanalysis, together with a patient, we create a new experience, a new intersubjective environment, and a particular range of states of mind that contain different states of consciousness termed by Stern et al. (1998), "implicit relational knowing." Stern and his study group who studied the process of change, indicate:

> If in the course of playing, the mother and infant unexpectedly achieve a new entire level of activation and intensity of joy, the infant's capacity to tolerate higher levels of mutually created positive excitement has been expanded for future interaction. Once an expansion of the range has occurred, and there is mutual recognition that the two partners have successfully interacted together in a higher orbit of joy, their subsequent interactions will be conducted within this altered intersubjective environment. It is not the simple fact of each having done it before, but the sense that the two have been here before. The domain of *implicit relational knowing* has been altered. (p. 909)

For example, a child is perched on a diving board at the community pool, looking over to his parents for an approving and confirming moment. He sees that the parents see him; he is thus invigorated to a new level, to go to the end of the board, and, looking again, sees the affirming response, the belief of the parents in him. The anxiety as he moves to the end of the board is juxtaposed with his newly emerging expansiveness; a look to the parent to see reflected back the belief that he can do it regulates his affective state enough and joins with his exploratory motivation enough to contain anxiety/excitement to take the plunge. The entire experience becomes a point of reference for future departure and expansion. This shared moment, this sequence of affective and intersubjective experience, though the child is doing it alone on the diving board, is now internalized as an increment of procedural memory of the child's confident engagement with himself and with his parents; his sense of self is now altered. Perhaps it is also retained as an explicit memory icon.

So too, in analysis, it is this stream of "present moments" that creates internal changes. It is in the moment when the patient looks or listens for the analyst's belief in him that the patient can indeed move into new territory, take the plunge into the unknown experience, allow an uncharted feeling, seize the moment in a fully affective, authentic way.

It has long been argued that affect is a more dominant determinant of behavior (and consequently, of illness) than are ideas and concepts (Ostow, 1999). The notion of various researchers, including the Boston Process of Change Study Group (Stern et al., 1998) emphasize the relative importance of unconscious affect over conscious insight, as changes in unconscious procedural memory and knowledge occur during moments of particular emotional meaning. These changes serve as indices of therapeutic process and emphasize the preeminent importance of the unconscious, as unconscious internal representation can contribute to procedural memory and to therapeutic progress without even reaching consciousness (Kandell, 1999). Much of what happens in treatment that is most meaningful, of creating new lived experiences and new procedural memories, is not a product of insight (Stern et al., 1998). This implicit relational experience becomes a new procedural memory. The formulation of a new model, developmentally and dynamically informed, organizes and makes more accessible current experience.

Certain shared experiences become signifiers of a much larger nonverbal process of an entire relationship. Implicit relational knowing, important in developmental psychology in preverbal time for infants, suggests important unspoken, shared experiences of connection throughout a relationship. The representations of these experiences is registered often in interactive patterns (procedural memory) with perhaps only an icon of specific symbolic (explicit or semantic memory) form.

The implicit knowledge of how to be with another, patterns established early in life, get redefined in psychoanalysis. The old patterns manifest in transferences, and it is not only the transference interpretation that is a mutative knowing, but the new lived experience alongside the old/understood recreation of the past. It is how we are able to make coherent these new lived experiences that creates a change in the patient, not only in how they proceed and know, but how they are conceptualized. Oliver Sacks (1998), a neurologist, in speaking of psychoanalysis, spoke of retranscription of the mind and brain being the fundamental activity of psychoanalysis.

Even when the actual experience of the analytic relationship does not come under direct scrutiny, it is still contributory to change relationally and implicitly. Of course, implicit relational knowing occurs for both the patient and the analyst. The past becomes reorganized, and the present is actively shaped in a new manner. Reassembling the present invariably changes the past. New experiences activate new neural firings, creating different spatial patterns in the brain (Freeman, 1994).

Time looks forward, memory backward. The more time slows, the faster it goes. When apart, the imaginary companion of the psychoanalyst in the patients' mind, and the imagined private conversations that occur as the process and relationship together are internalized, can begin to take the place of the imaginary companions of the symptomatology and the internal organizing assumptions. This shared experience is a new learning experience and assimilation; the new introject of the analyst will gradually become metabolized to be introspection and self-empathy, the personification of self-examination and self-awareness. While initially perhaps needing to visualize, or at times even to hear the voice of the analyst in order to evoke this experience, it will ultimately become more autonomous. This new memory can be used to mitigate tension or painful affect states, as well as to personify hope, and it changes the patient's mind and brain. Vaughan (1997) characterizes the analytic relationship as an affect-regulating function, among other things, that encodes the brain's corticolimbic system by a slow alteration of connection between neurons, allowing mastery over troubling emotional states.

We teach the past at least as much as being taught by it. The past is made tangible by our specific recollections of its instances, and by its reconstruction. We habitually take the old road, not always for the illusory mastery of repetition, but at times to see the same thing in a new way, revisited from a present life experience: the same thing now looks slightly but surely different.

We are always remodeling our memories, revising them as we review them. The stories we tell about our past become our past. Psychoanalysis is replete with transcription, day-to-day updating, and remodeling of the fundamental software of the mind. Memory is constructed/reconstructed/coconstructed simultaneously and continuously.

PART II

Developmental and Clinical Integration

*The novelist may be the last to know the theme of her
work, may even have avoided thinking about it too
particularly, lest, like happiness, it disappear on too
close examination or seem too thin and flimsy to live.*
                    Diane Johnson

*It has been asserted that we are destined to know the
dark beyond the stars before we comprehend the
nature of our own journey.*
                    Loren Eiseley
                    The Unexpected Universe

*If you do not expect it, you will not find the
unexpected, for it is hard to find and difficult.*
                    Heraclitus

*Reality has a way of hiding even from its most gifted
observers.*
                    Loren Eiseley
                    The Unexpected Universe

*The body is merely the visibility of the soul, the
psyche; and the soul is the psychological experience of
the body. So it is one and the same thing.*
                    C.G. Jung

6

Somatic Symptoms: Conversion, Psychosomatic, Somatic Action, and Somatic Memories

It is easier to fall ill than learn the truth . . . so take care of your maladies . . . they always have something to tell you.
M. Pavic

The sorrow that has no vent in tears makes other organs weep.
Henry Maudsley
19th Century English Anatomist

The unconscious speaks more than one dialect.
Sigmund Freud

It can be said that every muscular rigidity contains the history and meaning of its origin.
Wilhelm Reich

Moments when she came home to her body in ways she never had before—moments when she felt its aches, varicose veins and wrinkles so intimately and gently that she groaned with a happiness she could never describe. Fleeting seconds when Vivi knew that her body, in all its imperfections, was her own lived-in work of art. She lived there and she'd die there.
Rebecca Wells
Divine Secrets of the Ya-Ya Sisterhood.

Born equally of muted fear and hope, every psychologically based symptom gives disguised voice to the feelings it hides. A symptom both reveals and conceals, making very obvious to others what one is hiding from oneself, continually engaging what one attempts to flee. Thus, every symptom is a secret hiding in the open, a way to obscure from the self that which eventually becomes very evident. A symptom is an answer to a question its creator has not dared ask consciously, a story line with its own developmental history, its own psychodynamic scenario, with multidetermined defensive (repetitive) and compensatory (developmentally restitutive-reparative) intentions. Every symptom embodies the hope of taking uncertainty out of the future by freezing time, using a model of the past. The body is a Rorschach onto which fantasies, meanings, and significance are projected, both as a surface and as a cavity (Dimen, 2000). As an idea as well as a fact, the body is container and conduit of the emotional.

Symptoms substitute a paradoxical illusion of mastery: to cure an absence, to remedy the loss of mastery (helplessness), as well as to defend against emotional pain. Mastery of the original absence or toxicity is always impossible since it is no longer the past. Symptoms are an attempt at a cure, a local anesthetic. The story of the symptom includes the theory motivating the symptom, the psychodynamic scenario in which the manifest symptom is embedded, and the internal and interpersonal impact that begins long before it happens and ends long after it is over.

A symptom carries various enigmas: that every fear was once a wish; that we construct defenses so that we unconsciously sustain contact with what we fear; that we make the object of desire and fear the same so that we can run away from it and engage it at the same time; that fear guides toward, yet masks desire (Phillips, 1995).

Symptoms manifest as the tip of the iceberg of defensive structures and of compensatory structures. A defensive structure, such as denial or intellectualization, is designed to protect from painful feeling, or to maintain nonawareness of a painful aspect of the self. A compensatory structure is one designed to repair or regain a defect in the self, to fill in a developmental need, and undergoes a development of its own (Kohut, 1977). Structure refers to their stability and continuity over time, and that both defensive and compensatory structures undergo their own development over time.

Conversion Symptoms

Conversion symptoms have classically been regarded as psychic energy displaced (converted) from mental processes to somatic expressions in order to provide more acceptable expression for repressed forbidden impulses. The bodily expression, speaking in somatic lexicon, combines forbidden impulse and defensive forces. In this manner, psychic energy is converted into somatic expression, bypassing the repressive and condemning barrier of the conscience. Originally associated with hysteria and a fulcrum around which psychoanalytic theory evolved, conversion was historically a model for psychopathology and for the theory of neurosis.

In the conversion symptoms of Freud's original hysteria, in which the body substitutes for some essential conflict, the conversion becomes what Lacan (1966) describes as a "symbol written in the sand of the flesh." Breuer and Freud (1955/1983–1895, p. 57) originally demonstrated that remembering, with feeling attached, removed the hysterical symptom. That is, when mind and body were bridged by feelings, the symptom was no longer necessary to symbolically express conversion, or to somatically link the two as in psychosomatic symptoms.

While Freud founded his psychological theory on the biology of the body and traced psychic processes to their biological origin, he paradoxically and unfortunately moved to a more delimited focus on the purely psychological. The unconscious became the recipient of warded off affects, the storehouse of symbolic representations. Freud then became more interested in the content of the unconscious material. As such, the representational system became more exclusively that of language and its symbolism; somatic language became regarded as a displacement for unconscious processes. Language involving the body has traditionally been viewed in psychoanalysis as defense, displacement, or at best, regression from other fundamental affects such as guilt, anger, or anxiety. These expressions-discharge through the body were seen as avoidance of feeling and thinking within the analytic session.

Conversion is an active process, a somatic expression of feeling or conflict with unconscious scripting on the tabula rosa of the body. Whether the "stiff neck" that may symbolically represent a forbidden erection, the total body shut-down of catatonia archaically countering aggressive discharge toward the world, or such highly specific manifestations as unilateral ptosis (Krueger, 1978), conversion synmptomatology can occur along an entire gamut of psychopathology, not just hysteria (Rangell, 1996). Hysterical conversion is a nonorganic dysfunction of a body part or sensory organ that takes on an unconscious symbolic meaning and malfunction, though without physiological damage. Conversion disorders follow an idea rather than an anatomic distribution. Untenable emotions and unbearable thoughts are converted into bodily expression, usually in a symbolic yet simple way: if one cannot bear to see something, hysterical blindness results. Another example may be an impotence deriving from guilt, the somatic obstacle as penance for a desire viewed as taboo or illicit; or, in a more archaic psyche, impotence as protection from a fear of fusion with the partner in merging of the body sexually and losing individual identity or even dissolution of the self (McDougall, 1989).

Conversion symptoms and psychosomatic symptoms both share the failed integration of body self and psychological self experience. Both are attempts at adaptation while at the same time are defensive functions, both contain messages, and both *are* the message. The body is used to represent or to express fundamental affect states that have been insufficiently represented and differentiated internally, which it may have felt dangerous or unacceptable to communicate to essential others with reciprocity and understanding. This failed or disrupted empathy results in the exaggerated use of the body in order, adaptively in its intent, to bridge internally to otherwise elusive experiences. The integration (or failure thereof) of body self and psychological self follow closely with Freud's (1915) metapsychology of affect when he designated three potential transformations of affect: conversion hysteria, obsessional neurosis, and actual neurosis. McDougall (1989) added a fourth: a psychic foreclosure of mental representation in which an affect is stifled in expression without experience or recall. The adult version of this paradox is that while a psychosomatic symptom is an attempt to buffer or protect from emotional damage, it could also endanger one's life.

The feelings of the self are not readable when there are no corresponding words; the body must then express in its own language the feelings, tension, and conflict. Often bored and having little tolerance for feelings, these patients have a propensity either toward passive retreat, listlessness, and depression, or in pursuit of activity designed to dissipate tension, distract from an internal awareness of feeling, or to fill an emptiness.

Alexithymia is a difficulty in psychologically processing emotions (McDougall, 1989) so that individuals who do not accurately identify emotions, and have not distinguished among various specific feelings, cannot differentiate emotion from somatic or cognitive experience. They are not defending against feeling, for feeling is not registered, identified, differentiated, and experienced as distinct from action or somatic expression. Unidentified emotions remains undifferentiated, subject to experience and expression only when coupled with actions or somatic expression. Emotion may only be experienced when imbedded in an action sequence or somatic scenario. Thus, individuals who have not fully activated this developmental capacity due to lack of accurate and empathic coconstruction of experience with an attachment figure may be able to only identify broad categories of feeling, such as feeling good or bad, or may express a feeling within a somatic concept, such as feeling fat or ugly. Or the perpetual focus of these individuals will be on others, on how they are perceived, and on the incessant reporting of activities and interchanges.

In the early months of life, long before an infant has evolved to a mental representation of body image, and while the infant is still experiencing his own body and the mother's body as a merged unit, he has intense somatic experiences and somatically develops ways of relating to significant others (Stern, 1985). So much communication is by means other than language. For individuals who have not developmentally distinguished mind from body, and not differentiated feelings in order to either verbally communicate or mentally represent them, expression may remain in a somatic realm. One of the significant challenges for someone whose body self is ill defined or unseparated from a significant other, is to give voice and find a language for undefined feelings and underlying fantasies for which there are no verbal links. A significant developmental achievement is to create verbal links for mind and body, to bridge right (feeling) and left (logic) brain experiences.

An analytic patient recalled that her mother did not want her to come home for her wedding, instead to have it at her university chapel with only the immediate family attending. As Joyce described this, she noticed herself getting fuzzy, confused. She couldn't remember the details, and even wondered if this were an actual memory or something that she made up in retrospect.

We focused on the instantaneous disconnection and fuzziness, and as she regained her present ego state, we refocused on the specific feeling that seemed to trigger it. She had noticed that she was actually feeling hurt for the first time that she was not invited home by her mother to be married in her home town, in her own church. She described her experience. "It's like changing the radio station a little: when the voice over the radio is from a clear signal, exactly on the channel, it's like changing the channel slightly to not get it clearly and specifically; I instantly stop the feeling. My vision even gets a little blurry." She associated to having a high pain tolerance, that if her doctor told her that something would hurt, she would "change" the station. Rather than having a high pain tolerance, she now recognized this as a state change.

We explored specifically the beginning awareness of her blurry vision. She recalled it first occurring when, as a girl, she would see the hate in her mother's eyes. She visually blurred her clear focus to protect herself. Many times the mother would rage at my patient, occasionally hit her. Joyce thought she needed glasses as a girl, yet never had difficulty seeing clearly in settings with no emotional trauma, such as in her classroom.

Other patients may blur one or more of their senses as a disassociative conversion as a means of certain protection. One patient had had ringing in her ears at emotionally charged times, ultimately recognizing this ringing as a kind of white noise that would buffer the sharp piercing words of both parents when they were in alcoholic rages. She had been through many medication attempts and changes, none of which seemed to work because she had identified the ringing in her ears as a side effect of many of the different medications, resulting in their discontinuation.

Blurring, dulling, or averting sensory input as a type of conversion reaction is quite common in disassociative patients. Everyday variations abound in all individuals. For example, why does someone never look at themselves in the mirror when they are mad? A patient responded to this query, "I am afraid I will see someone who is not lovable. I am afraid of seeing my mother." This patient, who had suffered from migraines, the "hate headaches" directed at herself, spoke of the mother inside, from whom she constantly sought approval, yet hated. She was just beginning to recognize her identification with the aggressive aspects of her mother; the only way that she could participate in the power of her mother was to align herself with her. The contempt she had for this identity with her mother became directed at herself, contained within the migraine headaches. The past, intruding unbidden, seemed more real than the present.

Psychosomatic Symptoms

The body's language has many dialects, many subjective (as well as some universal) translations of psychic messages into dramas on the somatic stage. Every psychosomatic symptom embodies many elements: hope, attachment coupled with the defiance of intrusion; compensatory effort for what is missing developmentally; repetitively creating that which, paradoxically, is most detested; and as a defense against the painful and unknowable. Each psychosomatic symptom brings together mind and body. When experienced and expressed directly and fully, feelings form the bridge between mind and body so that psychosomatic symptoms are no longer necessary. Coltart (1992) noted that a psychosomatic symptom remains unconscious while at the same time disguised in somatic code.

Psychosomatic processes may be derived from complex psychic scenarios, internal "scripts" written in earliest attachment patterns and experiences, to later be enacted on the theater of the body (McDougall, 1989). The narrative of attachment patterns may be given form in the body's language of illness. If a parent is unattuned or unresponsive to emotional cues, but attends to physical problems, the child's effectiveness in eliciting response may center on physical maladies. If somatic disturbances, visible and palpable illness, physical accident, weight disturbance, substance abuse, or other visible forms of self-harm or physical neglect result in more predictable parental response, the attachment pattern that is effective becomes etched in the mind of the child. The success, or intermittent success of response, speaking to the most basic motivation of effectiveness and mastery in evoking responsiveness, heightens the probability and internalization of a specific interactive scenario of physical expression of need and distress. Farber (2000) notes how a crisis of illness and being cared for, most predictably with self-harm or repeated somatic symptoms, will mitigate toward a "career" as a medical patient with pain and suffering, attaining to engage with others via illness. Speaking through the body in self-harm may develop an identity as a mental patient, elaborating and verifying an internal organizing assumption of defectiveness projected onto the body.

Contemporary psychosomatic disorders have been viewed from two primary theoretical positions regarding cause and illness. Hans Selye (1946) saw disease as the result of physical and emotional stress, resulting in a physiological response from the continued exposure to nonspecific stimuli. Selye's theories have been reintroduced currently through psychoimmunology, the relationship of stress on the immune system and resultant disease formation. The other ancestor of psychosomatic medicine is Alexander's (1950) specificity theory: Just as certain pathological microorganisms have a specific affinity for certain organs or systems, so also particular emotional conflicts possess a specificity for certain organs or symptom profiles. The classic psychosomatic illnesses studied by Franz Alexander (1950) include bronchial asthma, essential hypertension, rheumatoid arthritis, gastric ulcer, ulcerative colitis, neurodermatitis, and thyrotoxicosis.

We have come to know that while psychosomatic illnesses are the expression in the body of some emotional process, they do not necessarily have symbolic meaning nor are they linked with specificity of conflict as was once believed. More recent research has not supported the theory of specificity (Stein, 1986). Stein emphasizes that the notion of specificity still persists, but emphasis has moved from a psychological causal specificity to a specificity within the individual that is quite complex and involves psychological, central nervous system, neurotransmitter, endocrine, and immune systems necessary to understand psychosomatic disorders.

McDougall (1989) has indicated that when an adult unconsciously perceives body limits as blended with an important other, if body memories of early psychic trauma are mobilized, the result may be a "psychosomatic explosion," as if there existed one body for two people. Psychosomatic illnesses may secondarily have the result of defining a formless or contentless experience, such as defining body boundaries by cutting or rubbing, or defining the body's internal content experiences by bingeing and purging. Some pain from illnesses, as well as pain induced by the individual, may be internally organizing, the sensory input affirming aliveness. A contentless state of boredom or emptiness may be countered by some specific pain or illness, as reassuring as it is distressing. The psychosomatic symptom also serves to delineate from an enmeshed other: The parent cannot control the body of the child with anorexia. With an overly intrusive parent who may seem to control the body of her daughter, or regard it as an extension of her own, a symptom such as anorexia specifically communicates the limits of the mother's influence. Her words do not make the daughter eat. The daughter affirms her unequivocal area of the privacy of her own body, and also insures contact with her mother, exaggerating the attachment (usually at a time of lessened attachment, such as beginning adolescence, leaving home, or when parents are divorcing).

Case Vignette 1

A 40-year-old man, whose mother died by suicide when he was 16, described his difficulty in mourning a just-ended passionate and torrid affair with a married woman. He was struggling actively and painfully with letting go of this woman, wanting to hold onto the relationship and friendship even after the sexual affair, ended by her, was over. He also complained of rheumatoid arthritis, diagnosed by his rheumatologist as a "reactive arthritis," resulting in his inability to move freely most of his adult life.

We worked in treatment initially on understanding his affair, of his motivation to engage in it, and on his considerable difficulty in giving it up. He focused on wanting an exclusive, special friendship with this woman, to be important to her. It became gradually apparent to both of us that the woman of the affair had served the function of missed developmental experiences of adolescence, especially of validation of his sexuality and manhood, derailed by his mother's suicide in his early adolescence. The mirroring and admiring of his adolescent self and sexual development, and consolidation of a sexually maturing body self with psychological self was reworked with this woman. Ultimately, he recognized needing to "let go" of his "tight grasp" of this idealized woman, ultimately of his mother, mourning his missed developmental experiences while allowing himself to experience his rage at both women for abandoning him.

As he allowed these feelings, his body could finally "let go" of his rheumatoid symptomatology. The relationship with the married woman of his affair had become the stand-in for his mother, as he idealized both in a similar way, and maintained hope of a better ending with the current woman, one in which he could end the relationship yet remain close friends, an adolescent emancipation foreclosed prematurely with his mother. This married woman, like his mother, embodied the obstacle of taboo and unattainability, and with the obstacle fully in place, he was free to desire. As he allowed full expression of feelings and integrated body self and psychological self, the psychosomatic bridge between body and mind was no longer necessary. His rheumatologist took him off of medications as his arthritic symptoms gradually yet totally abated.

Psychosomatic pain may be itself a reassurance of identity, of containment within a body delimited by pain, which then forms the basis of subjective experience and identity. The pain itself may be the communication of feelings and experiences that have not been desomatized in order to achieve symbolic psychic representation.

Somatic Action Symptoms

Various configurations of subjective experience are encapsulated by concrete sensorimotor symbols and actions that have a primary purpose of bridging the dichotomy between mind and body in specific and tangible ways (Atwood & Stolorow, 1984; Stolorow & Atwood, 1992) These actions involving the body may serve an array of psychological purposes from restitutive to defensive functions. Various forms of action may predominate to concretely link mind and body, to bridge left brain and right brain in order to maintain an internal organization and cohesive self-experience. Examples include the use of substances such as food, alcohol, drugs, sexual or physical activity, or some other substance, person, or activity to bridge this duality. In these physical or sexual action symptoms, the body is used to go back to the beginning, to evoke fundamental sensory perceptions and physiological awareness of the body self. The bodily register is a proxy for emotion, yet provides a way to primitively engage a core body self and regulate tension. Since these means are effective but temporary, an addictive potential exists.

For someone who has experienced a trauma and currently has an emotional trigger, feeling lost in the experience, trapped in a state of nothingness or depression, building a bridge from being marooned in the feeling state/right brain to connect via concrete bodily and sensory experiences to logical reasoning/left brain, the body may be the vehicle used to craft that bridge. Various sexual enactments, physical actions such as exercise, or the use of the body in other ways including cutting or bingeing on food are attempts to build a bridge to create a reunion with the body self. Aubarch and Blatt (1996) and Fonagy and Target (1998) agree with my prior findings (1989a) that self-stimulation, self-mutilation, and other action symptoms directly using the body become a way to regulate or establish the basic awareness of the body self, and to create representations of mental states/experiences via the body when a cohesive representation of body self and psychological self has been disrupted, or never developmentally established.

Someone lost and "stuck" in a feeling state (marooned in traumatically induced unilateral processing of the right brain), may create a bridge of sensory experience via the body to the left side of the brain. Examples include exercise, bodily mutilation, or other physical stimulation that creates a somatic bridge from right to left brain. Other anatomical and sensorimotor engagements include interpersonal dramas such as sexual actions or perversions, the link with a self-object of various genres, or simply the use of one or more of the senses. For example, when someone is bored or feeling empty, going outside to look at the sky, smell the flowers, touch the grass, hear a bird, and sip on a beverage engages all five senses, perhaps building a sensory bridge to reconnect internally and feel more grounded. Eating disorders are so appealing perhaps in part because the process simultaneously engages all five senses. Bodily and sensual experiences, and associated fantasies, can create association of right and left brain, an internal reconnection to change the state of mind, and restore balance of self, mind, and body. This bridging between mind and body, actually and metaphorically right brain and left brain, create (or restore) a sense of self. For some, the least tolerable experience is affect without an object, to immediately yet artificially couple it with food, sex, drugs, or alcohol to provide an external focus.

For an alexithymic or dissociative state, attempts to render these experiences into some defined awareness of fundamental grounding and sensory perception often results in somatic action symptoms. Stimulation of the body's senses creates awareness in an initial attempt at reestablishing cohesiveness via the body self. Other addictive behaviors may use some substance to stimulate the brain or to create somatic sensations to an intensity to register somatically, such as drugs or pain-seeking behaviors. Some somatic action symptoms consistently serve this purpose of providing form and sensation.

Case Vignette 2

Ann's hard work in analysis allowed her to recognize that her weeping eczema throughout early childhood expressed her own tears, a longing for a mother who reportedly never hugged or held her, who by report of family and friends did not hold her in the nursery the first 10 days of

Ann's life until other family members cajoled the mother into not abandoning her infant daughter. By report of family members, the mother was depressed, and also disappointed that the baby was not a boy. This skin irritation throughout childhood delimitated Ann's body boundary, reassuring distinctness and the resultant hypertrophied boundary of scarring outlined her own space. It also forced her mother to touch her, rubbing salve and medication on the eczema. In the relative absence of emotional responsiveness, she had continued that native language of her body, the syntax of physical malady recognizable by her mother, a nurse: the eczema of weeping skin, the asthma of crying out for her mother, and the gut spasm at times of separation.

As certainly as it was neglected in infancy, her mouth continued as her perceptual pathway and attachment insurance. Her exclusive focus on this sense organ drew an emotional curtain across awareness of all other senses. Her procedural memory continued to make eating the source of her most intense and gratifying experience, her original and continuing maternal proxy, the territory of her initial hunger for her mother's skin, taste, and connection.

She asked, "Why do I chose an area (eating at a specific time of the day) to lose control in order to create a sense of control in my life? I work all day long to not eat symptomatically and deny myself food: I am successful at maintaining control (not eating candy, etc.) during the day. I am the architect of my discontent. I choose a time of the day, as well as eating to seemingly take control of my life by specifically losing control at that time."

Ann's mother loathed people who ate too much. The mother's aversion to Ann showing any of her needs was perceived quite early. Ann recognized that eating too much was an engagement with her mother, who showed critical, predictable concern.

Even now in her 50s, Ann still struggled with the paradox of trying to create the sense of control by circumscribing this specific area in which to lose control. At certain times she would eat food for which she knew she had an allergy, and then have a toxic reaction. The conflictual battle was now internal between her body and the toxic insertion.

Ann also recognized her difficulty in conjuring an image of her mother when she was away from her unless she would do something exactly as the mother did, or to exactly replicate a pattern involving the mother to activate the image of her. She was visible on the mother's radar screen only in certain action sequences, such as illness, and thus could only see herself (and her mother) when replicating these same action configurations. She could evoke the image of her mother in the symptomatic use of food, a familiar and predictable attachment pattern of critical engagement.

Feelings, perceptions, and experience seemed tied to this early behavior, and she used food alternately to disconnect, and to attempt to
reconnect her mind and body, to push away from a significant other (her
husband) in doing the opposite of what he wanted (losing weight) while
preserving the bond, she believed, by avoiding anger via eating instead.

Many of Ann's phobias had to do with leaving and separation, such
as getting on a plane, or at times getting too far away from her house. At
the beginning of analysis, she continued a lifelong practice of rubbing
and scratching her forearms, often enough to cause rawness and bleed-
ing, always concealed under an elegant dress or blouse. She explored the
various feelings for which this practice had given expression: discharging
anger, an alternative displacement for frustrated sexual feelings, at times
to become more somatically grounded when she was disconnected. From
earliest memory, though not conscious at the time, the repeated scratching had also established a boundary: the scab. "The scabs were comforting; they were where I end." She also recalled experiencing satisfaction
that it was her area of privacy, causing frustration to her mother, as she
could not get Ann to stop scratching herself.

Ann had felt invisible to her parents, making it difficult for her to
then see herself. She particularly felt visible to her parents only when she
gained weight and they became critical, or when she had a specific illness. The failure to have her basic developmental needs met led to her
conclusion of badness and defectiveness, affirmed to her by her parents'
critical attitude toward her. Ann gradually recognized that she saw herself as bad in order to protect and preserve the illusion of her mother as
good, as well as to hold a hope of some remedy. Her belief in the mother's
goodness pervaded her fantasy and regard into almost her sixth decade.
For example, she still experiences surprise when her mother says something that is unkind or toxic to her. Though every experience she has had
for six decades should inform her otherwise, she has handled incoming
input by having two tracts in her mind dealing with her mother: hope in
one tract, experience in another.

Ann explored in analysis her excess weight as a way to be very visible to others; the irony was that in being overweight she was ignored by
others, essentially invisible to them as a woman, another layer of unconscious motivation. When she had lost weight in the past and became
thin, she felt invisible to her family, though more visible to others, and
this visibility of her womanly body felt threatening. As she pointed out
both the irony and the confusion of this, I indicated to her that it was
confusing only when she used others currently as her point of reference
and source of validation, an attachment pattern of considerable familiarity.

In one analytic session I asked how much weight she wanted to lose.
Then I asked how much her mother weighed. Astonished, she said, "The

amount I want to lose is exactly the weight of my mother: 140 pounds. The real person inside me is thin, has energy, is powerful. I have covered up that person with this other person."

I added, "Like your mother didn't see the real you, as if you were invisible."

"Now I see that is absolutely true. I thought previously that she didn't know the real me. It's hard to think so much of my life has been taken up with trying to be seen and loved by her. I've carried that judgmental, critical aspect of myself with me, like an albatross, all my life."

I said, "It seems you've carried your mother with you all this time, trying to get her to see your real body and real self, hugging you all the while."

"Yes," she said, "the hug I never got is perpetually there. Also, I'm thumbing my nose at her when she tried to get me to lose weight as a child, and I'm doing the same thing to myself now when I begin to lose weight. When I feel better, I gain it back."

"Perhaps when you would begin to lose weight and get anxious, it is like separating from your mother before you could get what you needed from her."

"That's possible. When I talk about eating it's as if there are two people inside me deliberating about eating. It's as if there is a powerful person inside me compelling me to do what I do not want. These two people are not in alignment. That judgmental, critical past is inside me too, like my mother. And then eating would relieve the tension to reinstate something familiar, her concern about my weight. If she were not concerned about my weight I'd be invisible to her. I never saw my father seeing all of me either, though I tried so hard to get him to admire me."

I resonated with her hope that her weight would protect from visibility, yet she was holding onto, preserving, even insuring the assumption of being flawed. She saw the multiple paradoxes, including that she would have to maintain the weight in order to maintain the hope that she was a thin (good) person.

As she lost weight, she became anxious, experiencing the separation anxiety from her mother, moving away from the familiar and comfortable home base within. Additionally, eating symptomatically instantly relieved the anxiety, as well as providing a symbolic nurturing. I indicated my understanding of how it relieves that anxiety by physically and emotionally reinstating a familiar place, a reunion with the mother inside her head. She remembered feeling invisible to her mother unless the mother was concerned with weight.

"I have made a person out of eating, a powerful presence that is threateningly powerful (especially since I am so big), but it is not comforting anymore. That person is angry, scary. I have given that person the power to make me sick. I know when I eat symptomatically now, and it's usually something that will make me sick, such as chocolate to create a migraine, or ice cream since I am allergic to milk. I can stop bringing a committee of people to the table with me to engage with them each time I eat. I was always mad and poked in the eye whoever wanted me to be thinner: my mother (who loathed people who were overweight), my father (who weighed me weekly at his office), more recently my husband, and now (at least as I perceived it) you.'

Her question then became "How can I get in touch with affection and love and keep it separate from sex?" She had attempted to cleave sensual and sexual under the cloak of obesity; sex became danger, making it safer to hide her sexual self. I indicated her desire to separate the two, making sexuality unavailable to herself, so the question now might be, "How do you reclaim your experiences and needs without having to partition off any part, to not abandon yourself and leave empty the space where those feelings need to be?" She recognized that she had to tell her secrets out loud to know them herself.

She acknowledged, reluctantly, that she had been filling in all the experiential space around the shadow to see what, in its absence and outline, was revealed. She acknowledged that she was also beginning to experience the pleasure of her body, of being inside her body more completely. She recognized her fear of sexuality and womanhood were it not to be camouflaged by excess weight.

She felt anxious with me as she lost weight. The remaining step in her analysis to lose the weight also threatened our separation. Giving up the mother melded onto her body would be giving me up as well, crystallizing the mourning of what might have been, as well as of what she now experienced in the analytic present.

Excessive weight and excessive thinness both may be enacting through the body a fear of sexuality and sensuality, the antipathy of intimacy, while at the same time, expressing the yearning for affection and attachment via food used as a nurturing selfobject, or in anorexia nervosa by denial of the need for food creating a body so emaciated that it screams for help. Excess weight renders one physically visible, yet sexuality invisible, a duality of conscious and unconscious conflict in each dimension; a shield for sexuality creating a barrier to intimacy, exaggerating the desire for food to fill emptiness and aloneness. By subjugating one's body, needs are disavowed and placed on others who want the individual to lose or to gain weight.

Somatic Memories

Although somatic memories are discussed in a subsequent chapter, the distinction between psychosomatic and somatic memory is important to make. Psychosomatic implies emotion within the body not yet integrated (desomatized) into feeling experience within the psychological self as distinct or pure feeling. In psychosomatic symptoms, emotion is experienced within the body, mediated through the brain, but never achieves independent status as a mental representation distinct from the body. Unlike conversion reactions, somatic memories are not symbolic and are not, like psychosomatic symptoms a somatic expression of affect, but are procedural–associative memories of actual physical experiences. The body, of course, does not store memory independently of the mind, but the experience, processing, storage, and retrieval of somatic memories are registered as somatic events, not divorced from the body, yet divorced from other aspects of memory such as affect, behavior, and cognition.

Procedural memory involves the body as well as the mind, and thus repetitions, at times misleadingly characterized as repetition compulsion, may occupy either the mind or the body, or both. Although Freud characterized repetition compulsions as destructive impulses in *Beyond the Pleasure Principle* (1955/1970) the intent is hardly ever destruction, but self-righting, a belated mastery. The repetition may be to attempt to create representation in a symbolic form that allows language and mastery, to break above the threshold of registered awareness of primitive nonverbal undifferentiated experience and sensation, to create a form to associate with affect, and to infer meaning. Physical illness, conversion symptoms, and especially psychosomatic illness are crystallized when there is disruption in interpersonal relationships, creating an internal disequilibrium. Loss or threatened loss can occur with important external people, important others who serve selfobject functions, as well as with internalized objects (Stephanos, 1980).

Developmental Considerations of Somatic Symptoms

The core of the self is developmentally grounded in body experience (Damasio, 1994). Body experience is an essential and fundamental aspect of emotion; emotion links an individual's mind and body. Emotions are both psychological and biological phenomena; only mammals have a limbic system, the mediator of emotions, and thus, only mammals possess emotions.

Freud called the ego first a body ego and psychoanalysis ascribed the body, and its drives and bodily events, as fundamental to the organization of experience. The problem developmentally is to unify the subjective experience of mind and body through the experiential bridge of emotion. A fundamental aspect of early development is the identification, experience, and accurate labeling of both feelings and body sensations, identified correctly by the caregiver and fostered in the child's verbalization (Krystal, 1988). Affects are originally experienced as somatic sensations, and evolve developmentally via the attuned relationship with the caregiver to be identified, distinguished, and articulated. This is the process of desomatization (Krystal, 1988; Krueger, 1989a). In doing so, feelings become experienced as feelings within a mental state, not as bodily phenomena.

Verbalizing emotion enables us to feel it as well as make it part of our self-regulating mechanism. Making feelings conscious, putting them into words, and describing them to other people, are all part of the mechanism for regulating emotion. This attachment is the means by which we regulate mind and body through the expression of emotion, beginning with regulating the baby's biological–physiological response and reactions. An essential aspect of early development is being somatically visible to parents, to be seen (and thus to see oneself feelingly) through all sensory modalities. This basic regulation of affect and state changes is the most fundamental function parents provide for the child in early development (Lichtenberg, 1998).

Empathically attuned verbal and physical responses by the caregiver serve to accurately mirror the infant affectively and physically to move toward language, and to reflect, capture symbolically, and master these experiences as a way of creating a specificity and subjectivity of distinct feelings with an evolving language. Stolorow and Atwood (1992) demonstrate that the extent to which an individual experiences affects as mind (i.e., as feelings) rather than as a body sensation depends on the intersubjective context and facilitation of the correct identification, labeling and synthesis of affective and somatic experience. This synthesis dissolves the boundary between mind and body at the same time as establishing different levels of distinction between body sensations and affective experience. In the absence of facilitation, feelings continue to be experienced internally as bodily content, as a body state or experience.

The failure of empathic attunement to physical and emotional states disallows one to identify, validate, and specify from an internal point of reference. Failure of this effectiveness of awareness and identification through intersubjective processing of emotions leads to a nonawareness of feeling. If psychosomatic symptoms are effective in eliciting responses, they may predominate. These limitations in articulating and communicating feeling create a defect in reflective self-awareness and affect regulation to soothe and calm oneself, as well as an inability to symbolize feelings and bodily experiences (Aron, 1998).

Affective states may fail to evolve to conscious, symbolically represented and identified feelings because of the absence of validating responses to either the somatic state and reality, or to the symbolic identification in feeling terms; additionally, the subjective experiences may be perceived as intolerable or injurious to the primary caregiver and thus are blocked (McDougall, 1989). The former situation has been described by Krystal (1988) as alexithymic, literally, "without feeling," an impaired ability to tolerate or process emotion, a disjunction between affect and language. The regression to or persistence of psychosomatic symptoms reflect degrees of developmental arrest of affect attunement. The dominance of these psychophysiological experiences becomes central in a regressive transference state, or especially in a disruption or rupture in an empathic bond with the analyst. At times they may gain a central focus when the patient is uncertain or doubts the analyst's ability to express authentic understanding and resonance with these central affective states, as well as when the patient's confidence in the analyst's ability for consistent attunement is shaken or disrupted (Stolorow & Atwood, 1992).

For some of these patients who are unattuned to their affective world, words may not convey their emotion or represent their internal experience, or they simply may not have the words or corresponding psychological representation for some affect states. Barth (1998) describes the difference between the feelings such patients name and the often inchoate affects they experience, and how they often go through long and partially useful analyses but make only minimal changes with some of their most painful symptomatology. This difficulty of putting some affective experience into useful language is subsequently shared by analysts. At times an artificial clarity or premature closure can be developed when the analyst tries to put unarticulated thoughts or feelings into interpretive generalizations or pattern matching of present and past.

Krystal (1988) describes how affects are initially experienced as body sensations and evolve into subjective awareness and states that then become verbally articulated, and this developmental transformation of affects undergoes differentiation and articulation, allowing feelings to be desomatisized. This intersubjective developmental experience of the caregivers' empathy and attuned responsiveness resonates with both affective and somatic states in an optimally accurate manner, mirroring the precise reality of the subjective experience, allowing for the distinct affective and body states to be articulated. This experience of effectiveness also defines and differentiates physical from emotional.

Somatizing patients with impairments in emotional regulation have difficulty in recognizing, attending to, and expressing internal emotions. They may be consciously aware of their bodies, but not aware of the bodily changes as part of emotion. In the most extreme version, they are unable to label the visceral reactions of their bodies as emotions. Their body physiology is highly aroused, though they cannot vocalize their emotional distress and attach symbolic meanings into a language.

McDougall (1989) uses the concept of foreclosure and repudiation from the psyche as an ultimate ejection of an experience from consciousness, a step beyond denial and disavowal, to depict an adult's psychosomatic rather than psychological expression of conflict and psyche pain. This foreclosure of psychological events, leads to thoughts, feelings, and fantasies becoming replaced entirely by bodily experiences. This explanation also describes dissociative phenomena in which the actual process of dissociation creates a different ego state for experiencing, processing, and retaining within a particular state.

Winnicott (1966) spoke of psychosomatic illness as a splitting of the psyche and soma in a regressive move toward earlier, more archaic experience as a defense organization, the depersonalization based on developmental failure.

Winnicott's attempt to distinguish the somatic dysfunction and the conflict in the psyche involves the hope of attachment to an important other through the illness via caretaking. Rather than being solely a defensive regression and a splitting of mind and body, a psychosomatic symptom is often a restitutive attempt to bridge mind and body that have not been developmentally synthesized into a unity. When based on developmental arrest rather than regression, the body and psyche have not been initially integrated in order to later be defensively split or foreclosed.

7

Action Symptoms

Actions, sensations, and states of feeling occurring together
or in close succession tend to grow together or cohere in such
a way that when any one of them is afterwards presented to
the mind, the others are apt to be brought up in idea.
                              Bain, 1872

There is nothing more limiting than actually doing something.
                              Adam Phillips
                              Terrors and Experts

Action: the last resource for those who do not know how to
dream.
                              Oscar Wilde

Psychological symptoms may involve variations of mental activity, defenses heightened or gone awry, or pathological defenses with or without
enactment. Action is not an integral component to most psychological
symptoms. *Embodiment* of a symptom is specific to somatic symptoms
or to psychosomatic phenomena. *Action symptoms*, however, convert
any significant emotion or its signal into a specific action scenario. Action symptoms involve some engagement of the body self experience simultaneously with the psychological self, though not necessarily in an
integrative way. Action symptoms can be to anchor or to avoid. The use
of action may engage the body self in affect regulation, to defend against
feeling, to cause state change, or to attempt integration of mind and body.

Action symptoms are unique, motivated by the hope that action creates change and remedies ineffectiveness; hope is built into the action scenario of averting or reversing emotional pain, bridging mind and body, and perhaps secondarily engaging attachment with an essential other.

In addition to a dysphoric feeling, any particular state, such as emptiness or boredom, can be transformed into action and dissipated. Action may engage the body to create a psychophysiological change of state, or may simply be a defensive move away from the displeasure of registering a psychological experience, and into a tangible bodily action and immediate effectiveness.

An action symptom attempts restitution of a missed or derailed developmental need through some substance (e.g., food, alcohol) and/or some activity (e.g., spending money, sex, a variety of body stimulations), while at the same time defending against painful affect by redirecting and dissipating it into action. Action symptoms are more than remembrance through enactment, and differ from action in that they serve only a defensive purpose; action symptoms are both defensive and compensatory. Action symptoms temporarily regulate feelings and tension states, create the illusion of meeting a fundamental need, and can serve as a symbolic and restitutive self-object function. An action symptom's external focus circumscribes, makes finite and specific, and masters a small portion of the universe to then temporarily create an internal sense of effectiveness. The very choice of the symptom creates both a tangible effectiveness and an invisible prison; ultimately the mastery reveals itself as an illusion and the process is limiting. Once a particular action symptom is chosen, it temporarily alleviates tension but may ultimately, become driven and habitual, foreclosing other options, and may gradually grow into a life of its own in an addictive process, eclipsing more and more of usual pursuits.

Action, perhaps faster than anything else, ends suspense and uncertainty. Though arbitrary and impermanent, it creates the illusion of resolving ambivalence by moving to one side of a conflict and acting on that aspect. For example, if someone is conflicted about intimacy, a flight away from the desire/fear is to move to a perversion, or to an affair, quelling the anxiety of intimacy with a partner. Action collapses the potential space in which feeling and fantasy (and, necessarily at times, uncertainty and confusion) otherwise reside. Inducing a sense of hope, an action scenario provides concrete and specific remedy. The alternative, such as the painful and vague feeling of a developmental hunger, is hard to describe or experience because it is so elusive, so intangible. Action symptoms crystallize the theoretical to a tangible, predictable hope, to developmentally supplement, by proxy, what is missing.

Developmental Considerations

Those individuals who have not developmentally consolidated a distinct, accurate and cohesive sense of body self, have concrete thinking regarding body self and psychological self that is self-referential yet not self-reflective (Krueger, 1989a). Their capacity for abstraction and representation of their body and feelings is only partially developed and differentiated, rendering experience not only unarticulated, but perhaps also unformulated. Some dimensions of internal experience cannot be expressed, because they remain unformulated, never having been resonated with to achieve a representation or symbolism. Focusing on fundamental body experience and sensation via action serves as an organizing function for a self that is vague, fragmented, or incomplete.

Lacking an ability to distinguish the nuances of self-state awareness, these individuals elicit self-representation and regulate affect via the felt experiences of their own bodies. Because a cohesive self-representation has not been formed, their representation of self must emerge from the body self experience, not from a symbolic representation of the body or psychological self. These patients are not primarily denying body awareness and feelings, for they have not developmentally attained, desomatized, and differentiated affect and bodily sensation in order to deny them; they have not as yet integrated mind and body enough to defensively split them. At the time of a current emotional insult, they may feel lost and disorganized, attempting an organizing function by directing focus on the first and the most basic organizer of ego experience and structure: the body self.

At these same times of insult or perceived empathic disruption, these individuals engage in action sequences (action symptoms) that in some way stimulate the body, such as pain, gorging, starvation, overexertion, risk taking, sex, wrist cutting, body mutilation, drug or alcohol use and abuse to subjectively *create* a sensorimotor experience of the body self.

Somatic action symptoms may attempt developmental facilitation via creating a transitional symbolizing function/object as a way-station to integration of mind and body, toward the true formation of symbols with "potential space" for fantasy. The somatic action symptom, such as ingesting or restricting food, may be viewed as a meaningful, attempted adaptation designed to address developmental needs. The entire scenario in which the action symptom is embedded allows understanding of the development quest; the approach from this aspect of motivation and attempted adaptation, rather than approaching from the side of pathology, often fosters collaboration in understanding with the patient.

Developmental deficits in these instances involve a developmental arrest of the body self as well as psychological self: The deficit of body self includes a distorted or incomplete body image combined with a vulnerable reliance on the perception of others, especially physical perceptions. The representation of self cannot be achieved symbolically, but must be through sensory experience involving some bodily stimulation. These distortions occur specifically in regard to the self, as these individuals are often quite intelligent, accomplished, and successful in other realms of their lives.

At the time of empathic rupture in a self-object bond, or the unavailability of a necessary selfobject, the individual attempts to fill the emptiness and restore the bond. An individual may attempt, for example, by an eating disorder to reestablish groundedness in body self experiences via the sensory engagement of eating, the sensorimotor stimulation of inflicting pain by gorging with food, exercising excessively, or starving to induce hunger pangs.

An individual with a defective or incomplete body self (and thus psychological self) is motivated toward completion and restitution of that basic defect (Krueger, 1989a). Kohut (1971) first explained these psychological transactions not on the basis of the underlying fantasy or drive, but on the structural nature of the underlying deficit. His formulations focused on the psychological self, but can be extrapolated to the foundations of body self as well, assisting us to understand self-restitutive (or self-*formative*) attempts according to developmental precedents, current physiological and psychological self object regulation, and fantasy elaboration.

If developmental need experiences have not been met accurately and consistently over developmental time to be internalized, an individual will turn to other means to seek self-organization, cohesion, tension relief, and vitality. For example, the use of money symptomatically, as others may use food, to soothe, to calm, to revitalize, to establish or restore an affective experience provides the illusion of control, of an immediate and tangible effectiveness. Over time, any threat to an individual's sense of cohesion leads them to the same pattern of action symptom to restore that self cohesion (Krueger, 1992, 2000).

When there is a developmental deficit of affective vitalization, or, alternatively, too intense a stimulation, which becomes traumatizing in itself, this action symptom scenario attempts to regulate tension and affect, and to seize control and feel effective in the only means seemingly available at the time. These patients describe their subjective experience as a feeling of being hopelessly lost, with a sense of losing form. Prior to the narcissistic injury, the selfobject had been functioning as a referent and regulator of form and boundary functions, including the experience of body intactness and shape. With the withdrawal or unavailability of that self-object, the patient precipitously loses a sense of form, because when the self-object's boundary-regulating function ceases, she must rely solely upon her own vague or unformed self-representation that does not provide an adequate vessel for a solid, cohesive, consistent psychological self. The incomplete development of body self can be illustrated by projective drawings of the patient's own body image as distorted, prepubescent, and often fluctuating with mood. For example, when the patients feel empty or depressed after an empathic rupture with an important person, their body image drawings would be considerably more distorted from two to four times larger than when they were feeling good and calm (Krueger, 1989a).

The Menu of Action Symptoms

How someone attempts repair or remedy of developmental deficit and the accompanying sense of "not good enough" may be to project it onto the body as being "defective" in some way. The body becomes a Rorschach to make tangible and give shape (and thereby, hope) to hungers and taboos for which there are no words or a language. Efforts can then be made to overcome "defectiveness" or inadequacy by exercising (compulsive activities), losing weight (anorexia nervosa), being more attractive (compulsive shopping), changing the "defect" (plastic surgery), or imitation (of movie stars, admired others). Various attempts to regulate tension, fill emptiness, or counter defect may be to strive for grounding in sensory bodily experiences: compulsive stimulation of the body (sex, cutting, substance abuse, eating disorders), Internet addictions, or other stimulations such as risk taking.

Related to compulsive overeating is the compulsive action involved in losing weight. To become preoccupied with losing weight substitutes one form of action for another. To get very busy at alternate actions involves the same processes as eating: to divert and alternatively focus away from feeling and internal experiences. The accompanying fantasy often is that if an ideal weight is attained, then there would be nothing to worry about. Thus, "weight" tangibly crystallizes a problem to focus on; then, the remedy, the hope, also becomes tangible: to be happy as soon as the number of pounds is lost.

Impulsive action can be adopted as restitution for the disorganization precipitated by a narcissistic injury and is typically directed toward the individual's body. Actions such as bingeing, exercise, or self-mutilation (Farber, 1997, 2000) are intended to stimulate or enhance some part of the body and create an acute awareness of body self sensations.

Compulsive shopping and spending is an illustration of an action symptom that supplements deficient internal regulation and arrested integration of mind and body. The individual who compulsively shops and spends attempts external enhancement of body attractiveness and desirability, hoping to address loneliness and emptiness by engaging others to validate their worth and desirability. This driven activity is often coupled with an expansive mood and fantasy that one can have anything and everything one wants. Augmenting the attractiveness of the body, such as in compulsively buying clothes or jewelry, may serve to validate worth and attractiveness via the desirability of one's body (Krueger, 1988a, 2000). The idealization and unconscious fantasies associated temporarily provide a vitalization and self-cohesion with regulatory and restorative power. Relying on other people for their supply of affirmation, enhancement, function, and esteem, they attempt to find a way to tangibly obtain the source or the promise of these emotional goods, and thereby to counter the anguish of boredom, emptiness, or deadness. The inherent hope of new clothes is the concretized promise of attractiveness of one's body to garner responses and reestablish a bond. Shopping and spending are restitutive and organizing efforts designed to create or restore a perception of body boundary and integrity, validation and affirmation-admiration of the body, and to establish contact with lost self-objects.

This activity is often organized around an unconscious fantasy that once contact is made, the person within that fragile body and self–self-object bond will be complete, and the central organizing concept of the self as bad/defective will be transformed. For some individuals, the most salient aspect of the shopping and spending is the engagement with the sales clerk. The exclusive attention and empathic perceptiveness to the shopper's wishes create a temporary replacement for the disrupted bond that precipitated the shopping excursion. Having developed the capacity for sensitive attunement to others, she can choose a clerk who can provide exactly the right receptivity and responses. One patient described an ongoing relationship with a particular clerk, for almost two decades, a kind of pseudoempathic bond predicated on spending money.

Another related illustration is shoplifting. The individual takes whatever is wanted, and creates his or her own rules with an attitude of entitlement. While this act may be motivated by unavailable financial resources, it is more often designed to take from the shopkeeper whatever one wants, a proxy for emotionally missed "supplies" (Kramer-Richards, 1996).

The narcissistic vulnerability of certain individuals is a common theme, in association with a precipitating interruption in the emotional availability of a significant person who provides some essential psychological function (i.e., a self-object). This change in the availability of or relationship with a significant other can result in the internal experiences of hurt, anger, and disorganization. The narcissistically wounded individual then attempts to control something specific, concrete, and external that directly stimulates or enhances the attractiveness of some part of the body. This is a dual attempt to regulate the affect of a fragmented sense of self, and to restore selfobject functioning.

Another genre of action symptoms includes fetishes with an attempt to be inside the excitement component while hiding the shame component of the conflict. The fetish may be used to link mind and body internally, while being used externally as a bridge for attachment.

Case Illustration

The following case demonstrates some of the common elements and the sequence often involved in the psychodynamic scenario of an action symptom:

1. Narcissistic vulnerability with developmental failure to consolidate a cohesive sense of self with internal point of reference;
2. Core unconscious organizing assumption of badness/defectiveness;
3. A precipitant of the disruption of an important selfobject bond compensating for that missed developmental experience;
4. Resultant fragmentation of the already compromised integrity of body self and psychological self; possibly involving a state change;
5. The compelling desire for affirmation of worth and desirability (to attempt restoration of what is missing via responses from others);
6. An attempt to tangibly give shape and form to what is desired in order to fill emptiness and to defend against hurt and rage;
7. The temporary effectiveness of the action sequence to regulate tension, and to effect a state change, leading to the action symptom becoming addictive;
8. The generalization of the item or activity used to become sufficient alone, as an icon, for a state change prior to ever engaging the item or activity.

Denise had been a collector all of her life. One of her earliest memories was of collecting china dolls, though she did not recall how she came to be interested initially in this particular passion. The essence of her passion for collecting was of being in control, of acquiring, arranging, and rearranging this small universe of possessions over which she as owner experienced entire mastery and fantasy. By acquiring, she felt that she could have whatever she wanted, and created in her own space an entire domain of effectiveness. Denise recalled being enraged at her mother when she would rearrange her dolls, and felt this as an intrusion into her space, her room, her universe, and ultimately by implication, her body.

Denise had been sexually abused consistently from approximately age 3 to age 6 by her sister, four years her senior, who had been abused during those same years by their nanny. When this was discovered, the nanny was fired, and the sister began therapy. Although this stopped the abuse by her sister, neither of them talked about the abuse Denise had experienced. It was not until she was 14 and began promiscuous sexuality that Denise began her own treatment and then recalled the abuse by her sister. Denise, now 43, has evolved expertise in her chosen field as a collector, and her collection has significant value. She continues to spend several hours each day arranging and cataloging her collection. Collecting activity persisted over time and now had transformed to compulsively buying by Internet auction, where she was regularly spending $8 to 10,000 per month from a trust fund. This activity and preoccupation took up much of her day.

Although Denise had been to six previous therapists, some involving several years of work, according to her, none had helped, and the entire process had seemingly inoculated her to therapy, eroding hope that she was treatable. However, she had not been aware, until we began working together, that she was dissociative.

Dissociation was her own way of creating and controlling her own space; she could leave internally by dissociating when she could not leave externally to escape trauma at the hands of her sister. My focus with her on staying with her feeling and experience, and of being aware of the process of disconnecting and changing states of mind, was initially interpreted by her as my attempt to take away her own private space inside her head. She acknowledged that the time she spent online spending via Internet auction was itself an extended dissociation, "zoned out" in front of her computer.

She had attempted unsuccessfully to curtail her Internet spending, but her own relationship to her internal authority was to decide what she "needed" to do, and promptly defy her own authority, rationalizing that she needed to compensate for feeling lonely, empty, or depressed. She would continue at this activity until she was either exhausted or out of money for her monthly trust allotment. The story of her shopping always began with the promise of the activity supplying what was missing, of feeling better. The actual arrival of the items she bought would create a momentary excitement as she touched and held these items: hope given life by proxy, yet a promise never kept.

I indicated to her at one point that when one is addicted to something, the hardest thing to do is nothing. She responded by indicating that she felt worthless when she did nothing. Collecting was the consistent arena of her life in which she seemed to be effective. She had spent her life evaluating things based on the impact it would have on someone else, to essentially give them what they wanted so they would give her back what she needed.

Denise had also been struggling with abuse of food for the last two decades. She described being unable to get out of her state of anxiety and obsessional rumination unless she took action: excessive eating and purging. When she was not with someone, she felt lonely and empty. Her addiction to action was a way of generating experience to register above her high threshold, to experience her body. Nothing short of action would calm her or allow her to exit her anxious, obsessional reverie. She could not think or reason her way out of her obsessional state, and could not understand it while in it. She could sleep only when she completely exhausted herself.

She ate when she was afraid to feel angry, or when she wanted to "zone out" her emptiness. At times she would use food as an attempt to reconnect herself by sensory awareness, to bridge mind and body. She collapsed the potential space in which feeling and fantasy reside when she used the action symptom of eating, substituting for feelings. She recognized that to not abandon herself, to not create the action symptom of eating was immensely confusing; to stay with the process of exploring and tolerating the uncertainty of her own feeling was a new and unknown experience. Eating, and the resultant obesity insulated her feeling and awareness of her own body and sexuality, in her mind rendering it invisible.

Denise has defined herself by needs and motivations not met, resulting in her conclusion of defectiveness, and as if significant aspects of herself associated with this sense of defectiveness needed to be kept in hiding. For Denise, the story of shopping is the promise of supplying what is missing, of feeling better. Hope is enacted, and then purchased in the emblem of new possessions; the actual touching and holding of the items did make her feel better for a short while. She described the initial urge to go on a shopping binge as a desperate yearning for something or someone, an emptiness so vague and formless that she felt baffled about its meaning and driven nature. The compelling urge was to "hold onto something" specific, concrete, palpable, or otherwise she felt she "would burst." As she grew up in her wealthy family, both parents were involved in business ventures, traveled a great deal, and left her and her older sister in the care of a nanny and housekeeper. Her parents gave her much materially, surrounding Denise with the best of everything, and always bringing gifts from their extensive travels and vacations. She reported being "programmed to believe I've always gotten everything I want." She recalled instances when she would go into her mother's closet and cuddle into one of her mother's fur coats, loving the smell and feeling secure inside as if her mother were giving her a hug.

By her 30s she shifted to purchasing through catalogs, as it felt better not to be distracted by interaction with others. By age 40, she began purchasing over the Internet, reducing her interpersonal vulnerability. She was retreating into abstraction, itself a mild form of dissociation, especially when she felt crowded by the memories of her childhood trauma. Her spending on the Internet focused on purchasing china dolls, spending many hours a day on Internet auctions, pursuing the euphoric experience that countered her emptiness. She rationalized that she was building a collection, disavowing how its pursuit had come to dominate her daytime hours. For her, the act of spending was of being in control, of acquiring whatever she wanted; arranging the collection perpetuated the mastery of ordering her own space, the antithesis of the lack of mastery she felt of her own feelings, and earlier of her own body in childhood physical abuse. The dolls themselves represented the return to her preabuse time, the innocence and relative safety she experienced alone with her dolls at that time, having total control over their bodies.

Denise reported that buying something, especially over the Internet and using a credit card was like getting it free. It was as if, for that moment, she felt satisfied, without any thought of future accounting or consequence. She indicated that during a shopping binge, she had recognized her lack of judgment, but at that time her all-consuming focus was on whatever she wanted; she was inside an impulse. Reality would be further removed on the Internet, as well as with a credit card, a symbol of a symbol.

Her symptomatic use of food as well as Internet shopping could, by now, change her state of mind. Cued by any signal of an uncomfortable feeling, dissociation now began with the *idea* of food or of approaching her computer. She recognized that her state change occurred before food ever touched her lips, or before she ever touched the keyboard. The recognition of the power of her mind to create a state change allowed her to disabuse the illusion of the magic of food or Internet.

Somatic Self-Harm

Those who articulate in self-harm use the lexicon of the body in action language to communicate with and about the self (Farber, 2000). The various symptoms of self-harm from eating disorders to self-mutilation creatively attempt to reveal (and conceal) that which cannot be formulated, and may otherwise have no discernable shape or form other than that of how the body speaks.

Behaviors ranging from self-harm, through risk taking, to substance abuse, may take on a life of their own to become addictive. All of these attempts at simultaneous self-regulation and defense involve a route through the body. These various activities and substances used to sooth and comfort ultimately fail as a true self-object/transitional object function, eluding internalization for developmental growth. Someone may use food in binges or eating compulsively, or abstain from food to regulate affect and tension, to feel euphoric, or to dissociate. These varied uses are not sufficient for internalization and developmental growth, as they are reliant on a external focus and on the action scenario.

The body becomes a transitional object and the individual remains within the external focus and tangible thing or activity. Abstract thinking regarding the self and body cannot be furthered within this scenario; they are stuck in the metaphor. While these individuals may be highly intelligent and quite advanced in abstract thinking and symbolic representation about many aspects of the world and people, they remain curiously unaware and concrete about their own body self and psychological self.

While "speaking of one's experience makes it real" (Farber, 2000) the lexicon of the body is used for experiences not symbolically encoded and not developmentally differentiated to be experienced, retrieved, or communicated in verbal language for these individuals. The body speaks through somatic symptoms or gestures, through movement and its senses. In addition to expressive and self-regulatory functions, some somatic scenarios may be the enactment of split off, otherwise dissociated aspects of the self or of experiences. The mind and body are unintegrated: these emotional tallies from inside of the cave of the body may be the encryption of an entire lexicon of experiences.

Various acts of self-harm may become a transitional space of personal autonomy, effectiveness, and control over the body in an otherwise threatening and hurtful traumatic world.

Self-harm that attacks the internal parent(s) both punishes and reassures, reaffirming an attachment bond that may otherwise be sagging or has threatened vaporization. Loewald (1980) noted that internalization is not only of the person, but of the interactional processes.

Action Symptoms and the Clinical Exchange

These experiences, spoken for the first time by the body and not by words, may be experienced other than as a somatic state of sensation only as they come alive within the analytic dyad, and as perhaps only the analyst can give them words. Often these experiences may be ones perceived in a sensing or visceral way by the analyst, reflected back to the patient, to have the patient further shape and refine the experience once having taken it back. Sands (1997) has indicated that patients communicate these unarticulated experiences by projective identification to the analyst in order to have them given back in a way that lets the patient know that the analyst has really "gotten it."

When any of the five motivational systems described by Lichtenberg (1989; Lichtenberg et al., 1992), are developmentally disrupted, action symptoms can be built around a basic developmental need, as attempted restitutive enactments of each developmental need. The five basic motivational systems are the need for psychic regulation of physiological requirements, the need for attachment and later affiliation, the need for exploration and assertion, the need to react aversively through antagonism or withdrawal, and the need for sensual enjoyment and sexual excitement. Each system involves fundamental and evolving components of body self and psychological self and their integration into a cohesive sense of self.

Though often quite successful and intelligent, these patients typically are paradoxically concrete in their ability to describe themselves, their internal states, or their feelings in a meaningful way. They experience a vague sense of incompleteness, emptiness, unhappiness, and a sense that something is missing. They constrict emotional expression, inhibit fantasy, and limit their capacity to symbolize and to play, and though perhaps quite articulate and accomplished, may feel lost when focusing internally and some may not even have a language for feeling (Krystal, 1997). Often there is a specific external focus of symptomatology ranging in presentation from a separation crisis to a specific action symptom or scenario, such as addictions to substances, activities, or people. Lacking a consistent, internally regulated image of a body self and its desomatization to a psychological self, they addictively rely on external feedback and referents, such as other people, possessions, or objects to supplement deficient self-regulation. The process of empathic failures experienced throughout early development may have resulted in an unconscious core organizing assumption of badness or defectiveness (Stolorow & Atwood, 1992), then projected onto the body (Plassman, 1998). Psychoanalytic treatment for patients with early developmental arrests is quite possible, but must address the psychodynamic scenario of the present moment in which the attempted restitutive symptoms occurs, as well as the developmental needs that underlie. A fundamental clinical focus is on the patient's awareness of state of mind, of being grounded in body self and psychological self experience in the present time.

The initial phase of analysis with such individuals is not of interpreting unconscious fantasies, of decoding symbolism, or even initially of interpreting defenses against anxiety enacted in the action symptom scenario. First, the analyst must empathically resonate with and convey understanding of the comfort and investment in their symptom; of its immediacy and magnetic power of tension reduction of the actual relationship; and security with the action symptom as a self-object function; of the difficulty and anxiety in relinquishing the effectiveness of the symptom itself, because it can instantly change the way one feels. Such symptoms often cannot be abandoned as a prerequisite to psychoanalysis, but diminish in intensity and utility over time. Consistent therapeutic attention and empathic listening must focus on the use of the symptoms: the motivation (the attempted developmental restitutive intent as well as tension reduction and defensive purpose), the specific and detailed enactment, and the patient's experience before, during, and after the symptomatic act itself. Focus of the body self and immediate sensory experience may be necessary as prerequisite to awareness of feeling. Then, the use of the action as defense, avoidance of an internal focus on experience to counter painful affect can be collaboratively explored. To register an emotion, one first has to take an internal point of reference and recognize the internal origin of experience. This internal point of reference is quite different from the accustomed external focus of registering on the radar screen of another, or experiencing within an action symptom or through action with a substance, person, or thing. To get inside an experience may not be an accustomed place to be, because an internal point of reference may not be a position usually taken. From an internal perspective, the experience itself must be registered: If developmentally undifferentiated, the rudimentary registration of physical and emotional precedes the differentiation of each. Finally, after registering an emotion, it must be differentiated into specific feelings. This sequence of experiencing a feeling may be stopped at any point, and when internal experience or feeling is stopped, in that space where feeling might have continued can be placed old content, obsessionality, or any number of action sequences or symptoms. The above sequence describes how a patient may not be able to respond to the question, "How do you feel?" Rather, how someone feels may involve the steps outlined as the process to internally reference, index, and differentiate feeling.

Because the patient may not have differentiated specific feelings, an analytic focus on both the somatic and affective experience is needed to help the patient develop an accurate reading and labeling of internal signals. This initial focus addresses an expanded awareness of internal experience that may have been neglected, deleted, or distorted. The experience of effectiveness and the process of empathic attunement can then become internalized by the patient as self-empathy and resumed developmental growth. The potential space between feeling and action, rather than being collapsed by fusion of the two, is created for fantasy, contemplation, and later symbolism.

In more developmentally advanced psychopathology, such as that organized around Oedipal issues, there is an integrated body schema, with more highly organized and dynamically/symbolically significant loss fantasies, such as castration anxiety or immobilization. Unconscious fantasies of losing vital body parts or functions occur in conjunction with emotionally charged relational interactions and Oedipal issues. In those individuals with more structurally intact psychopathology (e.g., psychoneurosis), the fantasies of loss occur without severe threat to a sense of self-cohesion. When body self cohesion and representation are basically intact, symptoms often occur in more symbolic, emotional, and fantasied ways than in action symptoms. At this higher level, actions are more aligned with fantasies, such as "acting out" the fantasy, rather than in fundamental action symptoms as regulatory and restitutive attempts to compensate for a vague or indefinite body self and noncohesive psychological self.

The psychoanalysis of action symptoms is not fundamentally a process of the decoding of symbols, interpreting unconsciousness fantasies or defenses. It is the understanding of developmental and transference phenomena based on a combination of nonverbal communication, adaptations, defenses, accommodation, and the patient's internal object world.

The analyst must resonate and reflect with the patient an understanding of an urge, of how powerful an urge for action can be, of how difficult it is to stay with a feeling and not act, and, further, to communicate that understanding to the patient. Nothing is more compelling than action to end tension and ambivalence. Looking at a decision as a process rather than as an action event may be an aspect of transforming an old story into a new one. The patient will not be able to immediately put action into language, and the analyst must understand that procedural memory is "remembered" (activated in kind), often involving action and enactment. The analyst not taking counteraction, or insisting on the patient talking in feeling language, allows collaborative engagement. Once in treatment, a patient has to be free to speak of feelings in action language, and for neither the patient nor analyst to take away play/work space in which to do it. For example, "I feel like bingeing" or "I feel like running away" must be heard both as an immediate expression of affect in action terms, not to be immediately counteracted or fixed, but to be understood as action language from one pole of a conflict, internal dichotomy, or state of mind. When a patient is free to speak action language, especially when it is registered and reflected in another, action loses its mandate. As one patient aptly observed, "sounding wild and out of control is the antithesis of being wild and out of control."

A contemplative pause between feeling/urge and action may be especially difficult when the two have been fused traumatically, or never differentiated developmentally. In addition, feeling and action may be defensively fused, or defensively remain fused because it obstructs the space in which painful feelings and fantasies would otherwise reside. Empathic resonance and understanding must move along with the patient, into the pain of staying with feeling not foreclosed by action, and creating a space within which self-reflection can gradually develop.

For our patients who select from the menu of action symptoms, who speak the lexicon of action language, such as using food as a nurturing substance, or money as an extension of power or denomination of worth, direct experience has not evolved to metaphor and symbol (though the action chosen may be quite symbolic). Focus on the body self and on immediate sensory and emotional experience is necessary. For a patient so accustomed to action, to instant relief of the tension of a conflict, or to registering experience by somatic action, delay and reflection may initially seem impossible. The difficulty of moving from a tangible, specific focus to an internal, intangible focus on experience and feelings is itself the analytic process. In this transition, attention can be paid to the specific detail of sensory experiences (taste, touch, seeing, hearing, etc.) and immediate feeling. The analyst and the patient must find their own mutually created language and metaphors to reflect what it is like for the patient to think, feel, and experience her own unique aliveness and humanness moment to moment inside her body and in the analytic experience.

We can deal with action and action symptoms in the analytic exchange by understanding the antecedent affect or state, the intent (motivation) and impact of the action to change the feeling or state. The feeling or state has a specific meaning and developmental history, all of which are important to understand. The action symptom has an historical and developmental significance, psychodynamic and symbolic meanings, as well as a direct physiological impact with its use. The common denominator of action symptom weaves together defense, tension reduction, and affect/state change.

8

True Body Self/False Body Self

Conviction is felt in the body.
              Sandor Ferenczi (1912)

The real person inside me is thin, has energy, is powerful. I
have covered up that person with this other person.
              A Patient

Only a fool wouldn't judge by appearance.
              Oscar Wilde

We shall not cease from exploration
And the end of all our exploring
Will be to arrive where we started
And know the place for the first time
              T.S. Eliot
              "Little Gidding" from *Four Quartets*

Winnicott (1971) used the term *false self* to describe the defensive self-organization formed by an individual as a result of inadequate caretaking and failures in empathy, with the infant forced to accommodate to the conscious and unconscious needs of the caretaker on whom he or she is dependent. The false self begins as the infant's own needs are subjugated and continues as developmental needs are omitted or annexed to a parent. The false self is a construction of the individual beginning in earliest childhood when certain developmental needs are not met, such as mirroring experiences being inaccurate or inconsistent. As well, distorted mirroring and toxic insertions may create perceptions and conclusions of inadequacy and defectiveness as a core organizing assumption. This false self is then maintained, despite evidence to the contrary, regardless of repeatedly successful efforts at obtaining validation and affirmation. Achievement and success may be dismissed with remarks such as, "If they only knew the real me," or "I'm fooling them." Success and other affirmations are relegated to the "pretend" mode (Fonagy, 1998), disavowed as inauthentic.

A false body self may be a component of the false self. A false body self is created by inaccurate, inconsistent mirroring responses, and the failure to empathically resonate with and accurately label the full contingent of body self experiences. To look in a funhouse mirror, or a mirror with parts blackened out, results in an inauthentic image. Empathic nonresponse, distorted feedback, compromised sensory stimulation, or shaming responses regarding the interior or surface of the body self may result in an assumption of shame, ugliness, or inadequacy. An overarching protectiveness/withdrawal may exist from infancy forward in such fundamental behaviors as holding, containment, and sensual enjoyment of the body.

These individuals describe the sense of never having lived in their own bodies, never having authentically inhabited them. Their bodies never seem to be their own, and do not become integrated as a seamless aspect of the self. In some instances, eating, exercise, or other self-stimulating physical activities are attempts to create a sensory bridge to feel and to inhabit one's body. A false body self is nonetheless an organization of a semicoherent, often fluctuating body self and image, yet inaccurate and distorted, such as being obese or misshapen, even when not so in reality. Often the actual body is constructed to fit with the false body self, such as literally becoming obese. Not being at ideal body weight is not the same as a false body self, though the two can coexist. An image of ugliness becomes a concretization of self hatred and self disgust.

Only by coming to know, talk in detail about, and experience fully one's body can one see that what was assumed to be a true body is indeed a false body self, that *real* was equated with *true*. In an analogous way, a patient comes to know a false self and all its assumptions by coming to know their true self.

The meaning of the body physically, the body self and its image, and the psychological significance of aspects of the body, take on their most inherent properties, perceptions, and subjective experience from the early relational patterns with others (Meissner, 1997a). Meissner (1997a) distinguishes *body* as the actual physical organism, *body self* as the psychic structure that forms an integral component of the self system, and *body image* as the set of images organized internally into body representations. Bodily aspects of self-representations and self-experience coalesce in the icon of body image. With normal development, body self and image are integrated and in synchrony. Body images are the representations of experienced bodily perceptions and sensations, the amalgamation of specific physical feeling states. In disrupted development, body image can fluctuate wildly and significantly with state of mind, as well as between feeling experiences. Body image is the mental representation not only of the physical self, but becomes inseparable from the psychological self representation including self-image and self-concept (van der Velde, 1985).

Schilder (1959) spoke of body image and implied a singular, complete body image and body schema. Both Fisher (1970) and van der Velde (1985) have challenged this assumption with recognition that body image as well as body perceptions are multidetermined and evolving, at times impartial and incomplete, and even sometimes distinct from body image. Body image can fluctuate markedly in these individuals depending on state of mind and affect changes over the course of a single day, with sequential body image drawings illustrating up to a fourfold change in size (Donatti, Thibodeaux, Krueger, & Strupp, 1991).

Body image can be disrupted developmentally by inaccurate or inconsistent empathic attunement and unavailability of optimum intersubjective experiences with caretakers, as well as becoming distorted with early traumatic experiences of bodily invasion and disruption of bodily integrity (Arvanitakis, Judoin, Lester, Lussier, & Robertson, 1993). The body image may become a target for enactment of pathogenic conflicts, the Rorschach of self-cohesiveness or lack of it.

Shame may reflect core fantasies about the self that may manifest in body image (Meissner, 1998b). The conclusions from unmet developmental needs and core organizing assumptions of the self, if they are of inadequacy and defectiveness, may be woven into body image as a component of the false self to become a false body self. As certainly as deficits and conflicts can be coalesced into a false self, these same deficits can be focused on the core ego organizer of body self. A body image may be accurate, however, and still be obese as well as the carrier of shame and humiliation.

Shame has contributed to the sequestering of experiences, including those of false body self. Shame experiences are often state specific, associated with the false body self. Current body image (the current, accurate perception of the body) may corresponding with the false body self, especially if one has become obese, misshapen, or even distorted through surgery. Current body image may be so painfully overlapping false body self as obese, distorted, and unattractive that body image may itself be defensively blurred or denied by only looking at a part of one's body in the mirror.

Current correspondence of body image and true body self begins a process of discerning each of these from false body self. The painful odyssey of recognizing and reclaiming the body self requires specific internal sensory and affective focus, somatic attunement, as well as aligning weight to match true body self with its corresponding body image. The more fully that the actual (real) body and true body self are experienced, the greater the distinction from false body self.

Body image as a component of body self is integral to the sense of self and self-organization. The self, as well as emotional processes, are always and inherently embodied and intersubjectively constructed and revised. There is no realm of thought, feeling, or action that can be conceived without bodily engagement and expression (Meissner, 1998b).

Case Illustration

Victoria was a 38-year-old married professional who had continued to feel unsatisfied with herself, preoccupied with weight, compulsive eating, and loathing of her large body even after her first analysis. Since leaving home 20 years ago, she had experienced a yo-yo pattern of dieting and rebound weight gain, and was now almost 100 pounds overweight. She felt unfamiliar with herself at times, as if the "big picture" of herself and her life were available to her only in small fragments. Thus she found it difficult to be true to her "self," as what she could see of herself at any one time was limited. Victoria's mother was a talented teacher who married late and gave up her career, centering her life around Victoria. While loving and nurturing, her mother became anxious and overwhelmed with any emotional challenge from Victoria. During analysis of her own painful inner states, Victoria began to recognize her mother's state of chronic, although unacknowledged, depression, extremely low self-esteem, and marked neglect of her body and appearance throughout Victoria's childhood. Her mother's self-neglect culminated in her death from metatastic cancer just prior to Victoria's first analysis, a cancer which her mother had kept hidden and untreated for almost a decade. Victoria's father was a reclusive, emotionally unavailable mechanic, who valued concrete "men's work," from which Victoria was banished. He seemed puzzled by Victoria and unable to relate to her, and appeared either oblivious to, or occasionally scathingly critical of, her developing feminine body.

Lacking this context of empathic containment and safety, she became characterologically good, staying at the center of compliance rather than pushing to the edges of assertiveness and expansiveness. Unresponsiveness to her developmental needs resulted in Victoria feeling an overwhelming shame and selfishness for having needs at all. Her solution was to not want or need anything; however, consciously she felt herself to be disgusting, selfish, and some variation of simply unattractive to physically ugly. Her dominant belief system was of being defective, which meant that she could never show certain aspects of herself to anyone, for fear of exposure and humiliation, as she had experienced with her father who would comment whenever she gained weight. Since her yearning for response remained unconscious, occasions of unresponsiveness from others, particularly men, were met consciously with barrages of self-criticism and disgust about her body, rather than disappointment or anger with the other person. Her perceived "defectiveness" thus became an explanation for why responses to her were absent or negative. This shame of defectiveness became the core organizing assumption of her body self and psychological self. She stated, "I've deposited all my sense of defectiveness into my body."

Victoria spoke of the puzzling, surreal quality of her childhood, and her unsuccessful search for concrete evidence of trauma or deprivation in her childhood that might account for her current difficulties. Now, as during childhood, she concluded that something must be terribly wrong with her. She spoke of a dull ache, an emptiness, like waiting for an event, only there was no event. The problem, she came to see, was that she was looking for "something," when in fact "nothing" had happened. "Nothing" was the mood of her childhood, the mind state so ethereal that it did not seem real to her, yet it was a very specific reality. We explored the "nothing" state of being, the worst state of all for her, because it lacked even the contours of turmoil or pain. Childhood memories about nothing began to surface. With exquisitely developed sensitivity, she would ask her mother, "What are you worried about?" Her mother's reply was always "Nothing." She would ask her father, "What are you doing today?" Again, "nothing" came back to her.

As Victoria came to recognize "nothing" as a subtle but powerful state, rather than just "reality,' she recognized why she had always needed "something" to worry about. She had filled the nothing space with many "somethings": food, significant achievements, degrees, awards, and at other times with worry. She realized that her mother had spent much of her time in the "nothing" state, interrupted by intense episodes of worry, usually about Victoria, whose worry in turn created both a union and a reunion, with her mother, and provided her mother with "something" to bring them together, so her mother could know how to respond and not feel lost.

Victoria recognized how she would disconnect from her body in these "nothing" states, and float away. "I now realize this is when my former analyst would fall asleep, when I would even get close to this material. I assumed I was boring, and had nothing to say." I reflected her last sentence, highlighting the "nothing' and added, "It's hard to listen to 'nothing' at times." She said, "I'd try to get out of that state by focusing on 'something' instead of 'nothing.' Worry filled the hole." After this discussion, she wrote the following poem.

THIS IS NOTHING
Nothing is a ghost crying through me
Too pale to grasp
Too real to imagine.

Nothing sweeps through me with aching familiarity
Erasing all feeling
And remembrance of being.

Nothing lasts forever
A heaviness numbing
And pinning me under its
Weightlessness.

Nothing is silence, surrender
A star never born
But extinguished.

Nothing creeps under my pillow and into my dreams
Until I awake
Feeling Nothing.

Nothing is a memory
Which has no container
A room without walls
A thought without words
Skin without touch
Tears without water.

Nothing lies waiting, as freedom approaches.

Always—there is Nothing to worry about,
For Nothing is the Matter.

Victoria felt both anxiety and excitement about the possibility of both of us seeing her more fully as an attractive, sexual, sensual woman. She initially could allow herself to feel good only for a little while. I pointed out frequently how she was stopping this new and unfamiliar experience of herself during a session, replacing it with either the familiar bad feelings about her body and weight, or returning to the "nothing" state, the empty deadness. Historically, worry had always rushed into the space, filled the void, but at the same time prevented her from being sucked into the "black hole" experience of her mother's depression. Thus it felt very dangerous to Victoria to give up worry. She needed to stay for some time with the experience of disgust that she had for herself and her body, and the terrifying succession of internal decay and defect, before she could allow a different experience. She felt as if a piece of her mother had broken off and stuck in her body. The deep shame she felt was partly the shame of not living up to her mother's ideal of total self-effacement and self-sacrifice. Inside and outside had become confused, a duality and dialectic both speaking shame. These intolerable affect states had been ameliorated by food, which could soothe intense feeling and palliate her aloneness. From the detached nothingness, she used food as stimulation to reconnect herself to her body, as a constant companion. Only food engages all five senses simultaneously. Food led to a secondary effect of being overweight, and "fat" served many purposes. She viewed fat as tangible evidence that she was loathsome and disgusting, which kept her distant from potential affirmations of pride and pleasure. Her excess weight made her sexually invisible, asexual in her own mind. She viewed being overweight as punishment for wanting positive responses, which she felt she was not supposed to need, in reality or fantasy. For her, fat served as the perfect predictor of negative responses in a fat-phobic culture. Such assumed negative responses for her were not restricted to aesthetics but crossed over to judgments about personality (selfish, lazy, lacking discipline), morality (gluttony, a deadly sin), and competence ("How could I manage anything/help anyone when I can't manage my own body"). Excess weight thus created a perverse effectiveness by reducing the field of response of others to a predictable disgust about her weight, and extinguished perceptions of her femaleness and sexuality. Her additional weight was always there, putting its arms around her, filling in the gaps. She hid her true self, and her true body self, in the camouflage of excess weight. Losing weight seemed a threat, because it would increase her visibility to others and to herself, as had occurred during her many episodes of dieting, and exposed an awareness of her painful yearning for affirming responses. Her rebound weight gains after every significant loss now made sense. Victoria recognized that she viewed food as a constant and predictable companion.

Victoria experienced the disgust of her body and the introject of her mother's body as an amalgamated "mummy," a vivid metaphor that appeared first in a dream about her dead mother as a "wrapped up mummy," and then in a poem that she wrote about a shriveled up "mummy" lying inside her skin. She described the experience one day of feeling warm, sensual, and alive inside her body, then quickly looking in a mirror to stop the anxiety and uncertainty of this new experience by confirming herself as fat and ugly. I asked her what specifically she looked at in the mirror to draw this conclusion. She recognized that she did not look at the whole picture, but focused in on her eyes becoming blank, like the blank eyes of her "mummy" mother in her dream. I wondered if the change of her appearance in the mirror was due to a state change, prompted by certain experiences that led her to the mirror, notably feeling sexual and sensual and expansive. She recognized that it was when she felt sexual and sensual and wanted me to see her feeling that way, that her state changed to one of shameful fear. Most importantly, Victoria realized that feeling bad preceded, rather than followed, the fat and ugly image of herself, and that stopping feeling good or pleasure immediately ushered in the dysphoria. The perception of a grotesque image of her body served to give her feeling a focus and logic, as well as an outside that matched her inside.

Victoria gradually came to recognize that the gray, dull feeling of "nothing" was a state of mind, occupied for long seasons of her childhood, and that she had been living in a prolonged procedural memory, a continuation-construction of a wish-fear. She could recognize the experience as a state only by re-experiencing it with me, feeling that she would never get out of it. The state was itself a procedural memory of what it was like to be with her mother, and was also her mother's state transposed onto her. She had wanted to fill up her mother, to enliven her emptiness, yet never could. Insight about the experience was not enough, rather she had to actually be inside the state again, to know the difference between now and then, present and past. Through repeated experiencing of these painful states, Victoria began to recognize state changes as they happened, and the distinct body image inherent in each state. The integration of psychic equality into an integrated self and mind (as a crucial developmental achievement between ages 6 and 9) had not occurred for Victoria. This duality contributed to her formation and maintenance of false body self, and the elusiveness of true body self experience and representation. Similarly, moments of experiencing herself and her body in an expansive, womanly, sensual, and sexual way were all initially experienced as pretend, not as her real self or true body self, but assumed to be a component of her false self and false body self. "Real" felt different and unfamiliar at first, and only gradually came to feel authentic. Her false body self had seemed "real" to her, thus could be distinguished as false only as she was able to inhabit and experience her body in the present, rather than remaining in the explicit and implicit memory of her old story.

Central to Victoria's pretend mode was a very early puberty at age 8. (Very early or very late onset of puberty may also be a possible influence on false body self development.) Body changes coinciding with this developmental phase felt to her like a little girl "pretending" to have the body of a woman. The sexual development of her body did not feel real, and this dichotomy seemed to add to her disconnection as well as to her false body self concept.

We continued to focus on Victoria's immediate feeling and experience, building a foundation of a body self through knowing, feeling, and differentiating various bodily and emotional experiences. Attunement to and accurate perception of her real body's somatic and affective sensations were essential in order to distinguish her false body self as "false." Being able to move within and feel her body in a visceral, sensory way was first an internal experience, then matched in a physical way as she initiated exercise and weight loss. She recognized not having been inside her body or fully experiencing her body before. "Now that I am getting feedback from my body, it's so different. In the past I regulated myself with my head, instead of what was going on inside. Having an internal frame of reference is so different. For example, a scale was my external point of reference, a lure, a powerful thing that invalidated everything I felt inside. Numbers were huge, emblazoned things that plagued me. What I weighed determined how I would feel the rest of the day. Now I can feel when I am in my body and how it's working. Dieting is an external point of reference too—dieting is doing what someone else tells you to do." We both recognized that how she would look and what she would weigh could now come from the inside.

As Victoria took residence in her body, she developed a deeper understanding of her 20-year struggle to lose weight. She said:

> I was always exhorted by weight loss programs to rely on inner cues, but I couldn't generate anything inside. I wasn't in my body, so I had no feedback about how losing weight felt. Different body weights didn't feel different from the inside. I had no idea how disconnected I was from my body. Before, my focus was all external: weight, diet, numbers, size, scales. I have always measured time by weight loss: how many pounds I can lose by Christmas, my birthday, etc. I went through periods of obsessive exercise, but I didn't feel it in my body. Nothing was translated back inside. Now I'm starting to actually get feedback from my body. Even sex is different now. Before, I was an observer, pleasing my husband and relying on fantasy. Now I feel right in the middle of it, fully inside my body.
>
> Part of my true self is my true body. I have to move from the external cues of diet and scales to sense within myself and within my body. I had to be inside my body before I could do anything about it. I had to love my body first before I could lose weight.

As Victoria's eating disorder faded away, dissociation was in sharper focus as food was no longer used as an emotional anesthetic. She was more readily aware when state changes occurred, so that we could explore in depth the psychoanalytic scenario of feeling and perception that preceded state changes. We grew to recognize that the state changes occurred at the very moments that she felt most happy, expansive, good, sensual, and hopeful. Stopping these feelings instantly instilled the familiar emptiness, with the expansiveness relegated to the "pretend" mode. The stopping of her good and expansive feelings was something she had done automatically with her mother, in order to extinguish any separateness that might threaten the bond between them. Her boldness and expansiveness likewise could not be shared with her father, who, she came to realize, was severely limited in his experience of emotion, and lived in a world of concrete and tangible mental operations.

Victoria revisited her overeating at various times during analysis, recreating the experiences consciously, describing her eating as deliberate rather than compulsive. She noticed the fundamental change in the way that she ate, the way she felt different and experienced her body as she ate, how she tasted and enjoyed what she ate. She created an increasing continuity of feeling good, in contrast with previously segmented experiences. She became aware of how restrained she had been in her life, afraid of boldness. As she experienced greater freedom, I spoke of how an animal living its entire life in a zoo does know of captivity (or of freedom). The cage is a virtual one, personally constructed. She added, "Yes, it goes with you wherever you go, reassembling itself. It is possible to be the author of the cage and not have the key to the lock. I didn't know how I'd made the cage so I didn't know how to get out. I needed a locksmith."

We could now be aware, in vivo in the analytic process, of the pain and subsequent state change that occurred when her mother or father was blank and did not respond. Like putting her hand over a flame after having been burned repeatedly, it seemed counterintuitive now to allow herself to dare experience and express herself, especially her best feelings. She indicated how she was starting all over again in a place where no one knows her. I indicated my understanding of the strangeness/uniqueness to be inside her own experience, to embrace her entire experience in a comprehensive way to know her true self and true body self. This new engagement allowed her to distinguish between now and then, between true and false. She met this response with silence for a prolonged time, fully acknowledging the welcome, frightening new experience.

We came to know that some essential experiences of pleasure and satisfaction were not simply camouflaged with their essence withered in the atrophy of disuse and awaiting discovery, but had actually not existed until now. She had felt inadequate and defective that she wouldn't experience pleasure with her body, even when doing all the things that were supposed to bring pleasure. Even after turning herself inside out with her eating disorder in an attempt to find herself, she was unsuccessful. She recognized that "fat" was a state of mind, now acknowledged as part of her false body self, though she had partially created her body in conformity, and was now transforming her body to no longer correspond to that state of mind.

As she left this session, she felt full and satisfied, rather than her usual "hunger." That night she dreamed of taking a box off the shelf of her pantry with snacks inside. She felt annoyed that the box was so large with only a few snack packets inside. The box was too big, disproportionate, misrepresenting what was inside. She took the few packages out and threw away the box. The dream, as she had already interpreted, was of excess packing (her false body self), that misrepresents what is inside (true self and body self). She would discard the excess to retain the essence.

Body Dysmorphic Disorder

False body self may underlie anxiety over breast size or penis size, body dysmorphic disorder with excessive concern over the size or deformity of any body part, excessive weight and "fatness," particular focus on physical symptoms or physical size, fantasies of physical impairment, anxieties about impotence, preoccupation with physical vulnerability, fear of aging and its manifestations, including physical helplessness. Those patients who have a core assumption of defectiveness of the body self and/ or psychological self, may locate their self-hatred in certain specific physical characteristics as in body dysmorphic disorder. This focus on correcting a flawed physical characteristic gives hope proxy by trying to change physical characteristics. The body is a screen onto which is projected a core organizing assumption of self. The dead space resulting from derailed attachment between parent and child, or from unmet developmental needs is a "deficit/defect" projected onto the surface (ugliness; preoccupation with bodily defect of a part of the body such as ugly ears) or projected into the body as container (such as a focus on being fat, deadness internally, or a fixed belief in internal pathology).

The preoccupation with a defect in physical appearance that is imagined, or a markedly excessive concern of an objectively slight anomaly, can "cause significant distress or impairment in social, occupational, or other important areas of functioning" (DSM-IV, APA, 1994, p. 466). Focus is usually on slight or imagined flaws of the face or hair, such as wrinkles, scars, thinning hair, asymmetry, or excessive preoccupation of the shape or size of a body part such as the teeth, ears, nose, legs or abdomen. Often coming to attention after repeated plastic surgery, with consistent dissatisfaction, or with concurrent depressions and unhappiness with life, complaints mirror the assumption of a defective or bad self. This false body self parallels a false psychological self.

I have seen several individuals in consultation with plastic surgeons, at times after numerous plastic surgeries including breast augmentation, liposuction contouring, rhinoplasty, face lift, and collagen injections. Often quite phobic about having any wrinkle lines, and even if having an essentially complete body image, they may focus excessively on all aspects of appearance, exercise religiously, or immerse themselves in passionate appearance-enhancing pursuits. Their total body self and image never seemed to be quite good enough, and the plastic procedures create a perpetual series of occasions for hope. They often ruminate about a perceived deficit or defect of their bodies, usually an aspect of significant social attribution and regard, or of any sign of aging and narcissistic vulnerability, planning the next plastic procedure.

9

Dissociation, Trauma, and Development

All life, all history happens in the body.
Rebecca Wells
Divine Secrets of the Ya-Ya Sisterhood

Health is the ability to stand in the spaces between realities without losing any of them – a capacity to feel like oneself while being many.
Philip Bromberg, 1994

I had at once been splintered into a million beings and objects. Today I am one; tomorrow I shall splinter again . . . but I knew that all were notes of one and the same harmony.
Vladimir Nabokov, 1920

We have so many words for states of mind, and so few for states of the body.
Jeanne Moreau

Anna O., a patient of Breuer and Freud's, suffered from a dissociative disorder (Kluft, 1992). Freud's biographer, Jones (1953) indicated that Anna O. had "two distinct states of consciousness . . . a case of double personality. The transition from one to the other was marked by a phase of autohypnosis" (p. 223). Freud shifted from dissociation as a significant theme in psychopathology to the concept of repression when he rejected the seduction hypothesis in 1897 and replaced the paradigm of original trauma with conflict theory.

Only recently has contemporary psychoanalytic theory revisited the dissociation-based theories of mind. Freud's move from the seduction hypothesis and traumatic realities to the preeminence of Oedipal and unconscious fantasy focused psychoanalysis on neurotic processes and the centrality of fantasy. This moved psychoanalytic focus and theory away from multiple self-states and vertical splits based on actual trauma and abuse, toward repression of unconscious wishes and fantasies, internal conflict, and a hierarchical conscious and unconscious process.

Freud initially used the concept of repression in what we now refer to as suppression: the everyday intentional, conscious pushing from the foreground what is difficult or painful. His later writings moved repression to a broader venue as a defense mechanism operating outside of awareness to keep or return painful material or emotion to the unconscious, and thus repression came to be used as an unconscious defense. Freud's original seduction hypothesis gave significance to Janet's findings of the relationship between trauma and dissociation, and the existence of unconscious personalities in hysterical patients constructed in response to traumatic events. Psychoanalysis began again to embrace the notion of "multiple selves" within self psychology, as Kohut (1985) noted the existence of simultaneous and even contradictory selves in the same person with varying degrees of importance and compatibility.

Although initially in psychoanalytic use, and still currently in many writings, dissociation was mistakenly lumped in with unconscious repression. Rather than the hierarchical, topographical model of the unconscious with its representative buoyed to the surface of conscious awareness, dissociation creates parallel tracts in the mind and in the brain. The parallel, and sometimes interacting and somewhat overlapping systems of dissociation are a hypertrophied process of the interacting parallel systems of memory, experience, and subtle changes of states of mind throughout the day. Normal overlapping lines of communication of these parallel processes become disrupted most dramatically at times of traumatic stress (Spiegel, 1994).

Dissociation is distinct from repression, in that with dissociation there is an initial failure to integrate a traumatic experience with the rest of the core personality because the experience is recorded in a different tract of the mind and brain. Dissociation creates a model of depersonalization and disavowal of the body, a model that becomes broadened to deal with other aspects of the self as segmented.

The phenomenon of dissociation, an alteration of consciousness, is distinguishable as an ego state from splitting, the dividing between a "good object" and a "bad object." Splitting does not involve a psychophysiologically altered state, as does dissociation. When present from early development, this failure to integrate bears functional equivalence to splitting, described by both Mahler (1966) and Kernberg (1975) as a primitive and pathological defense to deal with conflictual and incompatible affects, such as love and anger toward the same love object, a transitory defense later replaced by the defense of repression.

Dissociation is unique as a defense because it is the only defense that involves alteration of mind–body state, a defense that involves an instantaneous psychophysiological shift of state of mind. As a defensive process, it involves a particular type of psychical organization, based on a continuous process of segmented experiences and representations of the world. Dissociative organization can become a working model of an individual who has experienced dissociation as a primary defense from early in life, later to become an automatic defense, organization, and model. Increasingly, we have appreciated that dissociation does not inherently involve psychopathology, is not synonymous with fragmentation, has adaptive purposes, and may indeed defend against fragmentation (Bromberg, 1994).

Dissociation occurs in response to an external cue of danger or overwhelmingly stimulating affect to withdraw/dissociate from contact. This dissociative distancing represents a protection from danger. The dissociative retreat creates the illusion of having control over a trauma-inducing person, object, or feeling, creating a dissociative buffer insulating from contact with the perceived source of danger.

What makes the defense of dissociation so difficult to discern by both patient and analyst is that it manifests as imperceptible state changes. Other defenses manifest in specific content such as denial or obsessional reverie, and are observable (e.g., reaction formation circumscribes what it is avoiding by presenting the reverse image). All other defenses such as denial, projection, isolation of affect, displacement, repression, undoing, and others occur *after* the anxiety provoking experience that mobilizes the defense. Dissociation originally occurs *at the time* of the trauma. The immediate threat to the integrity of the self catalyzes dissociation, and by adulthood, dissociation has become automatic, not in conscious awareness, and is generalized so that any uncomfortable feeling may be responded to by dissociation, even feeling particularly good or excited. Dissociation includes the concept of encapsulation, a defense against the fear of annihilation (Hopper, 1991).

States of Mind

A state of mind is "the total of pattern of activation in the brain at a particular moment in time (Siegel, 1999, p. 127). A state of mind determines perception and processing, emotional tone and regulation, access to memory, mental models, and behavioral response patterns.

Within a particular state of mind we perceive, remember, feel, think, behave, and respond in a mode consistent with this state of mind. The degree of consistency and continuity between states of mind is a significant determinant of our overall sense of organization and continuity of self. The mastery and regulation of state changes often determines our effectiveness in the range of human skills and tasks in our repertoire. The activation of a state of mind is determined by history and meaning, self regulation, present context, and mastery by the individual in a continuum of states of mind based on developmental experiences. Within a self-state there is continuity across time as well as cohesion within the moment. A self state includes an internally organized cluster of expectations, attitudes, meanings, and feelings (Sroufe, 1997).

"State" is defined by the Boston Process of Change Study Group (Stern et al., 1998) as "the semi-stable organization of the organism as a whole at a given moment" (p. 907). Putnam (1992) defines state as the "psychological and physiological variables that occur together and repeat themselves, often in highly predictable sequences that are relatively stable and enduring over time. Each state of mind has its own ABC'S: affect, behavior, cognition, sensation. Each discreet and distinct state includes affect, arousal/energy level, motor activity, posture, mannerisms, speech, cognitive processing, access to knowledge, autobiographical memory, as well as sense of self.

Putnam (1998) indicates that

> [S]tates appear to be the fundamental unit of organization of consciousness and are detectable from the first moments following birth and are self-organizing and self-stabilizing structures of behavior. When a transition from one state of consciousness to another occurs, the new state acts to impose qualitatively and qualitatively different structures on the variables that define the state of consciousness. The new structure acts to reorganize behavior and resist changes to other states. (p. 25)

Affect and mood changes may be the best marker of state change.

Changes in states of consciousness (synonymous terms include *ego state, state of mind, self-states*) involve affect, behavior, cognition, and sensation. These ABCs are involved in whole or in part, a systemic alteration of affect (such as terror or shame), behavior (remembering by repetition), cognition (the image of the event, such as a flashback), and sensation (such as a body memory). These fundamental somatopsychic responses determine the access to memory (state-dependent learning and state-dependent memory), attention, the sense of self, and the experience of continuity in one's life. Affect regulation is the aspect of self-regulation, regarding to the capacity to modulate emotion and to access, organize, and bridge states of mind.

Siegel (1999) proposes that there are seven ways in which we modulate emotion and organize states of mind for self-regulation: intensity of emotional processing, sensitivity with a threshold of response, specificity in which emotional regulation determines the parts of the brain activated based on establishing the value of the meaning of the representation, windows of tolerance of arousal beyond which thinking and behavior can be disrupted if arousal is beyond certain bounds, recovery processes for arousal beyond the window of times, and access to consciousness in which emotion directs the activation of mind and establishes the information processing and meanings for an individual.

Nowhere are these states of mind as discrete and dramatically distinct as in the dissociative identity organization in which various states are quite distinct from each other, each with its core of identity, history, and experience. Bromberg (1994) asserts that dissociation is as basic to mental functioning as repression, and that dissociated experiences often are enacted in the analytic relationship as a way of being communicated to become "thinkable" and a subjection of reflection. Each self-state, if a discontinuous state of consciousness for some individuals, has its own perception, processing, memory, and style of relatedness to self and others (Bromberg, 1994). The states are coherent and distinct, though often camouflaged from awareness, yet hiding in the open.

These states of mind are different from feelings, defined as the subjective experience of distinct affects. Sylvan Thomkins (1962) presented nine innate affects including interest, enjoyment, surprise, fear, anger, distress, shame, contempt, and disgust. Each innate affect is governed by inherited genetic programs with psychophysiological representations.

When someone cannot escape a trauma outside, they can escape inside, partitioning off the trauma like the body walls off an abscess to prevent contamination of the whole: a state change. Dissociation is perhaps the only proactive defense mechanism; that is, when danger is anticipated, all the information pertaining to it goes down one tract, rather than throughout the entire mind. One dissociates not post hoc, as with repression and all other defenses, but as the event is actually happening. In the event of severe abuse, there is a complete corruption of the developmental milieu: in addition to trauma and assault on the body and psyche, there is also a dissolution of the bond with the parent or caregiver. Only dissociation can prevent a complete fragmentation of the nucleur self.

The mind as a linear model with linear dynamics of unconscious conflict expands to a complex system of multiple states of consciousness that only appear continuous, seamless, and unshifting. Each state of consciousness is relived or enacted in its own relational context. "If an analyst thinks of a person as speaking from different self-states rather than from a single center of self, then the analyst will inevitably listen that way" (Bromberg, 1994, p. 532). Tracking how someone goes into and out of self states is both linear (dynamically understanding the specific feeling, coupled with meaning of trauma-danger, and triggering a dissociative response) and, at the same time, systemic (within a structure of states of mind, a psychophysiological alteration of a self-state occurs as a unique defense in which the individual is unable to reflect on experience, rather than an unconscious avoidance of it).

States of mind include a range of specific states and experiences including degrees of relaxation, alertness, calmness, creative energization, contentment, anxiety, boredom, agitation, depression, nothingness, deadness, emptiness, confusion, and many others. A state of mind is a psychophysiological state, not a specific feeling. Depression, for example, is not a feeling but a multifaceted and multidimensional state of mind. Depression is a state of mind when uncomfortable feelings are stopped, and the numbing state change to depression occurs. A state of mind has its own developmental history, its own set of experiences, determines what is perceived and subsequently how it is processed. Schwaber (1998) suggests each self-state has an impact on another person with whom we interact, and their state on us. Nonverbal expression in analysis ranges from motoric body movements and kinetics to the more subtle and implicit nonverbal dimensions of state of mind.

State originates in the body, is biologically rooted, as it is a psychophysiological experience. State is regulated from the beginning in an intersubjective context, created between infant and caretaker, as it is between patient and analyst. Self-state is mutually regulated between two people, and mutual regulation of state is the central activity of mother and infant (Tronick, 1989). State of mind provides an organizing context, and determines perception and processing (Sander, 1997). Each ego state has a representational system that includes a self-representation and object-representation, a predominant affective tone, a particular somatic body self experience, and a cognitive organization paralleling the internalized self–other dyad (Davies, 1996). This representational schemata is a developmental organization that synthesizes all emotional, bodily, and other representations.

Our evolving understanding of the workings of the mind involves not only the unconscious, but of multiple levels of both unconscious and conscious processes, multiply organized and linked with different levels of meaning, understanding, and experiencing (Davies, 1996). This existence and experience of multiple self-states becomes seamlessly woven into different levels of experience of attention and alertness, experience and representation of somatic body self experience, and different levels of psychological self experience and state. Integration and dissociation become a continuum rather than awareness and repression.

Infant researchers such as Sander (1992) present the importance of state regulatory experiences of two people engaging in an interaction, whether of infant and caretaker or of patient and analyst. The basic organizing function and capacity of state, always experienced within a context, is ubiquitous and, he notes, "The concept of state is a concept of the whole that we often lose sight of in our attention to the par" (p. 583).

The Neurobiology of Trauma

As the brain develops, disruptions of neurodevelopment can occur from lack of sensory experience during critical times, or by disrupted neuronal activation due to extremes of experience, such as childhood trauma or abuse. Cognitive neuroscience with psychoanalysis concludes that thinking, emotion, and feeling are inseparable, are embodied, and that it is impossible to detach one from the other (Damasio, 1994; Solms, 1995). In psychoanalysis we traditionally think of the mind influencing the body; neurobiologists such as Damasio (1994) suggest that the influence and causality go both ways.

In hyperarousal, there is dramatic increase in norepinephrine release creating vigilance, heightened attention, and behavioral changes including irritability and with heightened motor activity and startle responses. When the symbolic or actual trigger to these fear responses is presented subsequently (such as a car backfiring in a Vietnam Veteran traumatized by gunshot) there is immediate activation of these same sets of responses. These specific indicators or reminders of the traumatic event have been generalized to related symbolic events. There may be further generalization in which the components of the fear response sensitizes an individual such that everyday stressors now elicit exaggerated responses such as hyperactivity and greater sensitivity, and a fear state that persists can become a "trait" (Perry, Pollard, Blakley, Baker, & Vigilante, 1995). The traumatized individual may be more easily moved from being mildly stressed or anxious to feeling threat and terror in more general circumstances and to more emotionality including behavioral and cognitive problems that stem indirectly from the original traumatic events (Perry et al., 1995).

The affect processing system, primarily the amygdala, is functioning from birth on, while it takes several years for the brain structures involved in cognitive information processing, primarily the hippocampal system, to mature (Vanderlinden & Vandereyecken, 1999). Due to this immaturity of the hippocampal system, the basic response to trauma in a young child younger than 5 years of age, is a freezing reaction, resulting in internal dissociation and changes in some basic functions such as eating, but with little other in the way of coping mechanisms to deal with overwhelming trauma. Children abused later in childhood can rely on more cognitive strategies and sophisticated defenses.

Patients may use an eating disorder or other addictive substance or activity as including a way of dissociating to create a trancelike state, to "zone-out," or to "blank out." Children abused at a very young age may have difficulty altering their eating disorder symptoms, as they have become autonomically conditioned and operate outside awareness. The immediate reactions of freezing or dissociation can occur to various cues internally or externally, especially psychological or somatic triggers linked to original trauma. Outside stimuli may be specific referents to the trauma such as a look, a smell, a date, or a specific setting that may activate a sensory-linked flashback to the trauma.

Stress or heightened arousal from any source may elicit memories, either somatic or symbolic, related to a trauma. The content from an altered state of mind is more readily accessible, even at times experienced as intrusive, when one reenters that state of mind. These experiences of state dependent memory parallel the state dependent learning involved in dissociative phenomena, and account for the partial or total amnesia for memories or behaviors while someone is in an altered state of mind (van der Kolk, 1994).

It is not meaningful, indeed impossible, to distinguish a psychic phenomenon from a somatic one when someone has body memories, or when the body is involved in experiencing the phenomenon of an altered psychophysiological state. A procedural memory does not feel like a memory, but real life; a body memory does not feel like a memory but a very real, perhaps exquisitely painful current experience. A patient may have exhaustively pursued medical reasons for these procedural somatic memories.

Intervention through psychotherapy or psychoanalysis can affect neurological change; a new set of experiences organized in a new model form their own patterns and pathways within the neuronal network, creating changes in the mind and in the brain (Vaughan, 1997). Traditional understanding and insight alone are not sufficient, however, because state changes and creating a new experience transcend dynamic, symbolic, and unconscious meanings, all of which assume a single state of mind.

When an individual operates on a dissociative paradigm it affects the process of thinking and perceiving regarding nontraumatic experiences as well, creating an all-or-nothing model of discontinuities due to segmentation. For example, Joyce (case vignette in chapter 6) intellectually knows the intrusive toxicity of her mother, yet still experiences surprise when her mother says something that is mean or unkind to her. Though every experience she has had for six decades should inform her otherwise, she handles continuing input by having two tracts in her mind dealing with her mother: the hope residing in one tract, the experience in another.

The vigilant readying for trauma's impact enhances its perception. The individual's lived experience of trauma in the past provides a venue of expectation in the present for new editions of the original situation. These expectations are ultimately substantiated by relationships and life, further etching the assumptions that suffering is ubiquitous and victimhood is inevitable. Often, feeling good is only a temporary venture into new territory, without familiar guideposts, with a return to the familiar dysphoria soon enough, the dread again verified.

Dissociation is the result of experiencing from within a particular state of arousal, anxiety, or terror, usually due to trauma, in which the encoding of an experience results in the record (memory) of that experience within that particular psychophysiological state of mind. In other states of mind, the access to all of the components of the mental representation of affect, behavior, cognition, and sensation may not be complete. A "catharsis" occurs when all four components come together to form a vivid memory which is therapeutically helpful *if* the patient does not recreate dissociation to experience this memory, but *instead* stays grounded in a present state of mind, allowing an experience of integration of all components of the memory of affect, behavior, cognition, sensation.

This vertical split of dissociation is contrasted to the horizontal split of repression in which more subtle forms of painful experiences are pushed out of awareness unconsciously within the same state.

Repression may only impact an aspect of a memory, such as minimizing or distorting its meaning or feeling to render it inert. In repression, the individual would remember the event, but not access feeling about it, or its current meaning or impact.

At the level of the brain, excessive emotional arousal in trauma shifts processing to the right forebrain only, where one processes only emotionally, and often is marooned in the right brain of affect processing having difficulty bridging to the left brain of rational thought and executive functioning (van der Kolk, 1998). When this dissociation of the right brain from the bilaterality of left brain processing takes place, an altered state of consciousness occurs, creating a separate tract of experience, as well as of memory. Accessibility to this particular state of mind and memory is most likely accessed by a similar trauma or induction of a similar emotional upheaval.

It is only in extreme instances of repeated trauma and dissociation, such as dissociative identity organization, that the distinction between dissociation and repression is extreme; more likely, dissociation and repression are along a continuum of troubling to traumatic affect (Tuch, 1999).

Dissociation Phenomenology and Dissociative Organization

Psychic trauma occurs when overstimulating and intensely affective events cannot be understood or integrated into preexisting schemata, and overwhelm the accommodation and integration of ongoing experience (Davies, 1996).

Dissociation partitions off trauma by a psychophysiological state change. Dissociation is perhaps the only proactive defense mechanism; that is, when danger is anticipated, all the information pertaining to it goes down one tract, rather than throughout the entire mind. One dissociates not post hoc, as repression and all other defenses, but as the event is actually happening. In the event of severe abuse, there is a complete corruption of the developmental milieu: in addition to trauma and assault on the body and psyche, there is also a dissolution of the bond with the parent. In severe instances, only dissociation can prevent a complete fragmentation of the nuclear self. Dissociation is a defense; it is not simply a defense against unconscious fantasies, affect, meaning, or memories, but is a defense against an entire traumatic event (Spiegel, 1991).

While once unrecognized, and later thought to be extremely rare, recent studies suggest that up to 10% of the population suffers from one of the dissociative disorders (Ross, 1991). Questions have been raised about how it is possible that esteemed, careful clinicians see a number of cases of dissociation and even its extreme, dissociative identity disorder organization, while others never see a single one. Kuhn (1970) indicates that scientific endeavors evolve through the development of organizing paradigms, not necessarily by a slow, steady accretion of new knowledge, but at times by a "scientific revolution" in which "an older paradigm is replaced in whole or in part by an incompatible new one" (p. 91). In this manner, scientists see categorically different entities "when looking with familiar instruments in places they have looked before. . . . " He adds, "Like the choice between competing political institutions, that between competing paradigms proves to be a choice between incompatible modes of community life" (p. 94). These differing, even competing, paradigms "see different things when they look from the same point in the same direction. Both are looking at the world and what they look at has not changed. But in some areas they see different things, and they see them in different relations one to the other. That is why a law that cannot even be demonstrated to one group of scientists may occasionally seem intuitively obvious to another" (p. 151).

The essential features of dissociative organization are disruptions or disintegration of the functions of memory, identity, consciousness, and cognition. Commonly recognized disassociative disorders include amnesia, fugue, depersonalization, and dissociative identity disorder. When present from early development, dissociation, rather than a disintegration of aspects of memory, identity, or cognition, is the failure to initially synthesize and integrate these functions. There are an array of dissociative symptoms including recurrent amnesia, autohypnotic symptoms such as spontaneous trances and age regressions, conversion and somatoform symptoms, and posttraumatic stress disorder symptoms. Most dissociative phenomena are hidden both to patient and analyst, are covert in their manifestations, and seamlessly blend state changes. Even when we have seen patients for some time, we may not be aware of the subtle state changes that account for the shift of perception, processing, and content that is unique to each psychophysiological state of mind. Dissociative phenomena are not borderline or psychotic conditions in and of themselves, or a borderline or psychotic character structure, though some at the more serious end of the spectrum may present as such (Armstrong & Lowenstein, 1990).

Ego psychological concepts of defense and conflict are essential to understanding the internal dynamics of dissociative defenses. Dissociation is a defense, adaptive at one time, to render inaccessible immediate affect and memories of trauma. Dissociation is a type of internal organization, in which compartmentalization of experience is based on experiencing and thus recording the process and content memory in a distinct psychophysiological states of mind. Because of the compartmentalization in a particular state of mind, the elements of a state of mind, such as during a trauma, may not be integrated into usual, accessible memory, or into a cohesive sense of self. Trauma ghostwrites personal narrative to inform self perception of being a perpetual victim, though not necessarily having conscious recollection of the experiences of trauma leading to that core concept of victimhood and suffering. Just as there are multiple levels and dimensions of consciousness, there is no one, simple *the* unconscious, but a confluence of experiences, interactive representations, and state-dependent memories. The linear model of psychodynamic conceptualization assumes a single state, or a modification of like-minded states without state changes having to be a conceptual focus. Dissociative organization involves a segmentation rather than full integration of body self and psychological self.

The consideration of state changes is a different level of conceptualization of the mind as a map with different territories (states). Rather than the mind as a whole being one territory to be explored, we became cartographers of the mind, examiners of the emotional bridges between states, as well as explorers of the detail within each state.

Specific memories that were traumatically dissociated are processed in different areas of the brain from nontraumatic memories (van der Kolk, 1994), and cannot be remembered in the usual way because they were never known fully in the usual way. That is, they were not integrated as conscious memories able to be retrieved as memories. There is no distinction within a particular state of past and present.

When a patient has a state change, the affect, perception, and transference immediately preceding the change may not be available to the patient. There may be discontinuities from one session to the next as well as within sessions: the detail, insight, and understanding arrived at during the prior session may no longer be accessible in the current session. The defensive purpose of dissociation of originally protecting from overwhelming feelings, memories, and fantasies may still be automatically operating as if the original trauma were recurring. Developmentally, dissociation is also quite adaptive, allowing remarkable accommodation that would be impossible if the trauma had not been successfully dissociated. By using dissociation in this adaptive way, a large part of the individual's personality can be entirely unaffected by the trauma (van der Kolk, 1986). Dissociation exists "both to obliterate and to preserve" (Davies & Frawley, 1994).

The knowledge of trauma is defended against, as the nature of trauma is unintegrated. The combination of defense and deficit make knowing and not knowing massive psychic trauma a consistent problem, of reality as a defense against emotional reality (Laub & Auerhahn, 1993). Knowing and not knowing take the forms of amnesia, fugue states, fragments, overpowering narratives, life themes, and metaphors in a patient's life as well as transference phenomenon in analysis (Laub & Auerhahn, 1993) The most common form of knowing/not knowing trauma is reliving rather than remembering, remaining in the procedural memory itself.

Self-Harm

Those who express self-harm through the body may be motivated to inflict pain or damage on their bodies or to disfigure them to establish a sense of control over the body, reclaiming ownership when it has been traumatically divested.

Cutting and self-mutilation of the body have been viewed as a concretized attempt to counteract the experience of self-loss (Doctors, 1999) and the concomitant threat of annihilation (Orange, Atwood, & Stolorow, 1997). Threats to self-cohesiveness or to overwhelming affect may be remedied by self-mutilation, often with a sense of vulnerability to interpersonal contexts. Tenuous self-cohesiveness may disintegrate into disorganization and a pervasive passivity of not seeming to author one's own experience, unless by subjugating and harming their body.

The result may be an attempt to reestablish this grounding in body self, to organize experience concretely, and to encode in bodily form, for example, in the act of cutting flesh, to experience the sensation of pain, of seeing and feeling blood. This simple act engages all senses: all vectors point back to the origin of experience, the body. This example of encapsulation of fundamental experience through sensorimotor channels may be a desperate attempt to recognize and assimilate body self and psychological self.

Self-mutilation, as exemplified by cutting, is often a concretized attempt to counteract the experience of annihilation (self-loss) when significant others appear assaultive or insufficiently affirming. Self-mutilation serves to distinguish and differentiate a boundary, and at the same time, to bridge the gulf between body and mind. If ownership or regulation of one's body is ever in doubt, cutting establishes the individual as the center of that control. In the face of feeling a loss of control, self-mutilation displaces intense pain and helplessness with the very specific act of subordinating one's body. Common to all of the above instances is the patient self-mutilating to counteract intolerable affect states. For each, self-mutilation is an attempt to concretize as well as communicate and articulate feelings. The return to an unsatisfying yet familiar experience and state of mind is preferable to the loss of self and annihilation. In this way, trauma and the repetition compulsion are specifically related to each other (Russell, 1986).

Various studies of residuals of sexual abuse refer to bodily perception disorders, difficulty with body regulation, and various somatization processes, illnesses, and symptoms. (Goodwin & Attias, 1999). As these authors note, a high incidence of self-mutilation, suicide attempts, and numerous self-destructive behaviors in adulthood are all correlated with histories of early physical and sexual abuse. Alexythymic reactions of total somatic numbing and somatization disorders appear frequently in populations with sexual abuse in childhood (Van der Kolk et al., 1996).

A specific trauma can serve as an organizing focus, a signifier of meaning for earlier situations and events, as well as a process that may not have words or a language. Retroactively informing, it becomes the software program of perceiving and processing current experiences and future anticipations.

Several studies have related eating disorders in women with a history of sexual abuse during childhood or adolescence, and the relationship prevalence has ranged from 57 to 70% of eating disorder women who have a history of sexual abuse (Finn, Hartman, Leon, & Lawson, 1986; Kearney-Cooke, 1988; Oppenheimer, Howells, Palmer, & Chaloner, 1985). This remarkably high correlation between sexual abuse and prevalence eating disorders emphasizes how earlier lack of control over one's body foreshadows the use of the body in attempts to achieve mastery via self-harm.

Psychodynamic Scenario of Dissociation

The process of dissociation in the clinical exchange often occurs in the following dynamic scenario. First, there is some specific feeling linked to or generalized from a perception of threat or danger. When the specific feeling is stopped or averted, an alteration of psychophysiological state occurs. All such threats are registered/perceived by the senses, and the dissociation is an uncoupling between the mind and the senses (Goldberg, 1995). Dissociation, originally a response to trauma, is a defensive partitioning of body self and psychological self, particularly the extreme sensations of physical pain. Body feeling is anesthetized and body memory is isolated by state change because the body, being the object of traumatization, then becomes itself a source of pain, guilt, conflict, or shame.

The disconnection of the acute register of pain is the mission of dissociation, which immediately, instantaneously, and, until an individual is aware of this invisible process, magically creates the illusion of dissipating any discomfort. The state change may range from feeling "zoned-out" or blank, to a distinctly different state such as depression, obsessional reverie, or rage. An individual learns to create various ways to reconnect the mind and body by some somatic bridge, to use the body to exercise, to take a warm bath, or to focus on breathing. Action symptoms of stimulation of the body, such as alcohol and drug use, or self-harm inflicted on the body, are often used as an attempt at bridging back to the body self as foundation of affective experience and organization. This reestablishment of connectedness with the basic foundation of experience, the body self, is a temporary reequilibrium, referred to by Goldberg (1995) as pseudointegration.

Because of this patterning of instantaneous dissociative withdrawal from sensory experience and intense feelings, these individuals have not become accustomed to residing inside their own experience, in their own bodies, or at the center of their subjective experience. Various dissociative symptomatology may predominate, such as feelings of deadness, difficulty with identity, versions of depersonalization and derealization, amnestic instances or episodes, or the more extreme out-of-body experience. All are originally a protection from an immediate perceived danger, a withdrawal from directly experiencing the senses and the body.

An individual becomes aware of dissociation only when there is a failure of the system of usual defensive organization and pseudointegration of mind and body that has predominated for most of their lives. Another pathway of recognition may occur when trust has been established in a clinical setting. The seamless process of dissociation is so veiled and imperceptible to the individual and significant others that it may be decades before recognition. Successful dissociative defenses, styles, and patterns become woven into one's lifestyle, and may be so concealed in habit to be unrecognized even by a spouse. There is social, economic, and cultural support and disguise for this type of psychological organization, which adds to its opaqueness (Goldberg, 1995). Often a dissociative individual has learned to use various stimulants (such as food, coffee), various activities, (such as exercise, warm baths) and other intense sensory experiences (such as a frantic lifestyle, external focus such as constant television or music) to provide a sufficient focus to maintain an internal cohesion and organization as well as a counter to internal dullness, deadness, or depression. Goldberg (1995) notes that creating a lifestyle to maintain distraction and attention to more than one thing at the same time creates an understandable explanation for any discontinuities in one's life, as well as of linear time. Many of the individuals may use a focus of food, alcohol, or drugs as a way to explain to themselves, or to unconsciously balance their perception of dissociation. For example, a patient may use alcohol as a tangible cause of state change and as explanation for brief amnesias. When closely examined, the state change begins just before the first drink was ingested, and she is surprised to discover that she has been creating an external happening to match and to account for the internal process. The detailed exploration of this scenario illuminates the power of the patient's mind to create what was attributed to the substance itself.

Usual experiences of every individual includes a continuum of ego states for which there may be some awareness, even of how to exit and enter different states, and what state works best for what endeavor. Creative artists become cognizant of which state to enter for a creative endeavor, which state to enter for conceptual planning, and what state of attention and concentration works best for each task from the alertness of business endeavors to relaxation for sleep.

The use of certain medications, such as pain medication or stimulants like Ritalin, serve a similar purpose as does ritual use of coffee or other stimulant drinks to create the continuity of a sustained single state of mind. The perpetual creation or perception of crises, even to the more moderate procrastination until a frenzied meeting of a deadline, all cre-

ate not only an external focus but the physiological tension that organizes within an orbit of a state change. The induction of stimulation by
external crisis, ingestion of stimulants, or other actions, as well as the
ability to self-induce states of arousal all maintain an internal balance for
the dissociative individual, the equilibrium of pseudointegration.

For someone well entrenched in a dissociative model, any feeling
may trigger dissociation. Paradoxically, particularly good feelings may
trigger a state change to return to a more familiar state of hopelessness,
despair, or depression. This model is not only a defense, but an organized
systemic pattern of dealing with the world, established early in life from
exposure to significant repeated, trauma or from dissociative parents, or
both.

In adulthood, dissociation is a seamless and automatic maneuver,
not in conscious awareness, triggered by its earliest couplings with signals of danger. It is a unique defense that represents an inability to reflect
on experience rather than an unconscious avoidance of doing so (Donnel
Stern, 1997). Rather than an unconscious preference, it is automatic and
involuntary until this process is very actively focused on by both patient
and analyst. It is unique among all defenses in a clinical way because the
change of state process does not appear to be objectifiable alone, and
insight and understanding of the system cannot occur in an altered state.
Because of this continued defensive partitioning of dissociation, the content of different states of mind, as well as the process of moving between
states remains unformulated, and one is imprisoned by this process that
seemingly represents a freedom of movement.

Dissociation astutely avoids certain experiences and memories, reflective thinking, and truly free play and imagination of the mind. Full
feeling, fantasy, and imagination within any one state, or among the plurality of states, are disallowed because this free play of the mind may
come dangerously close to, or trip on a landmine of trauma.

There is an inherent organization of discontinuous states of consciousness that overall give the picture of stability until either a sufficient
disruption of the system, or hypertrophy of a state of mind attempting
compensation or defense. Often by middle age, the perpetual vigilance
and continued alertness-awareness, and the tremendous daily drain of
energy by dissociative state changes become depleting to the individual,
who may then search for recognition and understanding of the ongoing
internal drama, or at least an external catalyst sufficient to provide a
focus.

While everyone experiences different states of consciousness, with
overlap, blending, or sharing between and among states, a dissociative
organization entails more abrupt and distinct states of consciousness.
Dissociative symptomatology becomes clinically recognized when the

discontinuity becomes direct and overt. Each of the dissociative phenomena, including amnesia, fugue, depersonalization, and dissociative identity are defined by manifest symptomatology that obfuscate the associated personality style or dynamics.

In addition to significant trauma, the repeated exposure to a primary caretaker who is dissociative renders the child vulnerable to integrating essential experiences in a continuous and cohesive way. This exposure and experience can create a primary model of the mind as dissociative, in that there are multiple unintegrated ego states rather than multiple states within an integrated self (Fonagy, 1998). With distinct unintegrated self-state experiences, state-dependent memory is a natural correlate; that is, the specific state in which the experience occurred must be reentered in order to evoke the memory, a state-dependent experience.

In some instances of extreme toxicity, the parent operates much as a virus does by infecting a cell, overtaking the cell's function for its own purposes, leaving the cell itself internally altered, damaged, or dead (Fonagy, 1998). A virus can become so integrated with the genetic component of the cell that the virus itself becomes part of the transmitted genetic material. The invasive organism is converted to a component of the cell, not perceived as nonself to be destroyed as the immune system might otherwise do.

Dissociation and Body Self Development

Bodily experiences that cannot be mastered by the developing body self and psychological self are by definition traumatic (Attias & Goodwin, 1999). Sexual abuse that occurs during childhood or adolescence when body self and psychological self are forming and integrating has disruptive effects at many levels on the resultant sense of self, and even fundamentally on body image. The various reparative and restitutive efforts may include eating disorders, somatic symptomatology, conversion disorders, fragmentation into multiple psychological/body states, or deliberate injury of the body (Attias & Goodwin, 1999).

So many of the symptoms that we encounter are essentially derived from an individual trying to reclaim her own body from having been traumatically dispossessed at critical developmental junctures, to re-create a compensatory effectiveness to regulate body states. Fantasy is not enough to restore hopefulness, effectiveness, and mastery as the trauma shatters necessary organizing fantasies. Ulman and Brothers (1988) spoke of the impact of trauma as the shattering of necessary archaic narcissistic fantasies, and their attempted faulty restoration as manifested systematically in the dissociative disturbances that create depersonalization, derealization, and disembodiment experiences. An action symptom may seem to be necessary: another lived experience to replace the lived experience of the trauma. Sadistic action toward the body, as well as sadomasochistic enactments in analysis may be an attempt to change the meaning or the outcome of past trauma, by repeating and scripting a different ending. Self-harm may be designed to attempt to reclaim ownership of one's body, to be the author of experience. In extreme instances, fantasies may develop into psychotic transferences indistinguishable by the patient from external reality, and focus on perception of abuse by the treating professional, revenge fantasies, attempts at validation of the perception of abuse, and even litigation threats or action. This attempt to rewrite a better ending to the trauma of an earlier life or to annotate or fill in the missed experiences may be about engaging the dissociatively altered reality as well as filling in the black holes of experiences.

The dissociation resulting from traumatic abuse, and the confusion of coexisting ego states based on separate and distinct bodily experiences may leave an individual without the necessary language or concepts to describe her experience. The experiences may be so state-specific that they are segmented, and these various segments may not be apparent to the individual, or at times to the analyst, and the various ego states may each be responded to as they occur, perhaps missing the overarching concept of the process of dissociation and the coexistence of multiple ego states that comprise a system of experience. At times the analytic experience may be parallel to the individual's experience of segmented, focused, and contained experiences that are demarcated, each responded to in content, missing the process of the dissociative quality and the discontinuity of time and state awareness. The sense of shame as well as the process of dissociation both contribute to the discreteness, distinctness, and failure to connect various distorted body experiences and other symptoms. When the patient is in a dissociated state, they cannot imagine, they cannot see metaphorically or symbolically, and there is no past, present, or future because they are not grounded in the present, so that time has no meaning. It is now what it has always been. Past blends imperceptibly into the present at these moments, and there is no difference between the two.

Patients have different representations of body self corresponding to the different ego or self-states, often fluctuating significantly with state changes. For example, a patient may feel quite good about herself, functioning and experiencing herself in a cohesive way, when, suddenly, she experiences disruption of an important attachment figure and the corresponding selfobject functioning, and instantaneously changes her state of mind. In an earlier work (Krueger, 1989a), I described the serial drawing of dozens of inpatients who were asked throughout the day to draw their body image corresponding to different needs, feelings, or states of mind that they experienced. Their body images would dramatically vary according to self-state: for example, their body image would be three to four times larger at times of particular upset and state change experience. The multiplicity of the self-experience, vividly illustrated in the vertical split of dissociation, has its corresponding representation in body self experience and image.

The evolving development of body self and body image and its integration into psychological self is traumatically disrupted by sexual abuse or other trauma. The violation of traumatic insertions challenges the developing sense of body boundaries and the clear cut "edge of me," leading to experiences of bodily vulnerability (Fisher, 1989).

Young (1992) has summarized the essential issues related to trauma to the body as calling into question the experience of "having a body" and "living in a body," disrupting the central experience of the body in human existence, a disruption that is undeniable in severe trauma which is inscribed in and on the bodies of the victims. The threat of injury, death, or disruption of physical integrity is an essential component to traumatic stress, and part of its definition. Bollas (1989) indicated that the traumatic impact of sexual abuse, especially incest, is to create a regression in the child's mind back into an unwanted, developmentally undifferentiated state, reversing the psychic differentiation from the mother. He indicated that this process occurs in childhood sexual trauma, incestuous and nonincestuous, and can disrupt ego functioning and ongoing development to comprise the child's capacity to feel, reflect, fantasize, desire, dream, and even comfortably think. Selma Kramer (1990) has elaborated on her findings of the two most important residues of incest being particular problems in learning related to powerfully charged resistances to remembering events and feelings associated with incest, as well as identifying with parents' distortion of reality and their potential injunction to not tell or know anything about the incident.

The relationship of attachment problems in dissociation has been addressed by Fonagy (1999) to indicate that a lack of resolution of trauma in the parents may be associated with the parent responding to infant distress by fear. When the child perceives the parent as frightening, or frightened and unpredictable, the child responds with detachment (Main, 1995).

Any fear or trauma in infancy and childhood brings forth the biological responses of fight, flight, or dissociation (Fonagy, 1999). The inconsistency of the parental response, including at times being frightened or frightening, may result in a child perceiving the need for soothing and comfort with accompanying arousal as a danger signal, prompting dissociation. A natural response to a fear or disruption of contact coupled with intensification of need, is to dissociate; this disconnection of affective state effects a temporary escape when physical escape is impossible. This dissociated internal state, the antithesis of association, creates an unintegrated, essentially incoherent internal structure. Fonagy (1999) indicates that this form of attachment creates a dissociative core of self-representation, the predisposition to future dissociative responses. The specific coupling of signals and events with this internal reaction become encoded as danger. These "triggers" are concrete and external as well as internal, and are coupled in symbolic ways to danger and can automatically create dissociation. A generalization of response occurs, so that ultimately even the signal of certain feelings create an automatic, unconscious dissociation as defense.

In this manner, the transposition of dissociative states may be transgenerational, such as of Holocaust trauma (Fonagy, 1998). This continued slippage across the internal boundaries of connected and nonconnected (nondissociated and dissociated) self-states creates a particular vulnerability to highly symbolic and emotionally meaningful stimuli, especially to attachment figures and the moods and words of those figures. Fonagy (1998) even believes that this dissociative core permits a more direct transmission of unconscious fantasy from parent to child, which adds to the exquisite vulnerability. For example, a kind of developmental trauma may occur in which a small child goes to a parent and experiences the parent as disconnected in some way, perhaps due to an altered state from drinking, perhaps because of extreme disinterest or nonattunement, or from the parent being dissociated. Rather than experiencing the mirrored and attuned self-object response of the parent, the child cannot engage the parent. This experience is like that of walking to a mirror, expecting a familiar reflection of oneself, but instead encountering plain glass without any reflection. The instantaneous response of, "Where am I?" replaced by the cognitive recognition of it not being a true mirror is not possible for the young child. The response is instead terror, the anxiety of nonexistence ("*Am* I?") when not reflected in the parents' eyes. When not seen by the parent, the small child cannot see himself or herself. The continuity of being in one's body and taking it for granted is disrupted. If these experiences are cumulative, and consistently unpredictable, it becomes impossible to take one's body for granted, to see and feel one's self knowingly.

Another common example is the child of a parent who is dissociative, drug or alcohol abusing, with whom the child has had to relate in different states, alternating between attachment and full detachment. This description entails the phenomenon of the use of the dissociative defense without the actual experience of trauma or terror, yet based on more than an identification with a dissociative parent. Rather than actual life-threatening trauma, it represents a specific genre of developmental trauma that creates a subtle form of dissociation.

If these experiences significantly alter the reality of one's self and body, this disconnection, or more appropriately, lack of a cohesive integration of body and self, can lead to failure to symbolically represent early essential, even preverbal experiences into a more meaningful and cohesive whole. Brothers (1998) refers to these extreme forms of dissociation not based on trauma as experiential black holes, noting that it is impossible to experience a sense of wholeness and cohesiveness when important aspects of self-experience are dissociated. Additionally, these aspects of self never initially integrated in development may read as dissociated. The ways in which a patient fills these formless, empty, and vague experiences of developmental nonformation become the identifiable symptoms. For example, if these patients attempt to fill these developmental holes by food, an eating disorder ensues; many of these patients describe a binge as a kind of dissociative experience, and often refer to "zoning out."

This lack of formed, differentiated experiential self may present as a deadness, an emptiness, a sense that something is profoundly missing. There may be an attempt to locate this deadness in a partner, a kind of symbiotic twinship in which the deadness is then attempted to be activated in the other person as originally attempted with the parent. Because there can be no subjectivity or objectivity of one's self, the displacement of this deadness or emptiness into another to attempt remedy or restitution is a valiant effort at creating effectiveness where none could exist otherwise.

Some of the factors that can produce disorganized–disoriented attachment in children include parental confusion, rapid shifts in state of mind of the parent, overintrusiveness in response to stress by parents, and dissociation in the parent (Siegel, 1999). These emotional changes of state are usually accompanied by physical reactions such as bodily tightening, stiffening of muscles, change of expression, behavioral change toward action, and internal disorganization. Somatic expressions often come into play when parents have unresolved experiences from their childhood that have involved a threat to their physical and psychological integrity (Siegel, 1999). For these parents who have difficulty regulating their own state changes, it is especially difficult to consistently regulate state changes in their children.

The child of a parent with altering of states of consciousness becomes extraordinarily perceptive, sensitively attuned to nuances of warning from the parent revealing any indication of an impending change. Often unpredictable, the parent's shift may be an entrance into a trancelike withdrawn state with frozen silence, or a trip-wire into a sudden onset of explosive rage. The resultant dissociated state in the child, filled with fear, rejection, and alienation is often deeply permeated with shame. When this child is an adult and procedural–associative memory activated creates a dissociated state, this shame, a deep humiliation within, is component of the experience. A repeated entry into these states of mind as a child is engrained in neural networks, and repeated activation becomes a trait of the individual (Siegel, 1999).

The cues serving as catalyst to these internal dissociations, the subsequent behavioral change and internal experience, and their connection to patterns of attachments are relationships in the present and past that must all be understood as part of a system. Shifts of state may be indicated in simple ways, such as the change of the use of the present tense to describe the past, a move from first person to second person pronoun, such as speaking of "I," then shifting to "you" when speaking about one's self, indicating movement from an internal point of reference to that of an observer. Shifts of state of mind may be a smooth continuity, seemless and invisible, or it may be abrupt and chaotic, as is characteristic of the first year of life (Siegel, 1999).

Dynamically and developmentally related to identification with the aggressor, an identification with the dissociated or altered-state parent can occur in which the child internalizes the parents' actual state as a part of her own structure (Winnicott, 1965). When the child is then confronted at moments with a frightening or frightened caregiver, she takes in as part of herself that caregiver's feeling and state, and comes to see herself as frightening, bad, out of control, or in other ways unmanageable (Fonagy, 1998). Fonagy believes that the child must externalize this unbearable image to maintain self-cohesion. This frightening image may be perceived in an altered state, going down an alternate track as state-dependent experiences with state-dependent memory. The cues creating a bridge to this state become highly symbolized, automatic, and instantaneous over time with repeated usage and entry into that state. These experiences are unbearable in a usual state of mind, and become so automatic that affect, tolerance, and differentiation in fact does not occur, because any affect then becomes generalized as a signal terror to shift to a dissociated state.

Either with the transmission of a dissociated state from parent to child, or the experience of the terror of actual trauma, the internal space within which one can fantasize, think, feel, and reflect on experience and its meaning is either collapsed or does not get formed. Fantasy life, and the experience of internal metaphor does not exist. The developmental transition to fantasy, metaphor, and symbolization is sidetracked to an alternate state which is fixed, specific, and concrete with collapse of the potential space for fantasy and trial action. From a traditional perspective, this transition may appear at best borderline, often psychotic. Most frequently the patient appears concrete, unable to symbolize or even to speak of themselves and the experiences and actions from an internal point of reference, other than perhaps around the organizing identity of victimhood and orientation to crisis.

Stolorow and Atwood (1992) conceptualize most elegantly another level of discontinuity of mind and body in which the individual identifies with an external, usually critical view of an essential caregiver incorporated as a self-perception. In order to safeguard a necessary tie to the caregiver, the child abandons his own internal experience largely because it is unmirrored, embracing the perspective of the caregiver to form an accommodation to preserve that needed bond. The perception of criticalness and shame is located outside one's own body in which one's body becomes the focus of shame, blame, criticism, and self-consciousness. A separateness of the mind and body then exists, and the body becomes the container of repugnant, humiliating, shameful, and disowned aspects of experience.

Case Illustration

Maureen, 43, had been traumatized at the hands of her sister between approximately ages 3 and 6 in a reportedly sadistic way, the passing on of the sexual abuse perpetrated on that sister by a nanny. When the nanny was caught and fired, and the behaviors were addressed, the abuse apparently stopped.

Maureen reported a vulnerable disorganized attachment with her mother, experienced as disinterested and unavailable, coupled with the trauma at the hands of her sister, with whom she had formed an attachment as an alternative to the mother. Having never connected to her mother in a meaningful way, she noted that her mother zoned out and was not responsible after her sister died; her mother "wasn't there." She found her father to be the most consistently attuned to her, but at the time of her sister's suicide, when Maureen was 14, her father immediately began an affair and spent little time at home. Maureen cut her arms and legs beginning at this time, continuing into the present. She cut at times when she felt most abandoned and filled with rage. She attempted to purge her rage by cutting herself, yet she experienced doing so as horrible and disgusting. These attempts at active mastery of self-injury by her own hand were also part of a scenario of dissociation in an attempt to become reconnected to her body via the sensory bridges of seeing, feeling, and smelling the blood, later feeling the pain. Hours later she would experience the shame of what she had done to herself in the dissociated state.

When Maureen began analysis, she increased compulsive eating. My attempts at mutual scrutiny of these action symptoms was paralleled by her husband's confrontation about her behavior and lack of responsibility. Her daughter had just turned 3, resonating emotionally with the initiation of abuse when Maureen was age 3. By dissociating, Maureen was also identifying with her mother by withdrawing from the active engagement with her daughter, as well as her physical absence by traveling more.

Her disorganized mother, prior to the trauma of the sister's death, as well as the depressed mother subsequent to the death, were both actualized in analysis, in the experience of disorganization, dissociation, and depression, as well as experiencing me, at times, as unavailable, detached, or preoccupied. The revival of these relationships and qualities also activated development from a time when it had been frozen and derailed.

Both her vulnerability and aggression had so permeated her sexuality that she had created a barrier of obesity, a protective shield so that no one would approach her now, not even her husband. We came to see in the early months of the analysis how profoundly dissociated Maureen was, by her own estimate spending 95% of the day in a dissociated state. The only time when she was not dissociated were fleeting moments in the analysis, and short periods of interaction with her 3-year-old daughter. She had devised a system of nannies for her daughter, and always had one "on call" for the expected abandonment.

Maureen felt that what would happen to her in the day seemed reactive, such as what she would see on television, or what someone would say to her when she was out shopping, a random event that would determine not only what she would subsequently feel, but what would happen to her for the remainder of the day or week. Equal only to her inaccessibility with my early interventions was her initial passive indication that she did not want to give up dissociation: She seemed to enjoy the dreamy, detached state over one in which she would be more aware of dealing with various feelings, most of which were unfamiliar and painful. She hated crowds, even interaction with others because of her complete vulnerability to them and being unable to determine exactly what may constitute an emotional trip-wire for a prolonged period of disassociation. This vulnerability seemed to relate to the boundaries between states, being permeable and readily crossed, for which her only protection seemed withdrawal. This vulnerability seemed linked to cues from others and from the unconscious coupling and internalization of her caregiver's mental state to form a "dissociative core self" (Fonagy, 1998). I would repeatedly ask variations of "How connected are you with your self right now? How grounded do you feel in your experience of this moment?" Countertransference awareness of nonattunement and difficulty tracking her signaled her dissociation; ultimately she and I would collaborate to recognize and address this process more actively (in other patients dullness, boredom, feeling lost, or confusion are countertransference markers of dissociation).

Much of the initial and midphase work was on increasing awareness of the process of dissociation, to focus specifically on this moment-by-moment flow of how her mind works, of associating rather than dissociating. To directly address the process of dissociation was quite difficult for her, as it required becoming grounded in her immediate experience, fully "present" rather than dissociated. Then, exploration gradually expanded to move back to the point of the signal feeling that triggered an instantaneous dissociation into an altered state, to explore the feeling and its ascribed present and past meaning.

This association of feeling and meaning in an nondissociated state is not free association, as free association may foster resistance and nonresponsibility for staying with a feeling or experience to fully explore it. Additionally, dissociation may look like free association, and one may mask the other. Focusing specifically on the process of disconnection itself and relating that process to the state and content that one gets lost inside, is the painstaking, meticulous work of the analytic task for these patients.

A Clinical Overview of States of Mind

"Staying present" adopts a self-reflective position about one's own state of mind in present time and as a continuity over time. "Staying present" and collaborating together creates a new potential (analytic) space to view, new couplings of meaning, and an evolving mutually constructed new paradigm. The concept of analytic focus on the process and context of dynamics, unconscious meaning and symbolism assumes a unitary centering within a single mental state. An additional perspective is on the system—the structural context of the self-states, and the continuity or discontinuity of the self states themselves.

The variety of ego states (states of mind) that we all experience are more extreme, sometimes more distinct and discrete in patients with dissociation. Each of the ego states may represent corresponding self-representations, each containing its own perceptions, ways of processing, and set of representations of self and other. For these individuals with a primary defense and working model of dissociation, empathic resonance, and usual interpretive comments are not enough. The initial and ongoing work must focus centrally on the process of the state of mind, of state changes, and the mastery of state changes. Focus on the content, meanings, dynamics, and symbolism within each state will not result in usable, integrative synthesis and thus not to developmental growth. Traumatically sequestered aspects of the self, necessary to segment and dissociate during childhood and adolescence, must be understood first by focusing on how "present" the patient is now in an unaltered state, to understand the distinctness of states of mind, ultimately to master and integrate state changes. The primary defense of dissociation, necessary for both adaptation and survival earlier, since adulthood may be the primary interference with both developmental growth and analytic work. A dissociative change of state is an immediate defense to stop a feeling; staying with the present feeling is staying with present meaning, state, and context. Dissociation reinstates another state of mind with its own perception and meaning.

While the patient may be focused in a segment of his reality and self, the analyst must keep the entire system in mind, acknowledging and resonating with the immediate experience, yet collaboratively focusing on how present the patient is, how a shift occurred to a particular segment, and how to "get back" to being fully present and survey the entire system rather than being immersed in one segment as the whole. The patient may initially not experience the segmented states of mind as separate distinct subjectivities. These various states, each with their own perception, experience, and motivation, can be quite confusing to the patient, even overwhelming, in their initial recognition. Analogous to different software packages in a computer, the ego's expanding awareness as a search engine creates a mastery of state changes. The primary need of the dissociative patient is not to reenter past trauma in order to resolve it, as this would require dissociation, the repetition of state change. The reparation and belated mastery of reentering an old trauma and writing a better ending to the old story, even a thousand times over, only creates the illusion of mastery. Rather, the patient remaining present, engaged in a mutually transforming relationship and collaboration with the analyst allows all of the important and necessary aspects of the past to come into the present, for understanding, integration, and resolution of past experience. This dosing, timing, and titrating of traumatic experiences is the antithesis of the past, as well as mutual collaboration in the present. In this way, both patient and analyst are able to find a voice for the inchoate, the unspeakable, the unfathomable, and to crystallize hope in a new context. This collaborative, mutual process is also the antithesis of both passivity and of subjugation to authority, restoring the active mastery and power to the patient from within. In so doing, the patient may reclaim her own body as well as her own experiences, integrating the two in a new model that does not require segregation. Dissociative self-remedies are no longer necessary. Missed experiences as well as shattered idealizations must be mourned.

To formulate dissociation as a defense as a regressive ego state, or of isolation of affect and repression, thereby equating it to the regression to an infantile state of mind would be both reductionistic and miss the actual mechanism of the psychophysiological alteration and change of state mind that occurs with dissociation. Dissociation does evolve over time to a more ubiquitous defense, automatically triggered with any signal of affect, positive or negative. In this way, it is analogous to a powerful addiction in which its use can instantly make any discomfort seem to vanish, not considering the consequence or the effect on the system internally as a whole. It is a promise ultimately never kept, just as any other addictive process involving an object, substance, or activity. Plunging into the mental content of a particular state of mind, without engaging the observing ego (the process of how connected one is to one's self in this instance), will result in pockets of seeming useful analysis, but an overall stuckness , paralleling the dissociative system in its segmentation. In a particular state, a patient may be unable to put words to that state, or even recognize initially that is a state change process.

The defensively altered state of consciousness of dissociation, adapted originally to overstimulation and terror of external trauma, may become more consistently utilized in a characterological way to create disturbances of alertness, memory, awareness, and even of segmented identity. While appearing as repression and regression, and especially splitting, these internal segments of ego states may never have been integrated in order to be defensively split. While the content of each of the ego states is extremely important, it is more important to understand and master the process of having and changing states. The content of free associations from within a particular state may create the illusion of a psyche accessed and working, rather than limited within a particular ego state. While seeming to be useful and productive analytic work, it creates the overarching awareness by both parties of stuckness, punctuated by sudden and abrupt changes of state that seemingly have no apparent emotional signifier or visible symbolic trip-wire. Analysis of the transference is important, but only after analysis of movement between and existence of ego states can be understood and mastered. Brenner (1994) speaks of the difficulty of engaging these dissociative patients in treatment, emphasizing that the most productive work comes in helping them transform depersonalized self-observation into more analytic self-observation.

Part III

Clinical Applications

The years teach much that the days never know.
Ralph Waldo Emerson

Everything in life that we really accept undergoes a change.
Katherine Mansfield

This "I" therefore allows us to enter an inaccessible magic space, a hitherto inarticulate space of intimacy and honesty earlier denied us, where voice, for the first time, has replaced silence.
Frank Bidart
Desire

We can understand the unknown only through metaphors attached to what we know.
James Thorpe

A word spoken creates a dog, a rabbit, a man. It fixes their nature before our eyes; henceforth, their shapes are, in a sense, our own creation. They are no longer part of the unnamed shifting architecture of the universe. They have been transfixed as if by sorcery, frozen into a concept, a word. Powerful though the spell of human language has proven itself to be, it has laid boundaries upon the cosmos.
Loren Eiseley
The Invisible Pyramid

10

Clinical Considerations
in Dissociation

The mind seems to embrace a confederation of psychic entities.
William James, 1896

You can't solve a problem on the same level that it was created.
You have to rise above it to the next level.
Albert Einstein

All is caprice: they love today beyond measure those whom
they will hate tomorrow beyond reason.
Sir Thomas Sydenham

When I play drunks I had to remain sober because I didn't
know how to play them when I was drunk.
Richard Burton

Mr. Dufy lived a short distance from his body.
James Joyce

The acquisition of knowledge in any field of science is shaped and filtered by the theories held by the observer. The six predominant models of
the mind in psychoanalytic theory are characterized by Rothstein (1986)
as structural, object relations, Lacanian, self psychology, interpersonal,
and Klein-Bion. Even adding developmental and intersubjectivity, these
core concepts of acquiring and organizing data are insufficient to explain
the systemic paradigm of altered states and multiple levels of awareness.

The mind as a system is more applicable for dissociation: A systematic overlapping network of different states of mind, each with its own perception and processing of experiences and attached meanings.

The assumption in clinical work that a patient's ego/self-state is singular is valid because most analytic work is done from an essential core state of mind of both analyst and patient. Dissociative patients, however, may have several states, sometimes distinct, sometimes within the session, and sometimes between sessions. Dissociative patients, having difficulty with continuity, may not experience themselves as the same throughout the entire day. Dissociation is a defense cued by a response to a particular feeling or sensory input that instantly sets in motion a change of state of mind, often imperceptible to both patient and analyst.

The notion that emotions, wishes, and perceptions are transferred from prior relationships and earlier development into the analytic situation and onto the analyst assumes a horizontal hierarchy of unconscious memory and process moving toward preconscious and then conscious experience and manifestation. Dissociation is vertical and parallel. Tracts of different experiences (states of mind) exist in parallel fashion in the psyche with multiple levels and states of consciousness. Both the patient and the analyst must be aware of the plurality of states of mind of each, and their reciprocal and intersubjective reactivity (Davies, 1996). Likewise, patient and analyst need to be able in a systemic manner to resonate, hold, focus, contain, respond, and organize multiple aspects of awareness and receptivity, consciously and unconsciously (Davies, 1999). These states of mind may have overlapping seamless edges, or distinct, crisp distinctions.

Current traumas, such as surgery or other bodily invasions may resonate with and crystallize symptoms associated with dissociated traumatic experience. Other occurrences allow that beginning awareness of dissociated experiences include the patient's child reaching the age of the beginning of the childhood abuse or trauma, or the evolution of such trust that both patient and analyst are ready to have these issues emerge in the treatment process. Only when someone feels fully secure can they be aware of how afraid they have been.

Dissociation as a Defense

Patients who use dissociation as a defense are not struggling primarily with conflict, or needing to make conscious what is unconscious, or even to understand the wish, fear, and compromise formation of conflict, but instead, need to focus initially on the continuity of their own state of mind, on "staying present," which refers to being in an unaltered, nondissociated state that allows a self-reflective position about their own states of mind and discontinuities of state. Being or getting "present" may be unknown or without meaning to a patient who is dissociative, as nothing about a particular state of mind may seem altered when one is in it. Additionally, patients may only be motivated to understand and emerge from states of mind that are dysphoric.

Vignette 1

One patient expressed knowledge that often she felt an internal deterrent to emerging from an altered state of mind, as that would result in the immediate dissipation of positive aspects and talents exclusive to that particular state. Exiting any state (whether exciting or dysphoric) at times had the consequence of blaming or shaming by others who read her lack of continuity between states as failure to keep promises and professional or personal commitments. Additionally, driven passions that disappear overnight, lack of perseverance, and inconsistency of response can be symptoms of state changes that may result in reactions by self and others of judgment, such as "having no 'stick-to-itness'" that become shaming.

She recognized that her entire experience previously had been to respond to and be focused on external events, and the attempt to focus internally, to recognize state changes was difficult. She also knew that a movement from a particular state would be accompanied by the loss of important abilities and skills, such as foreign language ability and other knowledge. She experienced certain attributes such as motivational stamina within a particular state of mind, state specific athletic abilities, and talents that did not overlap into other states.

She recalled a recent segment of her life of isolation due to specific, toxic trauma and her creation of a shielding dome of music. She wore a protective headset with only her specifically selected music in order to totally determine her input. As a young girl she used music as soothing selfobject to mirror mood and reflect specific feeling, to resonate with needs, and the lyrics to inform about what relationships could/should be. Her repertoire of songs would mirror and resonate with a highly developed specificity of internal attunement, though experienced in a segmented way until analytic work.

Dissociation is often prompted by any feeling, good or bad, intense or not, in a patient who regularly uses dissociation as a defense, just as someone who is obsessional responds to any significant affect by intellectualization. Affect as a catalyst to dissociate occurs in an automatic, instant way, so that the patient often is unaware of how the altered state

was entered, and of how pervasive this process has become. When dissociation has become this automatic, it is so camouflaged in the fabric of
daily life as to be invisible. Dissociation immediately disrupts the self-
state and self-reflective functioning.

A feeling is stopped automatically and imperceptibly with subsequent instantaneous state change, rendering inaccessible (at least initially
in the analytic process) the ability to reflect on the dynamics, process,
and meaning in the original state. After a state change, there is usually a
sense of being stuck in that state, but without awareness that it is a state,
or that there are other states of mind. It is a significant leap to be aware
of state changes, to put words to the state descriptively and dynamically,
and to not change states but stay with the original feeling.

Current experience rather than past memory is more important in
the foreground of analytic experience. What is important will become
activated within the transference/fantasy/experiential sequence within
analysis. We do not in any other area of analysis make specific efforts to
urge a patient to remember a certain content. The term *repressed memory*
does not apply to dissociation. The psychophysiological state change of
dissociation is quite distinct from the model of repression of unconscious
conflictual material and experience (Kluft, 2000). The simultaneous tracks
of state of mind, like different software programs on the same computer,
are a different paradigm from unconscious unavailability due to repression as a defense.

A fundamental task in analytic work with the dissociative patient is
to focus on the process of state change in the patient's unaltered state.
Being aware of how "connected" or "grounded" inside one's own body
and mind one is allows gradual awareness of its antithesis: dissociation.
Focus can then extend to include the specific feeling that triggers the
disconnection, as well as to observe the transitions between states. The
current instantaneous state change of dissociation can then become a
focus of the mutual and collaborative work. Understanding, labeling,
and experiencing the feeling that has served as a trigger for a state change
precedes exploration of how the feeling initially was coupled with danger or trauma, and how dissociation becomes generalized as a response
to a wide range of affect. The automatic defense of dissociation gradually moves from an event to a process.

Once continuity of an unaltered state can be established, exploration can move to the reading of a current affect as dangerous, a perception from past experience and past time. When a patient is able to consistently stay with a feeling, this process itself distinguishes present from
past, new story from old story. Dissociation blurs past and present as an
affect or its signal unconsciously triggers a state change to experience the
exact past content of a state. The resultant experience is of *being in* a

memory rather than *having* a memory. The creation of a continuous present state distinguishes intrinsically from past experience as well as from other states of mind, and allows reflection on the process of state changes.

The mutual and collaborative focus on this process of "staying present" and of observing the patient's experience together creates a new, actual space to understand, to symbolize, and to transcribe experiences with new meanings. For the dissociative patient, the enigma of seeing oneself as a system is a different dimension of awareness. The recognition of the energy expended in dissociation emphasizes one effect of dissociation on the system.

For these patients who have so routinely used dissociation as a defense, it has also become a style cognitively, behaviorally, and affectively. Their model of the mind has become a segmental one, in which they experience their life sequentially and segmentally rather than as a continuum. Their continuity is within a state of mind, or of the same state within a certain context or cue, but not as a cohesive whole. The richness of their system results in a curious linear, segmental experience of their conscious life. Often because of compartmentalizing different experiences of self-awareness, becoming aware of multiple levels of states of mind is often quite disconcerting. For someone who is distinctly dissociative, the essence of the analytic work, and the majority of the time of the analytic work will be that of working on "staying present," of creating a continuity of self-experience and of integrating the previously disconnected aspects of the self and awareness. This self-awareness becomes a significant achievement in the analysis rather than the prerequisite for it. The association of various experiences is the antithesis of dissociation of encapsulation and segmentation.

Mutual Regulation of State Changes

A central activity in the process of analysis is a similar joint activity of a caregiver with a child: the mutual regulation of state changes (Lichtenberg, 1998; Stern et al., 1998). The regulation of affect states and states of mind involves the understanding and mastery of allowing access to a particular state of mind without altering consciousness to do so. Perhaps nowhere is this more poignant than the regulation of mind state with creative artists and writers. Various authors have been able to establish states of mind in order to do particular writing. For example, Dame Edith Sitwell would lie in an open coffin as a prelude to writing her macabre literature. The contained solitude and dim, stale air of the coffin set the stage for a particular state of mind, a mental genre analogous to her writing (Ackerman, 1999). Other writers create states of mind to fit their intended work: Dr. Samuel Johnson and the poet, W. H. Auden drank colossal amounts of tea when they wrote; Willa Cather would read the Bible to set the right tone prior to her writing; George Sands would go immediately from lovemaking to writing; Voltaire would use his lover's back for a writing desk; Benjamin Franklin wrote while soaking in a bathtub, wanting to immerse himself in concentration as in water to focus his thought process; Coleridge used opium (2 mg) before a session of writing. The painter Turner liked to be lashed to the mast of a ship and taken for a sail during an incredible storm, later to re-create this experience on canvas. Diane Ackerman (1991) writes in a warm bubble bath with a pine plank across the tub as a writing surface to enter a suspended, freely creative state of mind. The number of authors who used alcohol are legion. Many writers become fixated on a piece of music as they write a book, and will play the piece again and again thousands of times during the course of writing; the music chosen induces an emotional framework to set the mood for the story to come alive.

There may be a corresponding or matching of state of mind of the reader with that of the author, in which the author guides the reader to a particular state through the senses: the music and voice of the words, the texture of imagery, and the rhythm of feelings.

In addition to the mutual and collaborative focus of the analytic experience, a patient may use the process of keeping a personal journal, of portioning a specific, consistent, predictable time each day to write, to focus internally and reflect on internal experience. This process of internal focus and writing or drawing about feelings and bodily sensations may access and integrate body self and psychological self dualities, in which experiences can be articulated and defined. Some patients have described this process as actively engaging in an internal rather than external focus, like holding a mirror to their internal experiences in spontaneously and creatively writing in a journal. The use of a transitional object, such as a book or other inanimate object from the analyst's office, may tangibly facilitate a focus on, and representation of, the process of the analytic work as well as the internal attunement. This is helpful in particular for individuals who have not yet developmentally consolidated a body and self-image, and may not have solidified as yet an evocative image of the analyst or of the analytic process. A collaboratively chosen transitional object may serve as an icon for this process and representation of the analyst as self-object to foster continuity and internalization. Similarly for the patient with developmental disruption so significant as to not yet have the object permanence of evoking an image of the analytic work, office, or analyst, leaving an item in the analyst's office may offer a temporary sense of continuity.

It may be useful information for the analyst, as well as a beneficial collaboration, to determine how long after leaving the session the patient can maintain an image to evoke the process of the analytic sessions, and of the analyst. The amount of time may serve as a barometer indicating the process of internalization, development of a structure internally to maintain a consistent and cohesive self-representation, and the autonomy of self through various affective states.

We must speak to the analysand about the strength of internal aspects of the self that protect by alienating others, including attempts to alienate the analyst, of other aspects internally that bear sadness or rage, and perhaps others fueled by anger that otherwise would have been overwhelming unless cordoned off and encapsulated. The awareness and experiencing of these self-states must be dosed, timed, and titrated collaboratively, but after the patient has the continuity of an unaltered state, and mastery of state specific experience and state changes.

In the analytic relationship, we must be eager students for each patient to teach us how delicate the balance is, how certain words can have teeth, can bite hard, or can prematurely pick away scabs. We must be aware that real feelings do not disappear, despite the illusion created by dissociation. We must know as well that the patient may not determine who he or she wakes up as, or what might flip the switch throughout the day for another expression, aspect, or self to be present.

The Clinical Exchange in Dissociation

Disarming the land mines of emotional couplings in the hippocampus that have been traumatically fused requires a new lived experience, new emotional and cognitive couplings from the immersion in the analytic relationship. Insight and understanding alone are not enough. Consistent focus and attention to immediate body self and state of mind develops an entire continuum of experience rather than the all-or-nothing segmental experience of dissociation. Therapeutic work with a dissociative patient must initially center on awareness of self-state and the process of state changes. Being present in an unaltered state and focused in a full integration of present state of awareness of mind and body is the antithesis of dissociation, in which a particular state/identity with its associated set of memories is activated and in the foreground, while some or all of the others are inactivated or "turned off."

In treatment, the most abiding principle is continuity of unaltered, present state, and in creating this new continuity to write a coherent, complete story, with no passages or chapters left out. This process of experiencing and integrating in current awareness from a constant unaltered state of mind and body may discover aspects of one's self not previously in awareness. Some experiences may never be integrated directly into the present because of the experience being recorded at a time before any cohesive experience could be registered; for example, much of the first three years of life when the central nervous system is unable to record explicit memories and events.

A patient may be so unaccustomed to conscious awareness of nonverbal communications, bodily movements, or facial expressions, that he or she may feel discomfort, anxiety, or shame when these experiences are initially in focus and verbalized. Consistent attunement to the body self as well as the psychological self can serve to associate rather than dissociate experiences in converging immediate somatic experience and emotional awareness in the analytic moment.

Concentration on body self experience may mobilize powerful resistances in the analytic work, including both shame and a fear of regression toward prior overwhelming experiences of trauma. This aversion may be to revisiting a distorted or fragmented body self, to the perception of the body as ugly, or to the fusion of somatic awareness and pain. Because feeling and action have been traumatically fused, or never developmentally differentiated the patient may worry that feeling will be the same as acting. There may also be particular times of day that require enhanced attunement to body self experiences such as times of fatigue, stress, hunger, or sleep deprivation. At these times it is important for the patient to address both physical and emotional needs, as in, for example, attunement to physical rather than emotional hunger.

The content, symbolic attributions, unconscious meaning, and even the dynamic flow of feeling detract from or obfuscate the alteration of one state of mind to another. Some specific feeling, whether recognized consciously or not, is the trigger that creates dissociative change of state (here and now always happens before there and then, so should always be considered first). Dissociation is both a developmental nonattainment (nonintegration), as well as a defense of the moment, occurring originally at time of some experienced or perceived trauma, recurring now in a moment of feeling, thus a form of response to signal anxiety.

Dissociation is almost always experienced in a passive way, as "just happening." For example, a patient expressed an inability to do paperwork, forgetting her clothes at the cleaners, losing her wallet. She indicated, "I tried to have my house nicely arranged with everything in order, documents and clothes put in order. But it was like the wind blows against me." She indicated, in closer scrutiny, that she felt somewhat "zoned out" as this was occurring. To focus on the feeling that induces dissociation as well as the shift of her state of mind is an active process, the antithesis of the passive victimhood implicit in being blown by the wind.

Within a particular state of mind the focal length is frozen, making it difficult to reflect or observe. Fullest recognition of sequential state changes must occur from an unaltered state. Having this fixed internal point of reference allows appreciation of relative movement of ego states. By comprehension of the process of dissociation as a defense, patients stay in the present moment and inside current experience, allowing the experience of all of the component parts, disavowed and denied feelings, experiences, and awareness.

As for every patient, psychoanalysis occurs within the present moment, not going back into the past unless it intrudes into the present. Feeling that is remembered is feeling that is present. Patients' difficulties have arisen due to their avoidance of the present moment. I have told dissociative patients, never having any refutation or disagreement, "It seems that almost every emotional difficulty that you've experienced in adult life has most immediately been due, not to the trauma of childhood and adolescence, but to dissociation." It is the focus on the process, the minute detail, frame by frame, second by second, feeling by feeling, that allows one to stay in the present, perceiving how quickly the present is lost due to stopping feelings and disconnecting from them.

In addition, one state of mind may serve as a defense for another state of mind. For example, a patient after considerable work on the process of state changes, stated, "The only thing keeping me from feeling the nothing/empty state is getting into an angry state, constantly being energized by anger. It drives me. If I got rid of all my anger, then I would feel 'nothing' again."

These individuals often seem ideal psychotherapy or psychoanalytic patients; they can free associate readily and richly, seeming to hold back nothing. Yet they may continue to free associate without integration. Free association may be used as a defense, or, what looks like free association may be simply a dissociative veering into another ego state. Following a dissociative shift, often there is an outpouring of vivid, prolific memory, suffering, psychosomatic, or body memory experiences. Plunging into state specific affective, sensory, behavioral, or cognitive detail replicates the process (dissociation) and content (procedural memories) of the past. In the analytic work, free association often only duplicates this haphazard and disorganized process, as a dissociative patient needs to give associations and organization root rather than flight. A new story is to remain very present, connected, and to experience feelings as their own, in the present moment, within an integrated, unaltered self state. The affective storms, the dramatic shifts in internal states or even identities, including flashbacks, perceptual difficulties, or extreme states of anxiety or depression in which one feels stuck, are all indications of the disruption of a dissociative system usually in balance. Goldberg (1995) states, "Because of the lack of true integration of psychosomatic experience into the life of the mind, the body and the instincts are unique and unknown to the thinking self, in a way that is more profound than that encountered in neurotic conditions."

A shift of attention may be used to calm and regulate arousal and attention states. Infants learn to do this, and parents learn quickly that calming can be effected by shifting attention, such as jiggling a set of keys to distract a crying infant. Distraction is a biological mechanism for self-regulation. This mechanism may be part of the adaptive utilization dissociative patients develop to simply shift internally from one state to another as a way of regulating affect and attention. A patient experiencing painful affect may shift focus to an item in the office, or to an aspect of the analyst or patient, a distraction to a tangible, specific referent. Distraction, zoning out, and other variants are on a dissociative continuum that includes more commonly recognized landmarks of amnesia, fugue, depersonalization, and dissociative identity organization.

A significant regulation of emotion is verbalization. Conscious awareness and verbalization of feelings are part of the self-regulatory mastery in an evolved recognition of affect and the mind–body synthesis of emotion. Those individuals who have limited identification and verbalization of subjective feeling have significantly more difficulty regulating tension and affect states. Talking about fantasies underscores the reality that it is not happening. Tolerating fantasy as well as ambivalence is a significant developmental achievement.

Dissociative individuals often fluctuate from internal emptiness or deadness to intense crises of affective storms, usually centering around some perceived personal injustice or abuse. This dissociative episode may result in retreat and isolation, fantasies and plans of retaliation and revenge at the perceived abuser, stimulation of the body in self harm in order to get reconnected, or action symptoms to reestablish the equilibrium within the subjectivity of mind and body.

Individuals who operate in a dissociative way may actively use a substance such as food or alcohol to effect state changes. It is often a striking demonstration of how the necessary regulation of state change is already internal to ask the question, "At what specific point when you eat/drink symptomatically do you notice that your state of mind changes and you feel different?" Usually the state change is the instant just *before* the food/alcohol ever touches their lips. The mood altering substance is recognized then as superfluous, a prop in a process. The idea of a binge, a drink, or a cigarette being sufficient to change the way one feels, emphasizes that we are always creating outside to match inside. Often we create outside to effectively make sense of and to give tangible form to internal experience, especially when it is not fully differentiated. This interpretative process can extend to helping a patient recognize how powerful his or her mind is, that the capacity and function to change the way they feel, to effect a state change, is *already* internal. The previous coupling with a substance, once obligatory and necessary, is now recognized as internal. The *idea* of the thing or substance rather than the thing itself creates a different experience. This empathic interpretative sequence can cleave the experience from the substance or activity, to demonstrate that it is no longer a necessary component in an otherwise addictive process aimed at state change. Mastery involves a paradigm shift of dissecting state change itself from a field of action sequence replete with dynamics, symbolism, and multidetermined meanings.

Grounding Techniques

Specific focus on atttunement to present state may be necessary for some individuals who have been detached from their bodies, or who are just beginning to be aware of a pervasive dissociative process, and have difficulty with internal attunement especially between sessions. Grounding techniques include variations of the following.

1. Asking oneself "How present am I?"
2. Going through a systematic review of the body and perceptions from it, of feeling, perceiving, perhaps even moving (such as tensing and relaxing) each aspect of the body from toes to head.
3. A systematic inventory and perception of each of the senses: seeing, hearing, touching, tasting, smelling.
4. Specific attunement to aspects of the body and the body function that may be calming such as a focus on and control of breathing, of various muscle groups, of body posture.

This specific focus may be calming and may effect both an awareness and mastery of immediate body experience. Patients have noted various ways of recognizing detachment or dissociation: awareness of very specific usual details of their surrounding, drinking water, controlling and varying breathing, attunement to someone else's voice, or a present orientation to self, time, or place. For some patients, a transitional object from the analyst's office offers a tangible bridge to reconstruct the experience with the analyst.

For the dissociative individual, awareness of certain emotionally significant experiences is hypothetical and deductive rather than having direct access to the experiences dissociatively disconnected and remaining segregated from mind–body synchrony. For example, when asked about a certain memory, a patient may respond, "When that happened, I probably felt sad." If asked about a certain event, the response might be, "I would have responded by. . . . " This deduction rather than memory of experience indicates being outside the center of their own feeling experience. Someone who has been abused as a child, but has dissociative amnesia for those events, if asked whether they were abused as a child, might respond, "Not that I remember." Anyone who has not experienced abuse would simply say, "No." This difference is quite striking, and can be illustrated by its parallel: If someone were to ask me if I had ever been to Antarctica, I would not respond, "Not that I remember"; I would simply say, "No."

Repetition versus Retranscription

Much of the work on the developmental impact of trauma has been in the reconstruction of the traumatic situations in adulthood analysis (Rothstein, 1986). The psychic trauma experienced in childhood or adolescence or recapitulated in adulthood in various attempts at mastery, serve as organizing concepts of the core self such as self-blaming by the abused, or creating a core organizing assumption of defectiveness or victimhood. The psychoanalytic position of understanding the repetitions of trauma and the repetition compulsion therein is captured by Furst (1986) when he indicates that reactions to trauma fail in their defensive purposes because they are belated, and this belated response is to the trauma being both past and complete without mastery, with mastery attempted in the present context. The repetition compulsion is a venerated and accurate depiction of psychic mechanisms, but a more fundamental reason why trauma gets repeated, rather than resolved, even in the analytic situation, is that the process itself is repeated: that is, the patient dissociates in response to some uncomfortable feeling and in this dissociated state the process and content are both recapitulated, making present mastery and integration impossible because of the dissociated state.

In the experience of trauma, the endless series of repetitions of traumatic material or the traumatic process resulting in victimhood do not lead to new learning, discharge, or detoxification of the traumatic experience. What may appear as an abreactive, as experienced from an altered state, is simply a repetition; that is, the "abreaction" of aspects of the trauma or the trauma itself as remembered is not enough. This repetition can even be retraumatizing, and dissociation is repeated rather than constructing a synthesis between mind and body, experience and expressed emotion, including bodily memory. A new story of remaining present and firmly anchored in the present experience, rather than dissociating even to a slight degree, is integrating, as all experiences come together in full awareness in an unaltered state. For the first time, mind and body, thought and feeling, memory and present experience are synthesized in the present moment and lived experience of the clinical exchange.

Vignette 2 (including a dissociative dream specimen)

Tim, a man in his early 40s, consulted me after moving to Houston. He had an analysis in another city for eight years and had felt stuck and eventually stopped two years earlier. He consulted me about how stuck he still felt in his life, his difficulty in being happy, and how futile it all seemed. He had done considerable analytic work with much insight and understanding centering around the impact of a particular accident in his life and development. Tim was intensely preoccupied with his bowel functioning, representing the control that he did not experience at age 12 when he had a freak accident. Most of his body was burned when a kerosene stove exploded at a mountain home during a family vacation. The meaning and symbolism of bodily control relative to his trauma were regularly in focus, and he continued to explore the significance regarding his trauma. He had begun our twice weekly therapy as if he were still in analysis, immediately going to the couch and beginning to "free associate." He focused on control and retribution. He would imagine the pleasure of traveling on safari, and immediately would stop his pleasurable fantasy to ask, "Where would I go to the bathroom, and would I have time alone?"

I interrupted him to ask how he was feeling at the moment just before he began to focus on bowel control and his trauma. He thought for a moment and then indicated that when he was pleasantly remembering a recent trip to a resort, and how he was feeling almost spontaneous, it was immediately replaced by concern about his bowels. I pointed out that at the very instant he was feeling spontaneous and good, he stopped himself and shifted to the content of control. He protested that it was free association. I indicated my belief that free association can sometimes be used to segue from feeling, or to stop a feeling outright, and that it didn't seem to me that he was really feeling free.

We then further explored the specific nature of the feeling that triggered that shift. He indicated that he had the fantasy while I had been talking moments ago of both of us standing up and his leaning on me. I asked him how that would feel. His response was, "Is this suggesting a dependency—leaning on you in the way I never did with my father, to get energy to move, or a solidarity celebrating with you my manhood?"

I told him I was more interested in his feeling associated with the fantasy before he moved to theorize. His response was that it felt like he was "watching something," and elaborated on that. I interrupted to tell him that this was an idea, and asked again how he felt.

His response was, "Comfortable, warm, relieving." That it was "okay to feel."

I responded, "The fantasy brought together the feeling and the idea in a way that you hadn't allowed yourself."

He was silent for some time and then spoke. "It allows energy and feeling to flow when I don't focus on constipation."

I said, "Or the other way around."

He said, "You mean constipation can be an inhibition, an inhibitor? The focus on my bowels a result of inhibition?"

"Yes," I responded. "Our connection in your leaning-on fantasy is a connection also of your mind and body, your thoughts and feelings, of being at the center of your experience rather than moving away to be an observer, watching from outside your body.

"I've been thinking about swimming," he said. "How good it feels to let myself be suspended and free and have all of me immersed in water and in the activity." I elaborated on how the sensations of swimming allow a full awareness of one's body, of water pushing against and outlining the entire body.

We subsequently explored the fantasy incorporating dissociation of "watching something" involving himself, and the predominant experience of watching himself from outside his body. He acknowledged the same experience in a session with me when he would stop himself from feeling and observe himself as if he were beside me, outside his body. While this may have been the transference of a critical parent, it was primarily and mostly for him the immediately dissociative defense of stopping a feeling and moving outside his body.

He later recognized that whenever he felt cold in the session it was when he had disconnected himself from his body. He became increasingly aware that some feelings served as the signal to shift a whole other set of experiences to the foreground: a state of mind in which he did not feel worthy, felt a void and empty, and felt fear as if he were a helpless child. Tim added, "When I feel little and scared and alone, it feels all or nothing." I commented that when he disconnects from his present experience and from feeling connected with both himself and with me, it feels like going back to an earlier time. He added that it felt like actually being small, and added that it was not like a snap or switch but more like "moving away." I emphasized that it was important to stay grounded in his present, unaltered state of mind and to allow his full awareness of the experiences of the trauma without actively dissociating into that state of being. He responded, "There is a difference in what you're saying about the scared feelings when they can come to me. I don't have to disconnect from them or go back to them." He recalled my earlier distinction between "having" a memory, versus "being in" a memory to avoid the here-and-now experience when dealing with trauma. Many times we revisited the notion that insight and understanding are the icon of an experience, not the software of the experience itself.

Tim indicated that he and his former analyst had spoken of this scenario as regression, and they were baffled by the seeming total disappearance of any ability of this brilliant, accomplished man to observe and to reflect during a "regressed state." His capacity to work effectively was precluded by the dissociated state being experienced as all-or-nothing, a loss of observing ego in the state the trauma occurred with the inability (interpreted by his analyst as resistance) to elicit any of the feeling from that earlier experience. I indicated that at that time in my professional life, the time period of his earlier analysis, I would have done exactly the same thing as his former analyst.

After months of our work, he reported the following dream.

> I dreamed I was in a house, like the Wizard of Oz. There was a tornado and the home was changing shapes. I was caught up in the tornado. The house was shivering, shaking, and I thought I would die. Yet I was also watching it happen. It set down in 19th century France. There was a beggar near a seaside covered market and a nearby town square that looked like my present century. His face was hideously deformed and he was bad smelling. It was like science fiction. He changed before my eyes to someone like the Star Trek captain, back to present time, and helped me so I wouldn't have to be a beggar. There was a courtyard with high walls, but part of one side was open, gaping. His body smelled, a putrid sharp smell. The smell stuck to me. Everyone was stone or brick, and I was afraid of being poor.

As we explored his experience of the story of the dream, and focused on affective and sensory details, he recognized that bad smells were his memory of his own burning and burned flesh. The high walls were not only metaphorically his defenses, as he first associated, but the thick scar tissue encasing his body, making it rigid and stonelike.

In the discussion, he recognized the tornado as a storm of dissociation to relocate to a different country (state of mind). Like the fire that ravaged his body, he was both in it and simultaneously observing it (dissociatively). For his teenage years he was in a depressed, hopeless state, feeling stuck, needy and isolated (a beggar, homeless) in a different country and in a different century (state specific memory, frozen in time). The present had changed, disappeared (dissociated) away. "My best friend had mental powers and supersensitivity about picking up the feelings of people, analogous to you. In the dream, he tuned in to be aware I was in this century, like you kept asking how present I was at the beginning of our work. He was an empathic person. He couldn't read specific thoughts but knew when people were sincere." He noted that being "present" changed the way he perceived and experienced his past, and of this traumatic, defining event. Much of his adolescent development, especially integrating an adult, sexual body was then possible in the analytic work.

Significant flexibility may be considered in the configuration and use of time. While Tim was able to do the necessary work at twice weekly sessions, adaptations of the treatment frame are often necessary for patients who have disorders of continuity. A sustained immersion in treatment is usually optimum for individuals who have difficulty with internal cohesion, and who segment aspects of their lives and their psyche. Daily sessions for at least four to five days per week are often necessary, and for a very few patients I have configured sessions at different points in the analysis with a frequency that allowed more immersion within a time frame, such as to schedule double and triple sessions, often toward the middle of the week, where the work done during those more intense times could be integrated by the end of the week in a single session for the weekend interruption.

Recreating the dissociation by focusing on the past and on memories experienced and processed from an altered state may be a defensive collusion of both patient and analyst to dissociatively translocate the painful intensity to the past. Often a focus on the memory of traumatic events with an abreactive or cathartic mission may also be a relief and redirection from the intensity of present moment experiences within the transference. Focusing on memories and defenses against remembering makes it "back there" and "then" rather than the full, powerful intensity within the transference-countertransference of the original trauma in a current lived experience.

This new, nondissociative experience involves the change of implicit memory and relational knowing (Stern et al., 1998). The process of new procedural and associative learning and memory patterns become generalized and modify structure both within the psyche as well as within the brain at the neuronal and neurotransmitter level (Kandell, 1999).

Affects are the organizers of self-experiences (Stolorow & Atwood, 1992), and the need is for caregivers to accept, confirm, validate, differentiate, synthesize, contain and regulate various affect states. When caregivers do not provide affect attunement and regulation, the child may dissociate or disavow affect, principally because it cannot be integrated or organized as part of self-experience (Palef, 1999). This distinguishes between disavowal and failure to *associate* affects that have never been raised into awareness to be traumatically *dissociated*.

A superordinate human motivation is the need to maintain an organization, cohesiveness, and meaning of subjective experience (Palef, 1999). In the absence of this affective organization in trauma, a substitute concrete, tangible focus creates an immediate meaning, cause, and sense of organization. These concretizations may manifest in an enactment, a symptom, a symbolic object, an activity, or as a substitute person or process that creates a temporarily organizing sense of meaning. For example, we often see in analysis that a concretization of a symbolic and substitute selfobject function, such as a perversion, an eating disorder, or other action symptom will vaporize once a solid bond and self-object transference is established, appearing again only when this bond is threatened, ruptured, or temporarily suspended by absence or failed empathy.

We daily make invisible decisions that become camouflaged in habits, our collection of repetitions. Repetitions may become repetition compulsions that attempt belated mastery, while attachment to the familiar as repetition is a part of the architecture of memory. Repetition insures that there is nothing new to forget, no new or different experiences to retrieve.

A patient who "keeps doing it until I get it right" reenters an old story to write a better ending. Even a thousand better endings do not work, for the process of reentering the old story recreates the old story. Psychoanalysis, as Freud (1914/1958b) suggested, is a process of repeating, remembering, and working through. Even more, it is a process of creating an entirely new story to be in, to contrast and differentiate from the ongoing recreated parallel old story, in order to juxtapose experiences, and for cleavage of past from present through insight and interpretation.

A theory alone is not enough to supplant lived experience; only a new lived experience can replace an old lived experience. Grief and mourning are then mobilized for lost hopes, shattered illusions, and missed as well as traumatic experiences as components of the analytic work. To grieve for the lost hopes is an important component of the analytic work.

The relational configurations and object choices of old, and familiar lifetime experiences have a particular pull, a familiarity that may disallow tolerating the anxiety of an entirely new and unknown pattern and choice. Another component of the pull to repetition is the loyalty to attachment figures involved in original scenarios and patterns, and perhaps the exhilaration of winning the love and affirmation, by proxy, of the original attachment figure.

The compelling desire, within an old and familiar model to both right the wrong and achieve belated mastery, as well as to disavow the painful aspects, even to nostalgically rewrite personal history, all form a compelling level of motivation to repeat. The longed-for outcome of the "someday" fantasy, creates expectation within a familiar pattern.

With therapeutic change, there is a particular threat of breaking attachment ties and identifications with childhood figures: though perhaps negative, they offer the certainty and security of predictability and unfamiliarity. Separating from or losing these accustomed object choices (the reiteration of childhood attachment figures) often manifests in significant anxiety, in terror of aloneness-loneliness, in dreams of erosion of foundation, and of unrecognizable change and transformation of people and faces. The more frustrating and depriving an attachment figure has been, the more vigorously the figure is often protected, and the more fixed and rigid is the patient's attachment to the figure, and to familiar relational patterns. This traumatically arrested development may be coupled with a very specific, concrete, and fixed reparative hope. The "curative fantasy" (Ornstein, 1991) represents a fixed hope that some very specific conditions and experiences that were missed in the past need to be provided in the present both for retribution as well as for developmental growth to proceed.

Recovered memories of abuse as true or false has been the source of much debate in this and other fields. The question of corroboration of the retrieval of memories from earlier years of childhood is not assumed as necessary with other developmental derailments, such as external validation of a narcissistic parent to confirm the narcissism of a patient. Subjective experiences of patients and reconstructions are often clinical conclusions, and are important as a relational collaboration effort. The psychic reality of each state and experience is what is important, and at times the historical reality may be indiscernible. The psychic reality brought to life vividly within the realms of transference in the present moment becomes our abiding concern. Sandler (1994) suggests that the retrieval of memories of abuse from the earliest years of childhood is at best the outcome of informed guesses. While we cannot ignore external reality, the reality of the present experience is both preeminent and sufficient. Rather than being intrigued with mysteries of memory, our most useful clinical impact is the experience, here and now, of becoming aware of states of mind and their regulation.

The specificity of the process of state changes allows awareness of discontinuities such as brief amnesias and the qualities and characteristics of more distinct states of mind. However, the memory impairment of dissociative detachment, the "lost time" currently in which the individual forgets what he or she has done, said, or been for a period of time may not be simply a reversible amnesia (that "lost time" exists but is accessible in a different state). Memory gaps may result from an encoding failure (Allen, Console, & Lewis, 1999). Dissociation as a defense changes a psychophysiological state with a significant emotional cue to dissociate the *content* of what immediately follows. *Dissociative detachment* is a term that refers to dissociation of *context*: The dissociative shift detaching one from the usual context and encoding of memory narrows or disengages attentional focus so that higher order processes and information about context becomes lost. In dissociative detachment, such as depersonalization and derealization, attention is narrowed or disrupted so that experiences may not be encoded in order to then be cordoned off, as in dissociative amnesia or dissociative identity disorder. The implication for dissociative detachment is that not all dissociative memory failure is reversible by therapeutic engagement with access to all ego states (Allen et al., 1999).

Feelings always come first, are the trigger for disconnection, and lead the way to reconnection. Not having a familiarity with feeling good makes it difficult to tolerate sustaining that feeling and state. The accompanying thoughts may include, "Do I deserve this?" "What is going to happen to end it?" "This can't last very long."

"Why do I stop myself from feeling good?" the patient ultimately must ask. It is important to focus sharply on this process, on the concurrent anxiety and uncertainty of being in an unfamiliar place. By moving back to the accustomed dysphoria, the separation anxiety from that familiar experience-identity is quelled. Familiar attachment patterns and figures are reestablished internally and externally. For example, the repetition of a familiar attachment pattern may also be reunion with the internalized parent.

A new experience may feel different, a state of mind that has no history and, as yet no associations. Relaxation and contentment may not be places previously inhabited, lacking a continuity with a past, the known, the familiar. The landscape has changed. All the familiar states, full of the familiar content, may not be accessible. A patient stated, "Eating is searching for something familiar. I've filled a lot of mental space with worry, anxiety, eating. The fear is that if I don't have anything to worry about, I won't know what to do, or even who I am."

As a patient moves from a dissociative model with discontinuity and segmented experience, to a model of continuity of the self and regulation of affect, intrapsychic conflict becomes evident, perhaps experienced as such for the first time. The patient has previously avoided the experience of conflict by dissociating one aspect, or by disconnecting from the conflict altogether to create the illusion that it is no longer there. A new discomfort exists of experiencing the tension of conflict. Bearing dysphoria and conflict without detaching or dissociating is integrating in itself the antithesis of repeating the traumatic experiences.

Dissociation can be the most abiding and powerful addiction that anyone can have because it is an instantaneous change of the way one feels. This process is faster, more powerful, and more effective than any addiction involving a person, substance, or activity. To not dissociate can become a more conscious decision, yet it involves the painful, ongoing process of recognizing, tolerating, and staying with feelings that perhaps have not been experienced for a lifetime. The internal regulation of affect state is a significant developmental achievement, and especially for the dissociative patient, is a fundamental nucleus of both analytic process and change.

We work in analysis to help patients recognize that they can always change their mind. A useful distinction for patients who have dissociative identity disorder is to examine the difference between switching (dissociating) and changing their mind (Waugaman, 2000). Drawing attention to the function that dissociation plays, and to changing one's mind becomes a viable option and alternative to state change. For someone who has operated in a dissociative model for a lifetime, there may be little familiarity with the process of changing one's mind.

The analytic process includes that of childhood remobilized, of unmet developmental needs and traumas activated within a newly unfolding story. Memories emerge without associated imagery or feeling, as well as flashbacks that seem disconnected, or even nightmares that seem symbolic yet enigmatically memorylike. As in any other treatment with any other patient, resistances occur, and dissociation is a defense. Understandably, patients do not want to walk down the pathway that would lead to remobilization of overwhelming traumas. The purpose of the treatment process is not to take the lid off trauma, but rather it is a way of creating a context of safety and manageability for the entire system, of collaboratively circumscribing focus and work. Dosing, timing, and titrating affective experience by awareness of present state of mind respects both the terror of regression and the dread to repeat.

As in any other psychoanalytic process which is developmentally informed and dynamically focused, the patient's entire internal system comes into increasing scrutiny through empathic attunement with the patient's experiences, perceptions, and feelings. Sustained empathic attunement is not enough until the listening process is extended to the systemic paradigm of state-dependent learning and memories. Memories of trauma (including the components of affect, behavior, cognition, and sensation) are not simply repressed as conflictual, or vertically split off as in developmental arrest, but are encoded during altered biological states that may be encapsulated in state specific experiences, accessed by attunement to state changes.

An awareness of an internal system of ego states is necessary, developed by the empathic awareness of both analyst and patient to the process, as well as to the content of ego states. The awareness of the addictive potential of disassociation is essential, of how instantly dissociation can create the illusion of making pain, a feeling, or a conflict go away. Empathy must be created in the analytical pair, internalized in the patient, to move hope to a new context of verbalization and create a new experience to replace disassociation-disavowal. Systemic thinking is the antithesis of segmentation; the antithesis of disavowal is empathy.

Traumas encapsulated in a state dependent memory system, and the developmental arrest of body self and psychological self, requires the establishment of significant trust in order to deal with dissociative defenses and the significant self esteem issues, often with a preponderance of shame. The developmental issues of the self are interwoven with resolution and integration of traumas. For example, nightmares may not be not only restitutive symbolic attempts to resolve developmental or current struggles (self stories in nighttime language), but at times partly the emergence of recurrent intrusive memory.

It may be difficult for the analyst to conceptualize a system of selves when one person is lying on the couch. The mind and body is a system with multiple parts, not all of which will be in communication with each other. This is in addition to, yet different from, the way of thinking of the object specific transferences in which the patient sees the analyst as an important person from his or her past, and even different from the selfobject transferences in which the patient regards the analyst as a part of or a function of himself, as validating, affirming, idealizing, or alter ego aspects of the patient.

Most commonly with these individuals, there is such a fluid and seamless shift among states of mind that they may not initially be aware of distinct states. If these individuals are regarded as if they have only one state of mind, or as if a specific state such as depression or emptiness is simply pathology to be eradicated, treatment may get stuck. Each state has its own story to collaboratively teach both patient and analyst.

Countertransference Reactions to Dissociation

Often when feeling is dissociated, the analyst countertransferentially may embody or experience those disavowed or disconnected feelings or states of mind of the patient. Resonating with dissociation as a process, the analyst may then feel disconnected, sleepy, bored, drowsy, tranced, lonely, or in some way "zoned out," paralleling the patient's process. Or, as the patient defends against feeling by dissociation, the analyst may become bored, the interaction listless, and the process seem to be stuck, with the mutual feeling that nothing is happening. Each individual analyst will register countertransference awareness in specific ways. This shared experience can even be passed on to a supervisor who registers it in a related way.

The awareness and formulation of bodily states may be the crucial component of determining feelings and sensation. It is essential not to leave the body out of exploration and conceptualization of the patient's state of awareness and experience. The analysis of the professional may not have addressed these fundamental connections of body sensations, body image, and body self functioning with conscious capacities and formulations, leaving little personal guide to this work (Jacobs, 1994).

In order to bring somatic states and the body self into analytic scrutiny, the analyst's focus and vocabulary must include body states, somatic awareness, shared symbolization, and metaphors of bodily development. Somatic communication must be translated into verbal narratives. The analyst's awareness of bodily experiences is both beacon and barometer to the patient's experience. For example, the analyst may embody a patient's sensations or expression, such as feeling the body tension, that the patient partitions from awareness. The interrelationship of the mind, body, and linking emotions provide the essential aliveness, the attunement necessary for a full immersion and understanding of various experiences of our patients who may dissociatively omit or disavow one or more of the above, or who may have had their integration derailed. Automatic responses on the part of the analyst may include denying or disavowing this experiences, focusing on the cognitive or affective components, or in not hearing or feeling these communications or sensations. Goodwin and Attias (1999) emphasize that direct communication and verbalization about the body and bodily phenomenon that are usually unconscious will counter depersonalization, and clarify regressions and fears otherwise unspoken, especially in trauma victims.

Both the patient and the analyst are embodied persons, not a composite of drives, forces, and psychological structures, nor a repository or passive agent of affect or events. Each actively create their shared, collective, collaborative story. The analysis is coauthored by these two active agents, focusing on the patient, and coconstructing both the history and present of the patient.

11

Embodiment in Psychoanalysis: The Body Self in Development, in Action Symptoms, and Transference-Countertransference

We fill pre-existing forms, and when we fill them we change them and we are changed.

Frank Bidart
Desire

All experience, thought, and feelings are embodied.

Feelings are first and foremost about the body, they offer us the cognition of our visceral and musculo-skeletal states . . . feelings let us mind the body.

Antonio Damasio
Descartes' Error

The body that is verbally inaccessible and developmentally undifferentiated needs access, description, understanding, even perhaps construction in analysis. Winnicott (1965) first used the term *embodiment* as synonymous with "indwelling," a seamless linkage of self, body functions, and the limiting membrane of the skin.

Embodiment of a symptom is specific to somatization or psychosomatic phenomena, and is distinguished from psychological symptoms and action symptoms. Psychological symptoms involve variations of mental activity, defenses heightened or gone awry, or pathological defenses with

177

or without enactment; action is not an integral component. Action symptoms convert any significant emotion or its signal into a specific action scenario. Motivated by the hope that action creates immediate affect and tension regulation, there is also hope of averting or reversing emotional pain, of bridging mind and body, and perhaps secondarily engaging an essential other. In extreme instances, the registration of feeling can only occur in an action sequence.

The core of the self is developmentally grounded in body experience (Damasio, 1994; Edelman, 1992). Empathically attuned verbal and physical responses by the caregiver serve to accurately perceive, mirror, and define the interior and surface experiences of the child, creating a specificity, mastery, and symbolization of feelings within an evolving language.

The extent to which an individual experiences affects as mind (i.e., as feelings) rather than solely as a body sensation, depends on the intersubjective context and facilitation of the correct identification, labeling, and synthesis of affective and somatic experience (Krystal, 1988; Stolorow & Atwood, 1992). A preverbal sense of boundedness, of being within one's own skin, the "core self" (Danial Stern, 1997) is established through interaction with attuned others (Aron, 1998). This synthesis paradoxically dissolves the boundary between mind and body at the same time as establishing different levels of distinction between body sensations and affective experience. In the absence of this empathic attunement, feelings continue to be experienced internally as bodily content, as a body state or experience, or registered only when embedded within an action sequence not differentiated and distinguished as feelings within a mental state.

Empathic attunement and accurate labeling of physical and emotional states is necessary to identify, differentiate, and desomatize affect, to develop an emotional literacy, and to experience effectiveness and mastery (Fonagy & Target, 1998; Stern, 1985). The failure of intersubjective processing of emotions leads to a nonawareness of feeling, or to the development of psychosomatic symptoms to bridge an unintegrated mind and body. These limitations in articulating and communicating feeling create a defect in reflective self-awareness and affect regulation, as well as an inability to symbolize feelings and bodily experiences (Aron, 1998) The rift between the mind and body, psyche and soma, may often be traced to its roots in a child's relationship to the mother's body. For example, the mother's disconnection with her own body and subsequent attachment pattern with the child can create a corresponding failure in the association-integration of mind and body in her child (Fonagy & Target, 1998).

Those individuals who have not developmentally consolidated a distinct, accurate, and cohesive sense of body self have concrete thinking regarding body self and psychological self that is self-referential yet not self-reflective (Krueger, 1990). Their capacity for abstraction and representation of their body and feelings is partially undeveloped. Though perhaps quite articulate and accomplished, these individuals may feel lost when focusing internally and not have a language for feeling (Krystal, 1988). Some patients have dimensions of internal experience not only unexpressed, but unformulated, because it has never been resonated with to achieve a representation and symbolism above the threshold of awareness (Daniel Stern, 1997). These experiences, spoken for the first time by the body and not by words, may be experienced other than as a somatic state of sensation only as they come alive within the analytic dyad, and perhaps only the analyst can give them words. Often these experiences may be ones perceived in a sensing or visceral way by the analyst, reflected back to the patient, to have the patient further shape and refine the experience once taking it back.

Lacking an ability to distinguish the nuances of self-state awareness, they elicit self-representation and regulate affect via the felt experiences of their own bodies. Because a cohesive self-representation has not been formed, their representation of self must emerge from immediate body self experience, not from a symbolic representation of the body or psychological self (Krueger, 1989a). The psychological distance required for developmental progress beyond a transitional object is unavailable at this concrete, nonsymbolic operational level and *symbolic equations* (Segal, 1978), usually involving action symptoms, rather than *true symbols* predominate. Symbolic equations differ from true symbols because they are experienced as the actual object rather than as emblem, such as the use of food by an eating disorder patient to become a self-object, a restitutive and defensive function, rather than simply a mental symbol of a nurturing parent (Krueger, 1988a, 1997). With a symbolic equation, there is no "as if" quality, only an all-or-nothing concrete experience. These patients are not primarily denying body awareness and feelings, for they have not developmentally attained, desomatized, and differentiated affect and bodily sensation in order to deny them; they have not as yet integrated mind and body enough to defensively split them (Krueger, 1989a). At the time of a current emotional insult, they may feel lost and disorganized and attempt regulation by directing organizing focus on the body.

Embodiment in Psychoanalysis: Body-based Transferences and Countertransferences

Body-based transferences and countertransferences manifest in the language of the patient's immediate felt experience. As a few examples: pushing away, holding, touching, turning away, hitting home, striking out, fending off, fed up, emptiness, fullness, or paralyzed.

The patient's implicit (procedural and associative) memory activated in analysis (that we call transference) may include metaphors of the body of dichotomies of inside and outside, of engulfment and expulsion, of each of the senses. Other forms of somatic communication can be observed as the patient on the couch, creates basic sensory experiences of touching certain parts of his body, of tensing and relaxing certain muscle groups, of holding or caressing as well as movements and gestures of stroking the wall, couch or fabric, and an endless number of facial expressions. Corresponding fantasies of movements, various actions, and various interactions between patient and analyst, as well as somatic and psychic memories of developmental experiences of the patient's past, all form part of the somatic transference (the body's procedural memory) of bodily experience in the analysis. The mutual and collaborative focus on the patient's entire awareness of both mind and body will directly activate and incorporate fundamental experiences, transferences, and countertransferences. For example, our patients may recall their bodily state of mind, how our voice sounded to them, how they felt soothed by our voice, while failing to remember the content of the discussion, the specific interpretation, or even vaguely, the subject of it.

Our own attunement to body-based states of awareness in the analytic work may be a quite neglected area of vivid clinical material. Careful attention to the detail of the sensual and sensory body communication and its associations may evoke somatic memories of experiences. Somatic memories are encoded, stored, and retrieved as a somatic experience. Examples are trauma, as well as experience prior to developing a descriptive language. Bodily based cues of somatic memories include body movement, sensory awareness, pain or pleasure, perhaps not even paired with conscious awareness or a verbal narrative. For example, Diane Ackerman (1991) wrote in *A Natural History of the Senses*, "Smells detonate softly in our memory like poignant landmines hidden under the weedy mass of many years and experiences. Hit a tripwire of smell, and memories explode all at once. A complex vision leaps out of the undergrowth" (p. 6).

Somatic countertransference reactions are just as relevant and informative as the usual countertransference reactions of feeling and fantasy. As analysts we must have access not only to our subjective affective states, but also to our bodily reactivity. Body self and psychological self each register both formulated and unformulated experiences, and comprise aspects of unconscious communication. Often the sometimes inexplicable and powerful resonances that occur between patient and analyst are mutually constructed and occur in a somatic arena. Harris (1998) illustrates this process when the analyst learned that she was pregnant before she actually knew consciously, as her patient was nauseated in the session and indicated odd feelings of heaviness and anxiety. Further, during the first trimester of the analyst's pregnancy, the patient's dreams, physical and emotional states embodied the analyst's own fantasies and experiences.

This integration of mind and body, of states, understanding, and coherence goes back to the beginning and builds on the foundation of experience, the bedrock of development. The developmental building blocks of a body self evolving to a cohesive psychological self may manifest in the clinical encounter in the earliest mother-infant transferences and countertransferences. These early body self transferences are the somatic and sensory memories of either physical contact with the mother, or the sensory contact needs and attunement that were lacking. These nascent sensory and somatic experiences frequently appear in relation to the body of the patient and the body of the analyst, often in seemingly metaphorical ways, in body-based language of the patient, and in sensory experiences of both patient and analyst (Wrye & Welles, 1994).

The reactions of both patient and analyst may result in a "torrent of anxieties, wonderment, sensuality, eroticism, and pleasurable and distressing somatic affect states, characteristic of the infant's impact on the mother" (Wayne, 1999, p. 24). Raphael-Leff (1989) states, "A close encounter with a baby throws us into the deep end amid the primitive wild things, by violating all the rules. Disarming adult defenses, a baby compels its mother or father to re-experience what it is like to be helpless, needy, frustrated, enraged, tantalized, abandoned, and betrayed" (p. 82). So too it is with early maternal transferences and particularly countertransferences in the analyst. The mother–infant dyad is a playground for sensory exploration and definition (Wrye & Welles, 1994) with transformation and interpretation of the child's body by being in such intimate contact with another (Bollas, 1987). Being lost in this original oneness, the blending of bodies, fluids, and sensations is a necessary immersion-merger in order to emerge with a distinct state of connectedness with another and concurrently with oneself. The adult patient compromised in this early development will have difficulty finding words for these wordless experiences. Additionally, this may be especially difficult, and different qualitatively, for the male analyst as opposed to the female analyst.

These earliest longings of experience to taste, touch, feel, smell, drink in the mother's skin and body become activated in the patient's transference experience, the procedural memory for what did and for what did not originally happen. At times these transferences manifest as fantasies and sensations of access to the analyst's body and the mingling of bodies in a sensual but not essentially sexual way, at times in a demand for physical responses by the analyst. For the somatic memories of ancient yearning for maternal sensory intermingling of bodies, the envelope of analytic containment requires both somatic and affective language.

Vignette 1

Ben, in his early 30s at the beginning of his analysis, indicated that he felt most connected with someone who would enact a particular enema scenario with him. He felt "at one," "being with my own kind," when engaging in reality or in an Internet chat room with a woman who would simulate a nurse giving him an enema. He scripted the scenario of her at first cruelly inflicting pain by inserting the enema, then of nurturing him as he released the contents injected. The caring so gratifying and eroticized reclaimed the only time he felt he had his mother's full attention: when she would give him enemas as a child. Here, her empathic response was nurturing and accurate: she was attuned, correctly, to the specific experience she was constructing with him.

He was concerned initially that I would criticize or, worse, not be able to appreciate his powerful and unique experience of intimacy with someone who gave him enemas. He felt "at home" during an enema scenario, that the Internet "cyberenema" or the nurse-dominatrix he paid to enact the scene would create the empathic nurturing he yearned for, the fantasy that she would perfectly understand him.

My countertransference experience of occasional barrenness, of feeling alone in the room was a resonance with his perceived abandonment and empathic failure of his wife, and earlier his mother. I shared his initial doubt of my capacity to truly appreciate the emotional power of the enemas, of the only true deep connection he ever felt with anyone.

Derivatives of this experience were noted in Ben's sensitivity to his wife coming into his study at home and rearranging anything on his desk, or leaving anything askew, all experienced as an intrusion into his space. He spoke of his study as the place he could work and play, where he felt safe, contained, held.

Ben emphasized how much he needed to be in control by not letting me talk at times, holding his hand up, asking me not to interrupt him. He felt as if he had to hold onto everything, to maintain a tension level in his body, to keep me out. As my responses were interrupted, blocked, or talked over, I commented on this process of inducing in me what it was like to be him, of not being heard, of having a build-up of what I wanted to release. He responded, "Now you know what it's like to be me." I said, "I get the feeling. Also, you're remembering in your body what it was like as a boy."

He said, "The only way you can get anything in is shoving it up my ass." He added, "I'm always afraid of what might come out."

Letting me in would be for him to be weak, not in control. For him, any interaction ended in his either being in complete control, or feeling defeated and weak, having things taken from him. He had to induce in me what it was like to be him, so I could experience it, name and conceptualize it, to give it back to him, to teach him what it was like to be him.

His professional life reflected this dynamic as well: as a money manager, he took money from his clients to control (to build up assets), always being afraid that if he did not perform well, they would take it back.

He attempted to divest control from me, trying to extend moments at the end of the session, not letting me speak or "insert" anything in him, yet telling me how bad he felt, hoping I would sustain my concern. He would ultimately succumb by feeling weak, tense, and ask me then for help, but only when he decided. He perceived me as taking something away from him as a precondition to attachment, the pattern of the mother–child bond via enemas. He came to recognize the pervasiveness of his procedural memory, experienced first in his body as tension, in incessant activity with inability to relax. He recognized how tiring it is to hold back wanting, the confusion of yearning for and fearing the same thing.

We came to understand that his erotic feelings, fantasies, and specific enema preferences were much less about genital sexual excitement than about being held, bathed, and being soothed physically, and of repeating hope and desire in its original attachment context. He desired to be in absolute control, to direct the intrusiveness, and to counter the experience of abandonment. He became aware of wanting an enema at specific times of empathic ruptures, of perceived abandonments and hurt, times that he felt alone and empty. He also sought enemas at times that he sensed his mother most needed to coalesce in her identity as a mother-caretaker, corresponding to the times when he felt empty, disengaged, or isolated from her.

His tender experiences with his infant son were recounted in exquisite detail, as he was primary caretaker while his wife pursued her graduate degree. The nurturing of his son further activated his own unmet needs, given new voice. He described the pain he felt for his son as he took him to get his first shots. He murmured tearfully, "I know" repeated again and again to his son as he was injected by a nurse. He heard me almost whisper, "Now you know both for him and for yourself." He felt his loneliness stabbing into the pent-up space of his body, and the gentle caring and holding as he was administered an enema. He felt both aspects in his body as he spoke; his tears concurrent with my own tears of joy for him finally being able to experience his own primordial yearn-

ing and emptiness in the embrace of his feelings/his son, our shared mingling of feelings/tears.

His son's shots echoed his own nonverbal experiences, the attunement
and holding as a shot/enema were given, and of the powerful hunger for
contact of holding and comforting. Ben indicated he felt that hunger in
such a vivid way because he knew he was holding himself as a baby when
holding his son, and felt it was like me holding him to say those words.
Together we found words for his desire of the somatic and sensory experiences of being touched, held, nurtured, and comforted by the "nurse"/
mother/analyst holding as experienced on the analytic couch.

Sometime later he mentioned his toddler son being cranky, with an
aversive response to having his mouth wiped. Ben described how he restrained himself from grabbing him to forcefully wipe his mouth; in doing so, he turned his head on the couch, pursed and tightened his lips,
frowned. I encouraged him to explore his own experience, what he was
remembering with his body through the words and vision of his son.

He responded that my question seemed to crystallize an image of his
mother grabbing his mouth and wiping it, "to show who's boss." She
would not allow his aversive responses, maintained a control over his
actions, and his body. He spoke of how comforting it was to control his
own body, still a foreign concept to him. He recalled his mother combing
his hair each morning so roughly and aggressively that it would make
him cry, as if no one in his family owned their own body. His younger
sister apparently shouted her aversive response with her anorexia nervosa,
inscribing with her body where she ended and the mother began.

The elaboration in the analytic process included registering and recognizing the somatic transference-countertransference, the reconstruction
of the earlier attachment pattern being implicitly remembered, and understanding the current precipitant of the somatic scenario. Alongside
this mutually created new story was intermingled the old story's wish,
fear, relational pattern, and hope imbedded in the earlier context. The
old story was interpretatively cleaved and mourned so he could inhabit
fully the present lived experience and new model.

A patient may have to speak in action or somatic language before
differentiating feelings. For some individuals, affect may be undifferentiated as well as unformulated, accessible through action and action language. This process cannot be bypassed: a patient engaged in action and
action symptoms may not be able to answer the question, "How do you
feel?" They do not know how they feel as they are engaged in action
sequences; the subsequent awareness and differentiation of feelings is a
stepwise process.

In this developmental hierarchy, emotion is not just "desomatized"
but is a developmental evolution with specific phases of recognition and

differentiation. The inability to articulate a feeling prior to an action symptom may not be purely a defensive response, but a developmental nonattainment that has to be addressed as a prequal to experiencing and articulating pure feeling. The first step is to move from an external to an internal point of reference, to inhabit experience; in this regard, evolving from action to action language is a developmental step. From internal experience, somatic and emotional can be distinguished, then a differentiation into the subjective awareness of feelings to be formulated, mastered, and communicated.

Somatic Transference/Countertransference Enactments

A component of early maternal preverbal transferences is the fantasy that repair and transformation can occur through physical contact, whether it is with the analyst or significant others (Wrye & Welles 1994). The patient seeking this experience in treatment has its roots in the earliest physical holding, containing, and need-meeting of the infant at a somatic level that was inconsistent or inadequate. These countertransference attunements may be difficult for the male analyst with the female patient, as these maternal transferences of necessity involve the fantasied female body and person of the male analyst. The male analyst may have unconscious feelings of confusion, fear, or loss in regard to these early maternal somatic transferences (Wayne, 1999) and defensively interpret them as the patient's Oedipal or homosexual strivings to place himself back in the body of a male. Or the analyst may remain emotionally or theoretically obtuse to these powerful, fundamental experiences.

The dreams of patients who give birth to infants, and subsequent dreams of caretaking and growth of the infant may represent fantasy parenting in the analytic encounter, and the birth of the new cocreated self. Various enactments of these primitive preverbal bodily transferences occur when words fail, or when symbols and metaphors, as well as physical experiences demonstrated are not put into words by either patient or analyst.

These procedural memories (i.e., transferences) of early preverbal and somatic experiences may manifest in the patient's experiences, dreams, imagery, metaphors, or enactments on the couch, such as patients rubbing, holding, touching their body, or in their experience of the analyst and the analytic space as metaphorically holding, soothing, containing, enveloping. Or, the implicit memory may be of disembodied words in dissociation: that "no body" is present in the room.

Transference and countertransference somatic experiences become necessary to recognize and verbalize experiences as yet without conscious icon or verbal narrative. For example, countertransference may be an awareness of various somatic responses in the analyst from state changes of sleepiness, arousal, restlessness, boredom, or of desires to hold, shake, cradle, or direct various actions toward the patient. When unrecognized or unverbalized, these early somatically based transferences may result in repeated acting out and action symptoms. Especially between opposite-sexed analyst and patient, these transferences may be defensively encapsulated in erotized form (Blum, 1973), avoiding necessarily more fundamental experiences.

Patients who are struggling to know and to master their own body-mind are exquisitely attuned not only to the analyst's feelings and words, but also to their perception of the analyst's bodily and sensory experiences both consciously and unconsciously. At times, resistance to analytic work is not to specific content, but to what the patient perceives as yielding ownership of mind or body (Gunsberg & Tylim, 1998). They state, "The qualities of the analyst's ownership of his or her own body and mind will largely determine a patient's ability to express curiosity about the analyst's body and mind and to share a mutual mind-body/body-mind field" (p. 134).

Looker (1998) describes the mind–body connection in certain enactments, indicating that "during enactment the mutually constructed verbal narrative has gotten under the skins and into the bodies of both patient and analyst so that it feels 'real'" (p. 256). What becomes registered in the body during enactment is the disjunction between mind and body from disturbed relational patterns or failed empathic bonds in an unconscious attempt to join patient and analyst.

Vignette 2

A candidate noted her experience of frustration when her patient was talking of engaging compulsively in various activities, going from activity to activity without any passion, immersion, or even attention. She spoke of her patient continually focusing on external matters, on decorating her house and going to various places to find the material and items. The candidate felt ineffective in finding a focus, to get the patient to give attention to her internal experience, or to engage with her in a significant exploration of feelings and meanings.

The patient seemed empty, flat, monotonous, and treated every association with equal nonemotional valence. The candidate described relentlessly and hopelessly trying to find the plot of the patient's associations, of her experience, but continuously felt lost, ineffective, and helpless. She complained that she could find neither thread nor theme, nor any manifestation of transference. I first asked the candidate for the detail, emotionally and physically, of how she experienced being in the room with this woman. She volunteered how her restlessness felt barely tolerable; she could focus on nothing with the patient that seemed meaningful. She felt disconnected from her body, alone in the room, unable to formulate anything that seemed to make a difference with her patient.

Knowing her skill and sensitive attunement, I suggested that we might consider her somatic and affective response as specific countertransference, a sensitive barometer to an equally specific transference being enacted. I suggested considering that the patient was inducing an empathy in the analyst for exactly what she was experiencing of questing hopelessly yet relentlessly for some focus, some container of recognizable shape and organizing meaning. That is, the process itself was the transference, the patient's *implicit* memory communicating the helplessness and ineffectiveness that the patient experienced in trying to give form and definition to her experience, somatically registered precisely by her analyst.

When this was conveyed, her patient was then flooded with *explicit* memories of what it was like to try to elicit from her mother a defining presence of meaning and form, and doing whatever her mother wanted (or what she perceived that the mother would respond to) in order to effectively elicit a response, just as she was trying to freely associate exactly as recommended.

The candidate elaborated on further examples in the analytic exchange that she now could see as procedural memory (transference) of the recreated "nothing" so pervasive in her childhood that it was impossible to capture in words alone. They focused more sharply on the various ways in which her patient had enacted attempts to create stimulation and awareness of her body self by touching and rubbing her body, the couch and wall. These nonverbal patterns of experience not yet symbolically elaborated were fully illuminated in the countertransference, ultimately verbalized in the analytic exchange.

The candidate noted that in a recent session the patient had spoken of feeling empty and alone, of having a vague kind of hunger before she left her house to enter another shopping expedition for things to "fill her house." The patient then returned home and entered a very hot bath in order to feel calmed, contained. While describing this incident, the patient was rubbing her arms, complaining of an itchiness that had been present for the last several weeks. The candidate and her patient found words to convey this somatic communication of encoded memories of yearning for the container of touch and embrace to counter the emptiness and hunger, and to find a meaningful attachment that might create a filled experience.

Mutual focus on the somatic transference resulted in the patient feeling calmer, to gradually desomatize feelings, and to find affectively integrated symbolic representation for the actions and metaphors of her body. The patient induced in her analyst what it was like to be her, so from that common ground of mutual experience the patient could know her experience better when the analyst gave the unfathomable back to her in words.

Patients' affective experiences and awareness may not be fully available for analytic scrutiny, interpretation, or integration. The integration of nonverbal and verbal levels of communication and understanding emphasizes the microscopic instances of patterned volume, rhythm, tone, and tempo that significantly shape the exchange of feelings and the cocreation of meanings of the previously unspoken dialogue in analysis (Knoblauch, 1997). Kiersky and Beebe (1994) have described the use of nonverbal cues in patient–analyst interaction as the basis for inferring and reconstructing the interaction structures that were nonverbally established by patients and their caregivers.

The transference-countertransference of the body self manifests through intuitive and sensing responses in our own bodies, in fantasies of somatic experiences, or in our movement mirroring that of the patient. When we are attuned to our own bodies, there is an intrinsic communication and correspondence as well with the patient's body self and psychological self. If we are to facilitate this awareness, bridging, and integration in our patients, we must keep "our own body present in the treatment room" (Looker, 1998, p. 258). Knoblauch (1996) states, "Too often, and particularly in past discourses regarding desire, the analyst's experience of his or her body has been isolated, constricted, dissociated, or inscribed as signifying unanalyzed pathology" (p. 238).

We have been trained in psychoanalysis to appreciate and favor the intellectual aspects of the clinical exchange more than the experiential. Often a somatic response is viewed as a displacement, thus a defense, from experiencing and processing intellectually. We have historically valued the word and intellect in ways that have maintained the gap between mind and body. Lacan (1977) indicated that psychoanalysis involves the real of the real body and the imaginary mind.

How the patient's state affects the analyst's state and response, the matching, resonance, and coinciding of states are important and sensitive countertransference experiences. This is especially true when preverbal developmental dimensions of the transference are in the foreground. These experiences may be particularly difficult for the analyst to attune to if the concept of changing states of mind, and dissociation as a defense is not in conceptual focus. The patient shifting an ego state, for example, registered in the analyst as sleepiness, may be read as something quite different unless state of mind is itself a consideration in addition to psychodynamics, symbolism, and unconscious process and content. The nature of the patient's somatic and mental state, the body movement and affect of the patient, the literal and abstract content of her words are all registered in the analyst in varying ways somatically and psychically.

The state of mind of the analyst resonating with the ego state of the patient is subtle and fundamental, an irreducible experience that is beyond words, and yet it may be conveyed in words and focused on as a process of how "present" the patient is at any given moment. Following this process of the patient being grounded within internal experience tracks how much the patient is internally centered, connecting both mind and body. Being very focused on the present, unaltered, fully experienced state and affect is even more crucial for patients who use dissociation as a primary defense (Davies, 1999; Schwaber, 1998).

Clinical Overview

While we are accustomed to using our own fantasy and feelings as a countertransference awareness, we often leave out our attunement to our bodies, and to the shared lexicon of isolations, enactments, and somatic states.

The dilemma for patients who have not yet fully integrated body self and psychological self is that they are unaware of what they do not feel, and cannot find a way to express not knowing. Interpreting unconscious process, symbolism, or underlying fantasies may not be useful until a core foundation has been established within the patient's internal experience. To recognize basic sensations, state of mind, to approximate an experience with words, a patient must have an internal point of reference to recognize basic sensations from an unaltered state of mind; once arriving at this way-station, analyst and patient may identify and differentiate feelings. At certain moments the most important function that we may perform as analysts is to register the patient's affective experience, and put into words this acknowledgement of what may be for the patient an unformulated or unsymbolized subjective experience (Aron, 1998; Daniel Stern, 1997). In this regard, empathy is an act of the imagination of how our patients feel if they could feel, a guide to certain experiences as yet an unimaginable by the patient. Additionally, the dissection of basic elements of motivation and experience may be incomplete without a guide to reconnecting and generating new meaning by collaboration, just as detachments without attempts at reengagement can result in developmental arrest.

The foundation of body self and early somatic transferences-countertransferences form the basis of developing gender identity, psychological sense of self, Oedipal integration, object relations, and ultimately the flavor and texture of intimacy. The challenge is to examine analytically how inchoate, bodily based feelings can be explored by two people, patient and analyst, using only words to formulate empathic resonance and understanding, and to cocreate a verbal narrative to metabolize deeply primitive experiences and projective identifications. The self that seeks embodiment and the body that yearns for residence in the mind integrate throughout development. For the entire compass of experiences occurring in the analytic space, words alone aren't important enough, as the "mind does not dwell entirely in the brain" (Ackerman, 1999).

12

Psychoanalysis: The Verbal Exchange

Only when you say the truth can the truth set you free.
Marianne Williamson

I have not so much trained him as created an environment in which he has wanted to learn. I have taken care not to dull his appetite for work by repetition or excess. It has been essential to our progress together that he remain fresh and keen.
Monty Roberts

Speaking of one's experience makes it real.
Sharon Farber

You tricked me out of feeling solitary by being others for me.
Clive Wilmer

Analysis as New Implicit Knowledge

To find a patient we must look for him or her in ourselves (though not letting ourselves get in the way), to see experiences brought alive, and then transferred into that potential space mutually created together. The analyst is a potential vessel in which the patient can live experiences anew, and with whom to create new experiences. A necessary part of effective attachment in the analytic process is the intersubjective experience of having made an impact on the analyst, of reciprocal knowing that affective communication is effective, in that it makes a difference, that the analyst has been affected, touched, changed, by the emotional expression of the patient (Aron, 1995). For example, patients who have been traumatized must know that the analyst can be a container of emotional pain and feeling without being damaged or destroyed by it. This containment, articulation, and regulation of affect by both analyst and patient can restore internal regulation of feeling and reestablish the protective shield of safety traumatically shattered.

For the patient to attend to the present moment, to be fully present, the analyst must also be fully attuned, aware countertransferentially (i.e., subjectively aware) of state, affect, somatic experience, fantasies, and responses moment to moment. Some of the patient's early developmental levels of experience and needs will come by way of fantasy, somatic transference, and selfobject transference, while others may be expressed through object-specific transferences. Simultaneously, the analyst is experiencer, onlooker, integrator, collaborator, and regulator. We experience with the patient, by witnessing the shared community of analytic exchange of two real people working together. The regulation of affect states may prevent the retraumatization that bumps closely against remembered experience. As integrator, we guide a collaborative search for core self experiences and organizing themes.

Something more than interpretation alone is necessary for psychoanalysis to work. Interpretation of the unconscious within the transference has long been considered the essence of the psychoanalytic process. The intersubjective process expands the focus to the patient's implicit procedural knowledge, the experienced ways of being with others (Stern et al., 1998). The difference that a lived experience makes, the implicit relational knowing, are all part of the "present moments" comprising the shared interaction between patient and analyst, creating a new organization internally for the patient.

Stern et al. (1998) note that patients who had successful treatment came to remember two kinds of events related to change. One is of special moments of authentic human interaction. The other is about the key interpretative interactions that rearrange their internal landscape. Most often, treatments that failed were terminated not because of incorrect technique or unaccepted interpretations, but because of the unrealized opportunity for a meaningful, emotional connection between the two people working together. Patients often recall these moments of authentic connection with particular clarity as a nodal or pivotal event in the analysis representing so much more of the process than could be verbalized or symbolized. The process is what happens while we are talking about something else; theory has never cured anyone. It is the "something more" that is the magical ingredient. It is what occurs between two partners in a relationship that makes a difference. This is as true for a psychoanalysis as it is for a marital relationship, a parent–child relationship, or any other partnership where implicit, procedural processes occur to catalyze developmental growth.

So often in creating a new story together, the patient presents something quite new, intriguing, or different, defying or transcending all categories of analytic responses, requiring a different new, creative, or innovative response from the analyst that becomes a new piece of the evolving story. If indeed the patient is developing a new signature, both the patient and analyst are responding in a unique, authentic, mutual creation that is different from anything the patient has known. This newly constructed and mutually realized "moment of meaning" (Stern et al., 1998) is an act of cocontribution of each that is highly specific to this patient and this analyst. It is perhaps at this moment that the two meet as persons unhidden by their usual roles, yet paradoxically still within them. This shared moment in the implicit relationship and the process of the work is not technical, habitual, routine, or rote, but is uniquely the voice of this pair at this moment. It comprises not only empathy but movement beyond the familiar for each.

The shared mutual and implicit analytic relationship is never symmetrical, for the focus is on the patient, but it is nonetheless real and is not entirely encompassed in the traditional notion of transference-countertransference. So much of what the patient implicitly knows and senses about the analyst is outside the realm of transference, and comprises the personal engagement, the process of two real people working together in constructing a new story for the patient and a new intersubjectivity and implicit knowledge for each and both. So much of both personal selves are revealed and have meaning and bearing on the analytic process. So many of these experiences, these "moments of meaning" (Stern et al., 1998) cannot be understood, or even helped by a usual transference interpretation. "What is happening right now in here between us" may in addition to the transferences, also be about the new, the different, the moving on within a new story. It may be understandable and conceptualizable *after* it has occurred.

The goal of jointly and mutually reconstructing past experiences with the patient is not to discover lost memories, or only to reconstruct a past, repressed event, but primarily to explore the meaning of a current experience, a current pattern brought to life in the present analytic moment.

So many of the patient's expressions of anger, boldness, assertiveness, adversive responses, fear, and other feelings may not be first and foremost a transference directed at the analyst, or a resistance to experiencing other aspects of feeling, but the message within the message itself: that finally because of this holding environment and the evolving trust and security, the patient can now fully experience and expose aspects never before allowed. It is just such a stance of empathic appreciation rather than the implicit judgment inferred in interpreting only defenses of underlying motivation of sexuality or aggression that allow the patient to further elaborate and understand his or her full experience.

Psychoanalysis is the art of seeing the contradiction and conflicts inherent inside someone's mind, the obfuscated assumptions, the invisible decisions camouflaged in habit, the expectable developmental needs given muted or distorted pleading voice, hoping to be heard. We suffer, as Freud indicated, not from conflict but from bearing it too little and too unconsciously. To raise the drama to the center stage of awareness, owning both sides of the conflict, such as the wish and the fear, or experiencing contradictory poles of a preconflictional duality, begins the journey to resolution rather than retreat or repetition. Above all else, psychoanalysis has the purpose of helping the patient not only have insight and understanding about how his mind works, but to evolve within this new story to be more fully real and human.

Part of normal development is the process of listening accurately to feelings by way of having them actively reflected in the mirror of parents and significant others. If distorted as in funhouse mirror, or inaccurate with certain portions of the mirror blackened (such as not reflecting the joy and vibrancy of a girl being exploratory, bold, and assertive, and instead shaping her responses into more loving and passive nuances of her actual feeling), then feelings are not desomatized. The body then continues to hold developmental (unconscious) longing. The urges within, pressing for recognition, perhaps find their voice in accidents, dreams, or slips of the tongue. These reminders of unfinished business, voices of the past and present amalgamated, occur daily to remind us of the rest of who, unedited, we are.

The past, rather than being in prepackaged forms seeking disclosure and attention, lies quietly waiting for reassemblage, reconstruction, and reworking of understanding into a new and present shape. The desire or pain, inevitably yet not inextricably the same, seeks not historical interpretation but present recognition and mastery. The desire-pain does not seek a container of symbolic understanding, but to break to the surface and receive oxygen.

In early development as well as in psychoanalysis, if one perceives the parent or analyst as unable to survive an attack, unable to be the object of love, aggression, pride, idealization, or any other intense passion, then one ends up doing things more intrapsychically, that is, alone. Many analysands feel that they end up doing their analysis alone, while the analyst may label this as "autonomous ego-functioning" and "self-analyzing function" of the patient. This may simply be reentering and repeating an old story rather than creating a new story together, collapsing the possibility of the new intersubjective experience.

The sense of self develops as a sometimes independent, sometimes interdependent center for the initiation, organization, and integration of experience and motivation. Lived experience occurs through internal and external perception, and the needs, desires, and wishes that play a part. We are never without motivation and experience. Affects manifest in the clinical exchange in concrete emotion (e.g., anger, affection, or sadness), in moods (e.g. milder depression, irritability, or crankiness), and in affect states, (e.g., rage, elation, or profound depression) (Lichtenberg, 1998).

The best ally in treatment, and the best entry into the patient's state of mind is the specific emotion. The cognitive capacity to be aware of and look at oneself is via discrete emotions, but one must be in a mind state that allows reflection upon it. In an affect state, the person's sense of self is lost in the affect and state. For example, you cannot impart a lesson or get objective with a child who is in the middle of a tantrum; you have to stand by, not withdraw, not get too close, yet help regulate the affect state to moderation. The story seems inescapable to the individual, not their own creation. It seems as impossible to escape this life story as it does to exit a dream; one cannot exit a dream within the dream, by simply writing an ending. Only by changing a state of mind, such as awakening, can a dream be exited.

The psychoanalytic experience is a unique, partially altered state entered in order to create a new story with the old story simultaneously activated. Suspension of usual action and social imperatives, the immersion in the process of one's experience, and the mutual and reciprocal interaction all foster individual and collaborative entry into a state of reverie.

To enter this suspended state and to create a new story with the analyst, the synthesis of a new life narrative can occur, to make sense of the old while at the same time transforming or creating a cohesive new plot. The old plot may be well entrenched and consistent, as in the experience of victimhood of a traumatized patient, or integrated fragments of plots for someone who has a more chaotic life history. A life story may have seemed so opaque simply because there was no end point, no internal ideal of "good enough" to create effectiveness. Without this ego ideal, nothing is ever good enough, and the abiding quest is for "more," yet more is never enough.

Ogden (1997) suggests that the analyst's sensitivity is shaped by the structure of the patient's conscious and unconscious internal object world and that an understanding can manifest in various ways in the analysis, in part through the analyst's attention to internal experiences including feelings, thoughts, fantasies, and sensations. These reveries of both the analyst and the analysand contribute to the analytic dialogue and the evolving story within the analysis. It is the task of the analyst to understand all three: the patient with all of the conscious and unconscious manifestations, the analyst himself or herself, and the intersubjective context of the creation of the new story. The interplay of both the conscious and the unconscious communication, the verbal and nonverbal, constitutes the ongoing music of the analytic process.

The use of the couch was originally designed by Freud to allow the patient to concentrate more on self-observation, and at the same time to create a context of being able to listen and be receptive to the totality of the patient's conscious and unconscious mind rather than being caught up in the distractions of face-to-face communication and responses. The patient's use of the couch, and the analyst's privacy, out of sight behind the couch, became components of the framework of psychoanalysis. This arrangement also does some important things that we now know as being vital. For the patient, a reclining position allows a greater breadth and range of thought than sitting (or, most pointed and focused, of standing). It also fosters an altered state midway between relaxation and attention, allowing the greatest synthesis and integration of psychological and physical awareness. For the patient who has developed exquisitely sensitive radar to read others, and is oriented to the responses of others, the couch frees focus from the analyst's responses to essentially require a more internal and sensory focus. For those who have become so accustomed to reading and responding to others as a way of calibrating their own response, and who have not fully developed their own internal point of reference, this initially may feel like being lost, devoid of unusual cues of interpersonal and social responses. It also allows the analyst to be free to listen internally, to resonate with the conscious and unconscious conveyances from the patient, to the full range of body self and psychological self experience. The use of the couch for many patients in once or twice weekly therapy affords the same possibility of the creation of the potential space for each to work in this way.

Of course, a couch does not guarantee the creation of an analytic process, nor is it a necessary prerequisite to one. Some patients have never lain down, or for significant portions of the work have sat up. Other patients may need to sit up or to lie down at certain phases of the analysis or for certain issues, and the possibilities of enactment and resistance are always a consideration. Rather than handling the use of the couch in a way that may be perceived as authoritarian, another point of view is to collaboratively analyze what would most facilitate or interfere with the work at a particular point in time. Sometimes it may simply be too frightening or too lonely for the patient to use the couch, and sitting up would facilitate the analysis, especially if object constancy is an issue. Or, as one analytic patient said after the second session on the couch, "You know, I've spent my entire life alone and dealing with issues by myself. I don't need more of that right now, I need to see you." Over time, we both learned together how absolutely correct she was, how necessary it was to see me seeing her. She needed to sit up and keep me in view in order to be able to sustain an unaltered state while expressing developmentally traumatic experiences.

On Symptoms

How surprising, even embarrassing, it is for a patient to recognize that their secrets have never been secret at all, but had been only aspects of themselves for which they have disallowed their own awareness. The secrets have been only from themselves. Their symptoms, those secrets hiding in the open, have been in evidence but not in awareness. The symptom both reveals and conceals from one's self. The glass against which their nose is pressed to take in whatever is possible, perhaps even illicit and forbidden, becomes a mirror in which they see the previously unseen, in themselves. They are protected from feeling by not knowing, the ways of avoiding knowing we call symptoms. At times we may mistakenly clothe a symptom (such as bulimia or paranoid) with the essence of a personality, as the protagonist of a story of fear and pathology, rather than as a sentinel in a story of hope and desire. In so doing, we focus on the pathological *result* rather than the developmental *intent*. We pejoratively give nicknames to clusters of symptoms, such as borderline or narcissistic, and obfuscate the person and their attempt to splint the missing link to the self.

We echo the voice as yet unheard by our patients. Their own experience begins to take shape and form, developmental needs become visible in their actualization and perhaps enactment, and their internal object world becomes transparent in the characters and dialogues of analytic interactions. The disavowed and projected versions of their secret self are induced in the interchange within the shared space created by patient and analyst. The symptoms, those previous ways of avoiding knowing, often begin to disappear as the engagement evolves.

A symptom is its own story, but it is told within a larger story, a happening of a lifetime in which the symptom may be an often-repeated compromise of desire and restraint. Many aspects of a patient's life are written into the code of the symptom. Symptoms reveal and conceal, splinting the missing link to self. Buried in private assumption, symptoms attempt to rewrite silent shames through public acclaim. To tell a secret out loud is to create a truth; this truth is constructed mutually rather than being extracted.

The desire for a more permanent solution and the wish to engage meaningfully with the analyst, as with other people, may be experienced as unsafe, possibly threatening, because of the patient's assumption that such a relationship would be as hurtfully unreliable as past experiences have been. Patients cannot give up their symptoms: a psychosomatic patient cannot stop having pain as a precondition of treatment. They must have a new story to be inside, mutually and collaboratively created with the analyst, before they can give up their old story.

As analysts, we must empathically resonate with and convey understanding of the comfort and investment in their symptom, of its immediacy and power of tension reduction, of the difficulty and anxiety in relinquishing its power and effectiveness to change the way they feel, of the addiction to the symptom itself, of its organizing function in identity. Such symptoms cannot be abandoned as a prerequisite to analysis, but they may diminish in intensity and utility over time and with understanding. Consistent analytic attention and empathic listening illuminates the use of the symptom, understanding of the motivations, enactments, experiences of the symptomatic act itself, and its change throughout the course of analysis. The experience and meaning of a symptom changes with developmental growth in analysis.

For example, someone for a lifetime has experienced anxious worry and suffering; they've got feeling bad down. Anxiety has been coupled with danger and trauma. Fear has predicted the future, and the only certainty has been repetition of the past. The pull of the old and the fear of the new inform invisible decisions that become camouflaged in habit, our collection of repetitions. To feel good, to be inside a new story together in analysis is to leave unknown territory and the effectiveness of its repetition, even if it has a destructive result. Just to feel good may mean being in new territory, beyond what is familiar, with no known landmarks, with a separation anxiety from the accustomed. This new anxiety is different. The uncertainty of expansiveness and awkwardness of feeling good are alongside the familiar restraint and perception of danger. To not create an obstacle and to have desire unobtruded creates its own anxiety. We provide a meaning for this new experience of a patient by setting the familiar symptoms in a new context: anxiety is now a signpost of moving ahead, an understandable trepidation in leaving the familiar. This retranscription of meaning is part of mutually creating a new story.

A patient very excited about her evolving talent as a writer sat down to write and said, "I got nervous and began doing a lot of different things other than writing." I said, "It's possible that your nervousness was excitement about immersing yourself in a long-awaited passion, and you read it as anxiety, as if there were danger." She then recognized the anxiety and her immediate distraction due to the unspoken assumption. This perception, coupling of meaning, and coping mechanism were part of the old story juxtaposed with the new.

How else can someone be aware of how far they have come in a developmental journey than to have a fixed point of reference, to validate progress at different junctures, to use the symptom again to *experience* it as different. In this example, the patient later briefly revisited her old anxiety as a souvenir of a place that she no longer inhabited. Cezanne spoke of a related process in art: "I don't paint things, I paint the difference between things."

A patient is never more aware of creating both a symptom and meaning than when she also recognizes that she creates both its presence and its absence. It is the enigma of recognizing that she feels most like a little girl at the very moment she realizes she is no longer one.

A patient has been author of her repetitious story, though feeling the victim of it, trying to exit it by writing a better ending. A thousand better endings later still creates the process of the old story. Invention has been sabotaged and creativity imprisoned by remaining in the old story, repeating the same story lines.

Analytic work for such patients with early developmental arrests must address the psychodynamic scenario of the present moment in which the attempted restitutive symptom occurs, the developmental deficits that underlie, and the often simultaneous defensive use of the symptom. The process of empathic failures experienced throughout early development may have resulted in an unconscious core organizing assumption of badness, defectiveness, or unworthiness (Stolorow & Atwood, 1992). Attempts at countering this core belief by unrelenting love, performance, and achievement all fail to eradicate this false self, seeming to further validate its authenticity. Such deficits in self-regulation mean that these vulnerable individuals rely on external sources to supplement deficient internal regulation. Through their reliance on others for affirmation, enhancement, function, and esteem, they attempt to internalize these sources symbolically by acquiring of material goods and money, or substances such as food, alcohol, or drugs.

The desire for a more permanent solution and the wish to engage meaningfully with the analyst, as with other people, is experienced as unsafe, possibly threatening, vulnerable to yet another empathic failure, to further activation of shame. The desire to be effective and to impose predictability, often accomplished by action symptoms, needs to be understood empathically, collaboratively, and nonjudgmentally. They cannot give up their symptom at the beginning of treatment any more than a psychosomatic patient can stop having pain as a precondition of treatment. Giving up an old model, or even the relationship with a symptom, would feel like an amputation, like removing part of their identity. They must have a new story to adopt and endorse before relinquishing the habitual.

As analysts, we must empathically resonate with and convey understanding of the comfort and investment in the symptom, of its immediacy and power of tension reduction, of the difficulty and anxiety in relinquishing the effectiveness of the symptom to change the way they feel. Such symptoms cannot be abandoned as a prerequisite to analysis, but they may diminish in intensity and utility over time and with understanding. Consistent analytic attention and empathic listening must focus on the use of the symptoms: the motivation, enactment, experience of the symptomatic act itself, the selfobject relationship with the symptom, and its change throughout the course of analysis.

On Free Association

Freud proposed that unconscious mental processes provided the explanation for psychic determinism, the notion that everything in one's psychic life is no accident. Utilizing the newer biological model, every psychic event, whether procedural or explicit, is determined by an event that precedes it by activating a neural network (Kandell, 1999). Psychological events such as free association, dreams, and slips of the tongue all relate to preceding emotional events, with the relevance and meaning to be understood. The idea that nothing internally determined happens by chance, and has meaning in context, is the purpose of having the patient articulate everything and anything that comes to mind without conscious filtering or censorship.

Free association creates a present experience of spontaneity and access to emotion and its expression, but also allows for the emergence of patterns and metaphors that link past and present. An old story, like a state of mind, does not feel or appear so when it is being re-created, as it feels like the reality that it is. A patient stated, "I can only see what's there when I let go of it." Free association is ultimately a paradox, because if a patient could free associate, he would not need analysis, and by that time he can associate freely, he is ready to leave analysis.

There are also a number of patients for whom free association is the antithesis of what is needed for expansion and change; those who are already loosely organized and tend to ramble need help to contract, focus, organize, and conceptualize their experience; those who are more disorganized and detached may need to create an intensity and emotional relevance rather than continuing to intellectually associate (Lichtenberg, 1998). The obsessive who needs the release of free association to allow what is internal to emerge, can also use free association as a defense, spinning away from an affect in order to elaborate further associations, all the while avoiding affective intensity and specificity. Rather than passively free associating, some patients may need to more actively focus on a specific feeling or sequence in which feeling resides in the detail rather than in the broad brush strokes. Likewise, action symptoms may require understanding the entire scenarios and pursuit of affect and motivation rather than continuation of free association in action language and events. For a dissociative patient, what may appear as free association may actually be a state change or a distraction to move away from a feeling.

For those who need to develop a more cohesive narrative, who need to focus more specifically on internal experience and ultimately develop symbolic organization, *saying everything* and *free association* can be qualitatively different. Saying everything about an internal experience is to more fully explore in detail the awareness and meaning of this moment's emotion, its developmental history, the dynamic scenario of its current foreground position, perhaps the interdigitation of procedural memory (transference) with new implicit relational significance (the new story). Saying everything is necessary for both patient and analyst to empathically immerse themselves together, allowing the patient, perhaps for the first time in his life, to be empathic with himself, to create an intimacy internally as well as with the analyst. In this mutual involvement, the analyst is witness/observer/interpreter/collaborator/coauthor.

Lichtenberg (1998) has elaborated in one of his principles of technique about the filling of the narrative envelope and the particular style of narration revealing organizational ability or difficulty, and demonstrating attachment patterns. For example, adults who as infants were securely attached give a coherent, organized account of their relationship experiences. Adults who had avoidance rather than secure attachment as children are dismissive and global, indicating, "my parents were great" without specific elaboration. Infants who were quite ambivalently attached as adults ramble with irrelevancies and obsessionality. Adults who as infants had disorganized attachment have fragmented, incoherent, and even dissociated affect and production now. Obviously each of the above patients will produce different qualities, content, and patterns of free association. For certain patients, expecting free association may be frustrating for both patient and analyst. For other patients, free association may be a divergence from needing to organize their experience and create relevance in their narrative.

Contemporary psychoanalysis and psychoanalytic therapy is unique in its balanced approach to experience the mind and the body, and expressing thoughts and feelings simultaneously activates both right and left forebrain. Psychoanalysis, used originally for the treatment of nervous disorders, expands into also being a treatment of the body; that is, a treatment for disturbances that find manifestation at the level of the body, enhanced by knowledge of the physiology of the mind and body connections (Goldberg, 1995).

Some of the most important experiences are ones that a patient will never free associate to, or stumble across an associative path on the way to another idea or feeling. Some experiences are so categorically different that a patient would never know how to free associate to get there, as the creation of new pathways and neural networks are necessary.

Neutrality and Empathy

The analyst positions inside the subjective experiences of the patient equidistant between the opposing forces of conflict (Rangell, 1996). This equidistance is not only internally between components of a conflict, and between id, ego, and superego, but also between the patient's internal and external world. Neutrality is not knowing what the answer will be, not having our own need for it to go in one direction or another, and knowing that there are many truths to tell without having an investment in which is most salient at this moment.

Neutrality is to remain equidistant from both sides of a patient's conflict or internal dichotomy in order to fully appreciate both components, such as a wish and fear, or wanting and not wanting the same thing, in order to understand motivations for each aspect. Neutrality refers to fully and completely listening from within a patient's struggle and internal dilemma to all components without omitting focus on any aspect. Fear is guide to the desire, and both must be understood. It is quite compelling to align with one aspect of the patient's conflict or dilemma, such as joining with the patient's attempt to overcome a symptom or maladaptive behavior, losing sight of the fear. This alignment with the component of the patient's internal position to developmentally grow and to get better disregards the part of the patient's conflict that is opposing growth and change, holding onto hope in an old context. This breach of neutrality frequently creates an impasse in the treatment of the patient who seemingly does all the right things and wants to get better, but remains stuck.

Accurate empathy is an aspect of neutrality, to be attuned to the entire subjective reality of a patient, even attuned to what the patient is omitting. To use an empathic listening position as a way of gathering information, the analyst must place himself or herself inside the entire experience of the patient, understanding and resonating with the patient's subjective reality. Empathy does not mean being kind, sympathetic, consoling, gratifying, or commiserating. Empathy describes a listening position, a particular way of listening from inside another individual's experience that permits appreciation from that person's own frame of reference. "Listening from the inside" includes an awareness of the patient's internal and perceived external systems and of the representational model to perceive and process body, psyche, and subjectivity.

Patients whose basic pathology lies in the formation and synthesis of body self and psychological self have helped us to better understand the nature of empathy through their particular sensitivity to it. It is by empathic failures in their earliest development that their pathology has been created—that their feelings, internal experience, and perceptions have not been listened to or accurately validated.

Patients may view an analyst as a part or function of themselves (i.e., selfobject transference); the analyst becomes increasingly important as part of the structure of the patient's self-experience. Illustration is provided by the description of the self-object transferences (paralleling early developmental phases) that become activated in the patient as the result of empathic listening: merger, mirroring, idealization, twinship, and alter ego (Kohut, 1971, 1985). The analyst becomes the personification of the patient's own listening and experiencing process and becomes a developmental organizer in the growth of the patient. Through dynamic understanding of this entire process, the patient develops self-empathy and self-structure as developmental growth ensues and empathy becomes internalized as part of self-regulatory capacity, ultimately obviating the need for symbolic substitutes such as action symptoms.

There are continued occurrences in the interface of the differently organized subjective worlds of the analysand and the analyst. Intersubjective conjunction occurs when the principles organizing the patient's experience give rise to expressions that are assimilated and closely similar to central configuration in the psychological life of the analyst. Intersubjective disjunction occurs when the analyst of significantly different background or internal organization assimilates material from a patient into configurations that miss or alter its meaning to the patient (Stolorow, 1995). The correspondence and disparity between the subjective worlds of patient and analyst can be used to promote empathic understanding and insight. When there is absence of reflective self-awareness by the analyst, such conjunctions and disjunctions can seriously interfere with the progress of an analysis. Stolorow (1995) indicates that while empathy and introspection organize the analyst's experience, the intersubjective psychological field is also the subject of scrutiny.

We know, and feel from behind the couch, that *objective* does not mean cold or uninterested, *neutral* is not noncaring, *equidistant* does not equate with no opinion, and *nonjudgmental* does not mean that we abandon judgment. Yet the analytic relationship is not symmetrical because it is no ordinary interchange of dialogue. As one analytic patient indicated after a thorough analysis of an upcoming important life decision, "At some point, I want your opinion and your trust that I would not be unduly influenced by your opinion. In fact, it would be a validation of your trust in me."

There are instances when neutrality can be distinguished from a position taken by the analyst in a particular context. An example would be to indicate to an anorexic patient that if we are to fully understand and resolve the issues motivating weight loss, it would be essential during the course of treatment to attain an ideal body weight.

It may even be useful at times to selectively suspend neutrality. A professional woman in analysis was struggling with her eating disorder, the resultant obesity, and her stuckness even after thoroughly analyzing both for a lengthy period of time. She mentioned one day, "I know you have to be neutral about my eating disorder and my excess weight, and you can't say what you think or feel personally." I responded,

> Then it might be useful for me to abandon neutrality and tell you about what I think and feel as a person and as your analyst. I hope you do allow yourself this final step of experiencing yourself as a complete, full-fledged woman with nothing the matter with you as we both see and know yourself inside and outside. I hope you will allow yourself the full measure of experiencing all of your feelings in each moment with no escape hatch of food or weight. I hope you will allow yourself to get to your ideal body weight, your true body self, so you will have the experience of living freely and experiencing yourself as fully as your remarkable capacity would allow. And I hope you'll stop using food symptomatically and you'll lose the weight during our time together so you an know the experience directly, not theoretically, and we can experience it together, and each of us can witness it.

While both of us were a little astonished (she perhaps a bit more than I, though I still can't be sure), and after a period of working silence, she quietly acknowledged her appreciation of my comments and feelings, and indicated she knew I was right. She knew how different it would be to allow both of us to experience and see her without her protective layers of defense and weight, and come to the end of a past that included trauma, danger, and shame.

Transferences

The organizing process of how we perceive, process, and attach meaning to people and processes in our lives is ubiquitous and outgoing. *Transference* is a verb; the model that is inferred from the patient's ongoing attempts to organize experience in the analytic relationship is called *transference*. Freud (1912/1958a) remarked that the analytic process does not create transference, but reveals it; Kohut (1971) indicated the same of the selfobject transferences. The "transferences" are repetitive ways of organizing current experiences based on past experiences. The object transferences and the selfobject transfereces are in a constant dialectic, and developmental evolution in analysis, alternating between figure and ground.

Freud (1912/1958a) spoke of the transference in psychoanalysis as a playground of repetitions of past experiences with important people. In this domain, unconscious and conscious conflicts will come alive to become vividly focused for both patient and analyst. At the same time a new relationship unfolds, a new story that is substantially different from the transferential one. Both the old and the new story occur simultaneously, with the foundation in the new story of trust, of collaboration, and of increasing insight and objectivity, even while being subjectively immersed in this interdigitating new and old story. Interpretations can cleave the old story from the new story, the past from the present, the old model from the new and evolving framework. The analyst is a coauthor, simultaneously immersed subjectively and objectively in both stories.

The mind is an open system with developmental arrest prematurely foreclosing aspects of the system. Analysis reopens that process, and the analyst become transference object and developmental object, guide to developmental organization.

As Weston and Gabbard (in press, a) note, "The transference" is a simplification of the many kinds of transference reactions a patient will have over the course of an analysis, reflecting the entirety of developmental processes and contents. They not that transference involves "the heightened activation of enduring patterns of thought, feeling, motivation, affect regulation, or behavior in the analytic relationship." This activation of neural networks of explicit and implicit (procedural and associative) memories in the clinical exchange offers an in vivo recognition and retranscription of patterns of feeling, thought, and affect regulation. Hope and motivation may then be moved from a past context to a present one, with current objectives and adaptation.

Both object and self-object dimensions of the transference are always present. What the patient wards off (the defensive) and what is needed to restore or maintain (the developmental) are in a constant dialect. Whether defensive or developmental is in the foreground determines in part the focus and availability of full engagement. For example, until fundamental developmental needs are securely in place, the patient may not be ready to deal with dimensions of the object transference as yet, because there is not a differentiated experience of the analyst as a separate other. On the other hand, repetitive, defensive interactional sequences may require focus on the object specific dimensions before other more fundamental issues can be approached. Dealing with each affects the other: When the self-object dimensions of the transference are dealt with to provide a foundation of self-experience and to establish an internal point of reference, movement into the object specific transference is less charged and chaotic.

How does the patient use the analyst to get better? These two dimensions of the transference continuum are complementary and interconnected, related and reciprocal, and the patient will let us know how, for example, how not to respond in an object specific way that repeats earlier experiences, to make the self-object dimension inaccessible. For example, the patient who needs to focus on recognizing and regulating basic affects and develop an internal point of reference, may experience the analyst who focuses on himself and interprets the patient's defensive avoidance of the transference centrality of the analyst as a replica of developmental experiences with narcissistically damaging parents.

Contrast the early description by Freud of the analyst being an inscrutable mirror, a surgeon operating in a surgical field of the patient's mind, to the version depicted by Susan Vaughan (1997) in which she indicates that in psychoanalysis she becomes a character of the internal dramas of her patients and collaboratively rearranges the furniture.

A patient must live the experience of the old story within the new story in order to tell the difference between the two, and ultimately to make the old story a part of the memory within the new lived experience. Procedural and associative memory become part of the lived experience of the new story. The internal experience and organization of a patient is replicated-created on the outside, casting others in the roles of the internal drama that parallels the internal organizing assumptions as they become played out in relationships with others. The mind is author of internal assumptions, producer of the individual life drama, and casting director of significant others.

With enough immersion and repeated new experiences with the analyst, and as the present and past are interpretatively dissected, these lived experiences crystallize a mourning of the past, including the old model. These new experiences alter neuronal connections in the frontal cortex in which meanings and emotions are synthesized; new couplings are created (Weston and Gabbard, in press, c). For example, a patient's mother asking "why?" rather than being an authoritative negative search for a mistake, now can be simply seen as the mother's style, perhaps her own uncertainty, and her way of maintaining a bond with a now adult son or daughter.

Models of relationships with others get established very early in life and become the software through which subsequent relationships are both perceived, organized, and processed. At least until adulthood or beyond, the software is not viewed as one way of looking at things, but as the reality, as the way things are. A fish cannot describe water; it can't get outside the system in order to do so. Through childhood and adolescence, with the exception of the occasional rare individual who sees beyond the system of the family, it is reality, not just a point of view, no "as if," no metaphor.

When someone experiences a terrifying incident such as a car wreck or being held up at gunpoint, and responds in a relatively calm and detached manner, only later on safe ground can they then add the experience of their full anxiety and fear. So, too, it is with the "safe ground" of the analytic collaboration that the patient can deal with issues that had previously been partitioned or segregated. Only by this connection and container of the analytic bond can the missed developmental needs of the past be fully experienced and mourned. One is never more aware of what was missed in the past than when now having it. For example, the patient may now, finally, be able to dare to allow the awareness (paradoxically through mourning) of the longings for body self experiences, for the reciprocity with the maternal body, and connection with hungers of all the senses. And finally, from within this new experience, the patient may be internally empathic, able to imagine, to symbolize, to be able to be introspective without compromise, with a belief system that does not contradict all other belief systems.

Interpretation

The role of interpretation, essentially of making what is unconscious conscious, is aimed at insight leading to a realignment of present concepts, a revision of mental software. This change realigns the patient's system, causing a reconceptualization of other aspects of one's self in terms of meaning and relevance in the present. Interpretation is the coconstructed generation of new meaning.

The emotional state of mind of the patient and foreground dimension of the transference determine the patient's receptivity to collaboration or interpretative comments. The feelings, meanings, actions, and assumptions of a patient are meaningfully subject to scrutiny only to the extent that the patient can actually experience them, not what we may impugn of unconscious meaning or symbolism, defensive reversal, or mechanisms that are metapsychological or abstract. To bypass or supersede the patient's experience would put the analyst in a position of authority, of determining ultimate meaning, as if the analyst were arbiter of the truth. *All we can do as analysts is to tell the patient our experience of him or her.*

Interpretation is more about illuminating, less about excluding or eradicating. There are times when interpretation cleaves the blurring of the past context with the present, catalyzes feeling, distinguishes feelings from states of mind, links mind and body, differentiates a new model from an old model. Psychoanalysis is a developmental experience and the psychoanalyst is a developmental organizer. An interpretation may be to understand more simply the context of what is being said: "What does it mean now?" "What is it specifically you are afraid of, right now, in this room, with just you and me?" "What is the age of this conversation?"

An enactment occurs when a patient's transference and an analyst's countertransference repeats or recreates an aspect of an old story (Jacobs, 1994). An enactment could be seen as the patient's effort to engage the analyst by crystallizing internal experience otherwise invisible. Enactments may be a best effort at conveying experience, perspective, and meaning within an old model, now presented within a new and evolving story. That a patient is able to create an enactment, to offer vivid, lived experiences, to induce in the analyst various responses not limited to empathy, may all be viewed as the noble intent of the patient's participation to convey experience and meaning. The patient is always telling us what he or she is experiencing, always teaching us what it is like to be him or her.

Every symptom, every enactment contains a nucleus of hope. It is up to the analyst to understand, to decode, to be able to know that the patient is engaging internal experience each moment. It is up to the analyst to find a way to focus together on that production, whether it is action language by the patient, a state of mind created within the analyst, a nonverbal, somatic communication, or a more traditional verbal offering. The goal of each session may not be insight so much as it is an immediate awareness, resonance with a felt experience, a mental state or body awareness with an attempt to collaboratively formulate experience and its meaning. As analysts we must allow ourselves to become who the patient needs us to be while at the same time holding solidly to our role in understanding the patient's mental state and internal experience within the shared space. We must allow enactments to teach us, to treat them as valuable information.

An interpretation is an attempt to find the words to say what the patient can't quite say, of giving meaning to what the patient hasn't given meaning to yet, of giving shape to what hasn't been fully felt. Perhaps more than the horizontal movement of unconscious to conscious, the vertical cleavage of present from past illuminates assumptions, defenses, and meanings no longer adaptive. To distinguish current experience from past, procedural and associative memory is a part of the process of coming to the end of the past, to make the past a memory rather than an active, intrusive, repeating presence.

I believe that our patients want us, as Anderson's (1998) patient did when she wanted her to "feel every step of this," to be with them in every experience. Both the patient and the analyst must be fully present, attending to each of their own as well as shared experiences, and the analyst must have the patient as the essential point of reference. Our own affect state must be in full resonance with that of the patient; the shifts of those states are vital aspects of our attunement. For the analyst to accurately recognize and assist in articulating affective states helps the patient to develop an internal point of reference. Affect evolves from somatic experience, through differentiation and subjective awareness of distinct feelings, to verbalization. Both somatic and affective internal signals that the patient may be neglecting, deleting, or distorting need accurate reading and labeling, and then retranscripted to current meaning and context. Some of those signals or experiences may be quite threatening, such as the experience of emptiness or of internal disorganization. Verbalization not only provides mastery via the articulation of feelings, but also, more importantly, facilitates the accurate perception and integration of body self and psychological self. The blending of affective and cognitive through symbolic and verbal mastery of the bodily and the psychic self consolidates a sense of self.

The analyst must respond contingently to the productions of the patient. A basic sense of causality thereby becomes established. It is the empathic immersion, resonance, and response of the analyst to the internal experience of the patient that provides a new framework of experience. The experience of effectiveness in the process of empathic attunement can then become internalized by the patient as self-empathy and resumed developmental growth. Ultimately, the individual can internalize the entire process for self-regulation from the newly developed internal center of initiative, affect, and esteem. The potential space between feeling and action, rather than being collapsed by fusion of the two, is established for fantasy, contemplation, and symbolism.

Both analyst and patient work together in defining the environment of the intersubjective experiences. Always, it is a dance of sharing, a movement toward understanding. Tracking by the analyst goes on in a number of parallel ways at different levels. The content of the conscious verbal topic that is elaborated, clarified, and understood is never to be disregarded. Lichtenberg (1998) emphasizes, "The message contains the message: what someone is actually expressing needs to exhausted before the venue is changed, and whatever is presented is tracked as communication, not as irrelevant and pushed aside to explore the deeper and more disguised" (p. 23). Another level is metaphorical, the unconscious and symbolic meaning of the unfolding process. Another is transferential, the procedural and associative memories of the patient activated at this moment with this analytic pair, to be imbued with new meaning. Still another, and perhaps harder to define level, is the implicit relational experience, the "knowing" of the shared mutual relationship that is occurring while other things are being talked about. At times, this implicit relational knowing is the subject itself, the focus of both patient and analyst.

The clinician intuitively senses these "present moments" of essential process, that everything is important, that hope and understanding are conveyed in a way of talking, in a nanosecond of response, with an imminent unformed developmental step and needing a verbal shape. Subjective time and experience must be packaged into a recognizable container, bound in an envelope of mutual recognition, often a repeated repertoire of responses that may become habitual.

Whenever a patient stops a current feeling by any defensive mechanism, the initial exploration of primary importance is recognition of the affect and experience that the patient stopped. The specific kind of defense (denial, disavowal, dissociation, etc.) as well as the content or model of the past activated to fill the void that current experience would have occupied, can then be understood in the context of the psychodynamic scenario that began with stopping the feeling. The consequence of stopping the present feeling is to instantly reinstate an old context of perception and processing. For example, when a patient is experiencing something quite new and different in current time, an anxiety/trepidation/uncertainty exists. The anxiety may be read in an old way, as a signal of danger, that something bad is about to happen. The model a patient uses can then be interpretively revised so he or she can recognize that current anxiety may simply signal uncertainty, of not having familiar landmarks, rather than being the emblem of danger as in the past. Staying with this new anxiety in order to become familiar with the newness is the change leading to amelioration of the anxiety, and ultimately to comfort and acceptance. To stay with the feeling, to see it through its course, and to redefine it in the present context, brings a new definition of subjective reality. Signal anxiety becomes retranscripted to become an affective icon of being in new territory, a validation of change.

Both patient and analyst can come to recognize the process of stopping a present feeling, instantly substituting an old experience with its own content, context, and meaning. For example, when either the analyst or patient become aware of the patient lapsing into a defensive position, such as an obsessional reverie, an exploration can begin of the specific feeling that patient had the instant before the defense was activated. The defense and content (here the state change to detached obsessionality) becomes a signpost of affect not felt, a deletion of present experience. To stay with the feeling, to see it through its course, can redefine subjective reality in the present context. The pull of the old must constantly be empathically appreciated and understood alongside the fear of the new, of how compelling it is to the patient to exchange the unknown and untried for the familiar. This new pattern of exploration, of staying with a feeling, can gradually replace old, automatic, and unconscious internal and interactive patterns.

Repeating or reflecting back to a patient only what is said is not nearly enough. Like imitation, it only approximates identification and understanding. To hear a patient, to resonate with their experience, to select what seems a central aspect of experience or feeling, and then to convey it is central in the empathic interchange. New meaning occurs when that primary feeling or experience is collaboratively explored by patient and analyst, forming a basis for new implicit and explicit learning.

A supervisee's patient spoke of the absences from his analyst, especially the regular ones on weekends, and indicated that he had no idea if she ever thought of him, and assumed that she did not. He grew angry to talk about how he had only his fantasies, just like being a child when he would have only a fantasy of his mother to relate to, rather than having his mother's actual presence. He could not imagine that his analyst even thought of him, since he could not as yet evoke an image of the analyst during longer intervals.

I suggested in supervision that she might consider saying to him something that would contain the idea that she understands how frustrating and even frightening it can be for her patient to lose the image and continuity of the work, even though she can carry the work in her head and reflect on it at times. This actual working model and reality is perhaps so different than anything the patient has known before that he cannot quite imagine it; having no object constancy disallows the fantasy of its presence.

All the present moments of lived experiences sewn together create a new pattern, a new way of relating, conceptualized in present time, and in a new context of meaning. Any new experience has an unknown future. Only the repetition of the past (that has no future) can be predicted with assurance. A new experience moving forward is both unfamiliar and somewhat frightening. This moment's anxiety to be tolerated and understood in time, precedes interpretation in terms of the past. The present and the immediate future are increasingly reorganized and created in the analysis rather than abandoned to repeat the past.

The unconscious compromises that a patient makes of trading freedom for safety, and aliveness for certainty, are the illusions shattered in analytic work. Freedom internally to be fully human, and the creativity of both inhabiting one's own experience and finding a voice of one's own may first be experienced within the analytic story. When you are looking for answers, someone telling you what to do isn't freedom. The illusion of an answer is someone giving advice. Ideas, of course, are part of an illness. Ogden (1997) indicates that a fundamental aspect of the psychoanalytic task is to help the patient feel more fully human.

Psychoanalysis has a bacteriocidal model, in which psychopathology is sought, resistance to its manifestation obliterated, revealing its pathological flourishing, and the pathology is eradicated. A bacteriostatic model looks at the healthy, the adaptive thrust of mastery, contrasting normal developmental stages and their facilitation with previous impediments and interferences, with the activation and facilitation of renewed growth and development in current intrapsychic and intersubjective arenas of experience.

Psychoanalysis has evolved from seeing the clinical exchange as the patient projecting onto the blank screen of the analyst, to seeing analysis as a partnership, a mutual and collaborative adventure. We then experience together the aspects of the patient's internal life, imparting new meaning to these events. Contemporary psychoanalysis is about seizing the present moment, expanding a here and now experience to increasingly live inside a full personal experience, created and conceptualized within a present context with the meaning authored by the patient.

13

Psychoanalysis:
The Nonverbal Exchange

He listened with an intensity most people have only while talking.

Lily Tomlin

And this I have learned: grown ups do not know the language of shadows.

Opal Whitley

Of course whatever determinism survives in principle does not help as much when we have to deal with real systems that are not simple, like the stock market or life on earth.

S. Weinberg

Until we can make room for the problem of subjectivity in our theory, we'll never be able to separate the singer from the song.

Whitley Spence

Nonverbal Dimensions of Experience

Some patients with early developmental disturbances may not be able to enter an analytic experience at the same level of consensual abstraction and reflection as other patients. Especially those who have not had sufficient self-object experiences to differentiate feelings, or even to desomatize emotion, have difficulty communicating aspects of internal experience

213

and affect by means of symbolic language. These individuals maintain an external focus, report action and interaction with others, and often begin treatment with an action focus such as missing sessions, complaining of no benefit, threatening to quit, and continuity action symptoms. They may feel lost and vague regarding internal focus, and to the analyst read as resistant. Their experiences of restlessness, ineffectiveness, and boredom are often induced in the analyst by similar frustration of ineffectiveness, even deadness or hollowness of the mutual experience.

Just as gender automatically shapes attributions and assumptions from an initial encounter, the patient's bodily presence in the consultation room nonverbally shapes an interchange. Expression through the body offers a rich melange of communication. The body language of movement, the boundary of skin, and the gut of private self all underlie the verbal exchange of the individual, of a self that is always and ultimately embodied.

Attunement to the patient's body, and our own as analysts, are barometers of the patient's experience. For some patients, this awareness may register only in action sequences or action symptoms that involve the body, such as tension, pain, self-harm, or exercise. These bodily attunements comprise an important aspect of empathy.

Verbal interchange is only one of the ways that meanings are communicated in the clinical setting. Nonverbal communications include enactments, body postures, facial expressions, voluntary and involuntary movements, position and position changes, looking and not looking, motor sequences of body alignment, alignment within space, and facial mirroring, to name only a few. Tiny changes in demeanor and impalpable dispatches, as well as the theme and grand gesture all portray procedural somatic memory for the blended music in the dance of the analytic pair. There is value in attending to implicit memories as they emerge in enactments and nonverbal sequences within the analytic space. All of these dimensions of nonverbal as well as verbal may be included in an informed psychoanalytic repertoire. This attention to meanings of the implicit nonverbal dimensions of the interaction include the simple and literal as well as the more abstract and symbolic.

For example, the patient's procedural memory of nonresponsiveness creates an expectation of the same from the analyst. Often an early memory depicting such a model scene or expectation is one of the internal experiences of aloneness, emptiness, devitalization, and the context of isolation and deadness of one's self with the nonresponsive caretaker. The expectation of what will happen currently is based on the experience of what has happened in the past, and may even cocreate a current nonresponsiveness. The communication of withdrawal, frozen rigidity, and muteness may be a pre-symbolic, nonverbal way of relating experiences that may need to be put into words by the analyst, a construction (when there is ample evidence) of the model scene with a caretaker where this attachment pattern originated. An interpretive attempt to articulate "nothingness," or to connect random or chaotic symptoms to demonstrate the relationship between early experiences and current feeling, personifies the hope of a coconstructed narrative to understand experiences, to regulate affect, and to create a new context of meaning in which self-cohesiveness can occur. Once these earliest relational patterns are discussed, significant feelings and memories often emerge around these experiences, and the patient may feel understood in a way never before experienced.

Listen to Daniel Stern (1990) describe the transition from nonverbal to verbal language for the young child in *Diary of a Baby:*

> But there is also a dark side to language. It has enormous disadvantages, especially compared with the nonverbal system already smoothly functioning . . . words cannot handle global experiences well . . . language is . . . clumsy at noting gradations between its categories. Action—expression and gesture—is fast. Language may split thought away from emotion. It breaks apart rich, complicated global experiences into relatively impoverished component parts. And, most important, some nonverbal experiences (like looking into someone's eyes while he or she is looking into yours) can simply never be captured into words: at best, they can evoked by words. (p. 16)

For so many of the developmental struggles and deficits, something must be created from nothing. The analytic task of giving verbal shape and form to preverbal and nonverbal experiences, especially those not even experienced due to nonempathic caretakers, are dimensions that go beyond unconscious meaning, symbolism, multi-determined content, and understanding of defenses. Winnicott (1986) suggested that the fear of breakdown in the adult patient is the fear of returning to an unintegrated, even nondifferentiated state that has already been experienced, the unthinkable anxieties of going to pieces, falling forever, having no orientation, or having no relationship to the body. The failure of the primary caretaker to developmentally reflect and confirm the infant's bodily experience, as well as to differentiate from her own (Wyman-McGinty, 1998), may be expressed in a number of nonverbal ways and be carried in somatic memory by each of us (Wyman-McGinty, 1998).

The most fundamental sense of effectiveness and control is of one's body. Various psychosomatic symptoms reflect a body seeming to act on its own, adding to the ineffectiveness already experienced emotionally. As well, other individuals use their body in order to effect control over feelings and self-states, to register an experience concretized within the body, or to experience some mastery and effectiveness by body proxy.

Especially for those who do not experience full ownership of their body, the body becomes the instrument of attempted ownership of various aspects of the self and of effectiveness. Since emotions are integrally involved with bodily experience as well as being the inherent link between mind and body, when the individual owns affective experience, there is ownership of bodily experience (Summer, 2000).

Summer (2000) emphasizes that for patients who have lost ownership of their bodies, such as by physical trauma or verbal abuse, an attempt to retrieve it may be by masochistic submission, the repudiation of all desire, or by self-directing pain or extreme stimulation in order to feel alive. These retrieval attempts, adaptive in their intent to reclaim ownership of the body, do so within the earlier context of deprivation or abuse, replicating the segmentation of mind from body.

The imperative of a patient to fill space with activity, to evoke or perceive directives from the analyst may make it difficult at times for the analyst to maintain an empathic immersion. Demand of the analyst to "do something," or "say something that is helpful for my life's problems" often induces a sense of ineffectiveness in the analyst. The analyst's challenge is to use these experiences as an initiation into the patient's own internal state, to inform an empathic attunement to the patient.

Many of these experiences are nonverbal and unformulated. The analyst must be the skin to contain, the eyes to see, the ears to hear the unspoken. A foundation of self is constructed by a patient through somatosensory experience, in which the analyst transferentially becomes, among other things, the mother's body, from whom come words experienced as soothing and encompassing, through which the patient can experience a self (Fenster, 1999). The body of the analytic work gives shape and existence for the patient's differentiation of form and defining presence.

Those patients who have difficulty forming an attachment in the analytic experience, unable to verbalize significant aspects of their experience, or who are significantly affectively constricted, may, by their very disengagement be activating a procedural memory of a protective disengagement to originally avoid trauma or its repetition (Kiersky & Beebe, 1994).

"Listening" for Nonverbal Material

In the beginning, developmentally, there are no words. Words are not necessary for the original self, the body self, or early communication. Before language exists, we communicate at a nonverbal, affective level: facially, posturally, gesturally, affectively, sensing, touching, and holding. Verbal language is a relatively late acquisition ontogenetically and phylogenetically. Even in the adult, nonverbal communication accompanies every word. Nonverbal information emerges steadily from the patient in analysis. Posture, gesture, body rumblings, voice changes and quality, as well as silence, are all means of expression available to the apparently immobile patient.

Attention to a patient's behavior is not new; however, the understanding and decoding of nonverbal behavior has traditionally been in structural terms, that is, as manifestations of sexual or aggressive drive-derivatives, or in other object-related terms. Transference material has been understood, until recently, in the model of object-differentiated, object specific transferences. What has been omitted in our conceptualizations of this behavior is its preverbal and nonverbal origin. The simplest explanation deserves consideration first: that nonverbal behavior is communication with a significant nonverbal implication. Just as we now consider self-object transferences to arise from this developmental time frame, we must also be alert to the affective and autonomic communication from a patient (Krueger, 1990).

Nonverbal behaviors are rich in meaning and history and are indicators of motivation, fantasy, and dynamics. Gesture and movement predate speech and reveal basic and powerful affect.

Gestures and movements may be scrutinized for the following characteristics:

1. Unity of movement, and affect
   Position of the body and interrelationships of the body (position of hands, arms, feet and legs in relation to the rest of the body)
   Coordination of verbal and nonverbal movement in regard to timing, intensity, and change over time
2. Associations of the patient to movements and gestures
3. Kinesthetic patterning and meanings in terms of the transference
4. Symbolic content
   Symbolic reenactments: Movements that recreate an object or self-object relationship

To decode various actions and movements that embody unarticulated and unsymbolized experience, requires leaving no detail to the imagination. The body has its own dialects, its own channels of memory. The body of memory, the body of fantasy, the body we create, and our actual body each may be different with issues initially outside awareness of the body, actual and perceived.

Fundamental emotions may remain embodied, and the perceptions are communicated in concrete physical terms: heaviness, weighted down, dullness, deadness, lightness, buoyancy, floating, lifted up. This somatic language is often a counterpart to using the body in action symptoms, with corresponding action language.

The analytic setting contains symbolic equivalents of an optimum caretaker–child relationship: consistency, reliability, empathic attunement, specific and defined boundaries, focus on the patient, acceptance of what is otherwise alienating, and a holding environment. These factors are important in the treatment of all patients, even those with more organized and developmentally advanced internal structure. The body self as well as psychological self must be integrated in the developmental foundation and structure of self-awareness and evolving cohesiveness.

One function of the analyst is to accurately recognize and assist in articulating affective states and to help the patient develop an internal point of reference. Affect evolves from somatic experience, to differentiation of types of affect, to verbalization about them. Verbalization not only provides mastery by articulating feelings but also, more importantly, it facilitates the accurate perception of body self and image, perception of psychological self, and integration of the two. The blending of affective and cognitive, bodily and psychic self, consolidates a sense of self. In the clinical exchange, both patient and analyst must stay attuned to and grounded in the rich bodily experiences and imagery of the patient. It is by somatic experience and its specific sensory bridges that the patient emotionally creates a connection and amalgamation between right brain feeling and left brain thinking.

The emergence of material rooted in the preverbal period is easily obstructed. It is undifferentiated and unstructured since it existed when there were no mind–body or distinct selfobject differentiations, encompassing basically the first three years of life. Although some verbalization begins in the second year of life, the major expressive behaviors are motoric, mimetic, and gestural. As verbal and cognitive capacities increase, the experience shifts, and the capacity for verbal and encoding mastery heightens. Still, by age 2 to 3, a child has limited language to shape and master internal and external realities.

Additionally, the patient's sense of helplessness and ineffectiveness can be addressed by detailed attention to the simplest somatic and emotional experiences prior to higher level verbal and symbolic concepts. A basic approach for an individual coming from a severely growth-inhibiting environment and having distortions in the perception of emotional and somatic experiences and communications may be to focus initially on the accurate reading and labeling of signals, both somatic and affective. Attunement to these internal signals that a patient may be neglecting, deleting, or distorting may be quite threatening, such as the experience of emptiness or of internal disorganization. As this close attention by both analyst and patient concerns the patient's internal experiences, the patient may fear re-experiencing the disappointment and emptiness of earliest empathic failures.

As the analyst responds contingently to the productions of the patient, a basic sense of causality becomes established. It is the empathic immersion, resonance, and response that provides a new framework of experience. The experience of effectiveness and process of empathic attunement can then become internalized by the patient as internal attunement and self-empathy. Ultimately, the individual can internalize the entire process for self-regulation from the newly developed internal center of initiative, affects, and esteem. In this manner, the healthy development of body self and image as well as psychological self can resume.

Eckman (1999) has demonstrated how nonverbal communication links behaviors and the autonomic nervous system. He showed the link between each of the six basic emotions (happiness, surprise, sadness, anger, fear, and disgust), with a very specific set of muscle contractions of the face. Additionally, when someone is trained to move their facial muscles in a particular configuration of one of the basic emotions, the autonomic nervous system responds accordingly. For example, if someone is asked to mimic facial expressions of surprise, the autonomic nervous system changes linked with surprise will occur. This has even been demonstrated for imagining those particular muscle contractions and emotions creating the corresponding autonomic responses. Additionally, when someone contracts facial muscles for a particular emotion, with corresponding autonomic nervous system responses, the subjective feeling of that emotion accompanies the facial expression. Beebe (1999) has indicated that this correspondence mirroring is an aspect of empathy: by matching the facial expression of another person one re-creates the body physiology and subjective state within oneself, as mothers do in mirroring the emotional state of a child. This attunement to nonverbal cues is not only a component of mother–infant interaction and analyst–patient interactions, but also a component of adult interactions.

Nonverbal communication is not just about communicating feeling, but also about unconsciously activating response patterns in another that includes cognitive, behavioral, and affective responses (Eckman, 1999). An example is that certain staring can activate aggression in others. For patients who cannot verbalize feeling, a question may be, "How does it make you feel like acting?" A patient may also include a countertransference awareness to specifically elucidate a confusion, a wanting to run away, a wishing to soothe, an anger, an urge to pedantically educate, a gut churning, a mental image.

Avoiding unbearable feeling can be distinguished from not perceiving or labeling a feeling. Additionally, some individuals have difficulty telling how they feel because feeling is coupled with emotional flooding.

Some of the difficulty with patients who are not attuned to their own affective experiences, or who do not have fully differentiated affects, is that they often have difficulty perceiving as well as communicating non-verbal cues. Their difficulty ascertaining and expressing nonverbal cues may be as impaired as their experience of feeling emotions.

At times the intensity and severity of somatic symptoms that a patient may develop in the course of analysis may be frightening to both analyst and patient. While we must always know by medical consultation that these are not of physical origin or consequence (Muecke & Krueger, 1981), a compelling countertransference response is to want to fix, to refer, or ease the degree of somatic pain the patient experiences. Listening to the subtle, literal, as well as symbolic language of body-based experience is important to the immediate affective material within an attuned state of mind for both the patient and analyst. Dreams, symbolism, rich associations, and a compelling desire to focus on the content may too quickly engross the patient and analyst before expanding awareness of the immediate experience.

For the patient who uses dissociation as a primary defense, the inclination to dissociate cognitive awareness from affective experience could result in occurring in a somewhat altered state. In these dissociative exits from the body, a patient may end up being very well-analyzed, but have maintained the dichotomy between mind and body, left and right brain. The patient's attunement to the here and now, to detailed aspects of feeling as well as to content, to state as well as to theme allow a gradual increasing tolerance of painful affect. How long one is able to remain within a feeling before activating a defense may be the best barometer of this process. At these times of defensive retreat, as well as at times of intense conflict, action is a compelling course, immediately ending ambivalence. Nothing seems to end ambivalence faster than choosing one side of a conflict or dilemma and taking action. The illusion sustains itself until the action is revealed as defensive avoidance of both affect as well as of tolerating the tension and dissonance of seeing the entire scenario of both sides of the conflict or dilemma. Embracing a conflict as such puts one in a different position internally from residing alternately on one side or the other.

An illustration of such action language is an aspect of work with quite gifted, extraordinarily successful, or famous patients. Patients who are specifically outstanding in some areas such as beauty, wealth, sexuality, intellect, athletic ability, or fame, have additional stimulation in that they are challenged and besieged daily by people who want them, court their favor, or want to associate with them in some way. Additionally, they have these ready avenues of garnering responses and affirmation to expeditiously find seductive, temporary solutions to emotional needs. For them, it is quite difficult to sustain and tolerate an immersion in the necessary experience to analyze unmet, continuously enacted developmental needs. Wrye (1999) spoke of her countertransference response to a patient's ability to "find magical solutions that made the analytic path decidedly unglamorous."

A patient's early, preverbal longings, needs, and fears will emerge in the course of an analysis, and both somatic and psychological will find varied expressions. These feelings are inevitable in a full analytic experience, and cover a spectrum of development. Some sensations may be omitted due to the unavailability of an adequate language, seem so inchoate and frightening that they are best avoided, or become clustered together under the rubric of sexuality, and may be read as erotic transference within Oedipal themes (Wrye & Welles, 1994).

However, when closely appreciated and differentiated, these unconscious sensory experiences may be in the realm of somatic memories of unmet needs of preverbal physical contact and attunement with the primary caretaker. An example with disrupted attachment is a dead space between child and parent where pathological or perverse ridges are created. Green (1993) described the attempt by the child to repair the psychic hole left by mind–body dissociation with compulsive sadomasochistic fantasy.

Implicit Dimensions of the Analytic Exchange

Contemporary psychoanalysis has undergone paradigm shifts of metapsychological and clinical theory to embrace developmental psychology, neurology, and cognitive science. Cohesive models based on a complimentary articulation of theories incorporate these principles into treatment, as the new analytic relationship transforms implicit procedural and associational memory of interaction to recodify the sense of self.

Stern et al. (1998) and the Process of Change Study Group of Boston emphasize that interpretation as an element in bringing about change in explicit knowledge is matched in an equally powerful way with "moments of meaning" as the key element in creating change in implicit (procedural) and associative knowledge and learning. Changes in "implicit relational knowing form the central analytic task, and mutual regulation of state of mind of the patient is the central mutual activity."

The broad domain of learning and intelligence of implicit knowledge involves intuitively knowing how to proceed in a relationship (Stern et al., 1998). The "moments of meaning" are those times/interactions in which something of importance happens, particularly bearing on the future. At these particular junctures, implicit knowledge of each partner

gets authored by creating a new meaning intersubjectively, mutually changing each, as well as the relationship. Stern et al. (1998) believe that this
process may not require interpretation or and may not even be made
verbally explicit.

These moments of experience in the domain of implicit-relational
knowing, the building blocks of a new model and its internalization, are
the nonverbal events from infancy to the present moment that have to do
with the experience of being real, bounded, human, and present. These
are interactive moments and sequences that create the process of "moving along" in treatment (Stern et al., 1998), knowing that one knows the
"unthought known" (Bollas, 1987), illuminating the "unreflected, unconscious fantasy" (Stolorow et al., 1994) and making conscious the "past
unconscious" (Sandler & Fonagy, 1997). This mutual regulation, matching and interchanging experiences create implicit representations that are
unconscious, but not necessarily because of being under some form of
repression.

While the nonverbal communication and experiences occupy the
background, and some specific verbal focus occupies the foreground, it is
often the enveloping melody of the implicit unspoken communication
that occurs between sentences and in the word shadows of feeling and
trusting attachment that stimulate change.

Changes that occur due to the analytic relationship involve changing procedures and implicit associations rather than solely, or at times
even prematurely gaining insight about symbolic meaning (Fonagy, 1999).
Insight through interpretation and implicit learning through experiencing a new and different relationship are both operative, alternating in
importance from patient to patient as well as moment to moment from
each patient (Gabbard & Weston, in press, c). The aims of psychoanalytic treatment, as elaborated by Gabbard and Weston, are the changing
of unconscious associated networks, especially those relating to dysfunctional affect regulation and interpersonal patterns, and altering conscious
patterns of affect, thought and motivation.

Transference may be viewed as the activation of various representations in neural networks. These schemas or networks activated associa-
tively link explicit memory (facts), episodic knowledge (events), procedural memory, affects and motives (Weston & Gabbard, in press, c). The
activation of these representations and associative networks bridge with
current affective and cognitive experiences. This concept of transference
makes it a working process of perceiving, processing, and experiencing
that is linked to experience in the present moment of analysis. The mutual exploration of perception and meaning can be explored and
retranscripted within the current context of the new relationship. As a
developmental process, the analysis will involve many "transferences" in

the course of treatment, as transference is the active process of perceiving, processing, and organizing in present time.

An interpretation is to speak to what is most psychologically urgent, not only of transference, of making conscious what is unconscious, but of using a wide angle lens to articulate a developmental experience. The analyst as well as the process created are subjects for internalization. The analysis of the transference is the analysis of developmental experience and the use of the essential other of the analyst with attunement, containment, and internalization of the experience to facilitate development. The analytic relationship is reciprocal and bidirectional, though not necessarily symmetrical. The analyst is both transference object and developmental object as analysis reopens the closed system of the mind. Interpretation is simply the expanding of awareness or sharpening a focus to create another phrase or sentence in a new, evolving story.

For example, listening to analytic theory of aggression as being a fundamental drive may result in casting in pathological terms some of the very essential motivations/developmental needs of assertiveness, boldness, and especially of adversarial needs. For the patient whose expressive and affective range has been shaped into conformity or shamed into submission, interpretative recasting of adversarial and affective expression into developmental necessity is a liberating process; core organizing assumptions of badness and defectiveness can be transformed in this process.

Creating new procedural memory directly impacts fundamental patterns, including primary attachment, compensatory responses, and defensive responses established early in life. Recreating a procedural memory in the analytic exchange does not feel like a memory to the patient. Even though it is "transference" to the analyst it is reality to the patient. That the procedural memory is activated is ongoing process in the new analytic story. Retranscriptions of experience and assumption begin as a foreign language in an unknown region, and gradually move to confusion, the discombobulation of old and new mixed imperceptibly. In this process the outside becomes inside to the patient.

The outcome of psychoanalysis may be less dependent on the nature and structure of the psychopathology of the individual than it is on the fit of the analyst and the patient as persons in an evolving relationship. The fit is not an all or nothing, present from the beginning, or spontaneous occurrence, but is a process, a mutually crafted series of experiences forming a relationship whose purpose is the work at hand.

For patients who have had developmental injuries or deprivation, a tenuous bond at best initiates the work, and often considerable work must be done in order for the patient to allow vulnerability and openness to use the analyst in a way to further both the process and the individual development of the patient. The analyst becoming an essential (usable) self-object is an important and necessary initial phase of the work.

Initial trepidation, distrust, and dread to repeat past failed empathic attunement gradually gives way via empathic resonance and immersion in the analysis to a provisional cohesion of the self, enough to establish a foundation for further growth and work. These individuals who are vulnerable and have a tenuous sense of self and esteem often, during the initial phase of treatment, withdraw into a self-protective shell, or experience hurt and anger during the initial course of treatment.

Fonagy (1998) indicates that the main theme of the analytic process is to enhance the reflective ability of these individuals who have compromised developmental capacity to self-reflect. The analyst must not presume an understanding of feelings and interaction, such as labeling a feeling and assuming that we are speaking of the same phenomenon as the patient when we each speak of "feeling." Feeling is the uniquely subjective perception of emotion. We deal with actions and action symptoms by understanding the antecedent affect or state, and the intent or motivation of that action in terms of changing a state or feeling, or in regulating tension. The analyst must recognize and label feelings, dynamic scenarios of feelings evolving into action, and how feelings lead to actions or action symptoms.

The analyst continually addresses the affect, this moment's experience, to highlight the differences between here and now, there and then, the new story and the old story. This may be even to emphasize the difference between the patient's feeling and our feeling, their perception and our perception, the shared and the different realms of experience (Renik, 1998). Throughout the analytic experience, retranscriptions of meaning and conceptualization using a developmentally informed new model distinguishes past perception and processing from the present.

The analyst enters the analytic space to be curious, to suspend disbelief, and to subjugate personal values, and to enter the entire subjectivity of the patient. The flexibility and fluidity of the analyst is crucial in mutual exploration of expanding reflectiveness and evolving meaning from the patient. Subjective awareness and objective awareness develop simultaneously. Relatedness is at least as salient as autonomy, and each, in their fullest evolution, may be the same thing after all.

In the newly evolving analytic story, new dimensions of articulation occur of previously unexperienced, unformulated, and unfelt states and experiences. Opportunities for newly constructed collaborative meanings both understand and redeem foreclosed experiences of intimacy, aliveness, and passions. Transferences, with their corresponding and complementary countertransferences may illuminate body self experiences, nonverbal dimensions of procedural and associative memory, as well as explicit and object-specific meanings. From the sensuality of preverbal contact to the antithetical dead space of dry, alienated, bored variations of nothingness, the old and new stories comingle in the analytic movement. At times the empathic bridge is not enough for the patient; for example, when a lived experience is so powerful the patient will have to *impose* it on the analyst and *induce* empathy to insure that both occupy the experience together.

Our patients will always tell us what is most important, what is therapeutic and what is not, and what their needs are. This may be spoken in simple, straightforward language, in somatic language, in enactments designed to demonstrate an internal experience, in the shadow traffic of transferences, or in the interchange in which there is activation of internal relationships for the patient in which the analyst plays a part, and the patient plays a part, and then later talk about it.

The previously untreatable patient may be one who has been unheard at the level of developmental need expressed, who is unable to be understood or to comply with presently available analytic theory or methods, and who may best be understood in a different model or amalgamation that may offer optimum understanding and responsiveness.

Patients know what they need, though perhaps not in conscious, logical, or day time language. They try in every way possible to let us know what it is like to be them, to activate developmental deficit and conflict, and to illustrate what has been, for them, adaptive functioning. To respect the old story and honor the newly evolving story is the mutual quest of both patient and analyst.

14

Creating a New Story: Retranscripting the Mindbrain

The door to the past is a strange door. It swings open and things pass through it, but they pass in one direction only. No man can return across the threshold, though he can look down still and see the green light waiver in the water weeds.

Loren Eiseley
The Immense Journey

One's destination is never a place, but rather a new way of looking at things.

Henry Miller

Treat a man as he is, and he will remain as he is. Treat a man as he can and should be, and he will become as he can and should be.

Johann Wolfgang von Goethe

Caninante no hay camino se hace camino al ander.
(Wanderer, there is no path. You create it as you walk).

Antonio Machado

Coauthoring the Clinical Exchange

The universe is made up not just of atoms, but of stories. In the creative interface of the patient's and analyst's inner worlds, certain experiences, such as those arising from early development, are without words or be-

227

fore language. Others, especially of trauma, are beyond metaphor. To navigate, especially to retranscript these developmentally changing stories, we must be ready for paradigm shifts. The integration of metapsychological and clinical theory, incorporating developmental psychology, neurology, and cognitive science, are all applied to the simplicity of human motivations in the complexity of lived experiences in clinical exchanges.

Much like a blind man given vision after a lifetime of having no visual memory to inform his perception, the coupling of body self experiences and psychological self awareness may be a new correlation of the senses. This coordination of senses, experiences, and the meanings that we attribute are all part of the process of creating our world. Just as visual memories inform a perception, a pattern of existing knowledge must inform understanding. A pattern can exist for one individual and be completely recognized, while invisible to someone standing alongside. What one is agnostic to depends on what we have come to know both by learning, training, and the attachment of meanings.

Part of the experience of storymaking is the feel, the safety, the trust, the ambiance of the room, and the resonance of voice as well as words with internal knowing of the receiver. The roles of storyteller and listener, as each takes turns with patient as protagonist in both, unfolds on the shared lap of the analytic experience.

Psychoanalysis is a system for discerning hidden patterns of coherent meaning, uncovering and decoding unconscious fantasies, and interpreting defenses that become actively engaged in daily life, and discerning that the language itself is meaningful rather than only symbolic (Ogden, 1997). It took us nine decades of the first 100 years in psychoanalysis to get the notion that the message contains the message, as Lichtenberg (1998) has pointed out, rather than only containing the "real meaning" camouflaged or layered beneath. The message must be understood as a full and valid communication and exhausted before the venue is changed. The immediate communication and experience of the patient yields initial understanding before looking at what the patient is trying not to say (a defensive focus), or what the patient really means in terms of past repetition (genetic focus) of what is not said.

It is not nearly enough to illuminate and articulate patients' negative assumptions, unconscious wishes and manifest defenses, even to reconstruct compromised experiences and contexts. For patients who have developmental arrest, we must help them create and formulate a new model within which to understand and incorporate new experiences. The creation of this new model, this developmental container of present day, is hope personified.

The hope of the collaborative immersion is to clarify, illuminate, and cleave in the present analytic story experience and organizing concepts of it from the past. Making conscious what is unconscious and demarcating present from past become complementary. Every interpretation has not only a horizontal axis (conscious and unconscious) but also a vertical axis, in which the experience and the present moment are distinguished from simply reliving or repeating the past. The past and present are never more distinguishable than at the moment of juxtaposition.

The elements of an analytic experience are the two subjective experiences of patient and analyst, and the cocreated intersubjective field. The intersubjective field is mutually, though unequally, created. No two analyses, like no two relationships, are ever alike, or even fundamentally similar, though developmental stages, phases, and scientific principles prevail throughout.

It takes two people for an empathic immersion to occur. The analyst must move beyond his own position to inhabit the experience of the patient, to see how the patient feels, senses, perceives, and processes subjective and intersubjective experience moment by moment, frame by frame. The meaning that is attached and the past story that the patient has created, imposing itself transferentially, are all part of that understanding. It also takes the patient allowing that experience, using the analyst in a way that allows both to be inside the simultaneous old and new stories.

As we attempt to study someone else's mind, we become part of the field of study. Whether tracking bodily, affectively, relationally, developmentally, systemically, or in other ways, mutual inquiry and construction of one person's individual reality is the result of the encounter of two subjectivities. Each of the components, from developmental to unconscious motivation, is mutually discovered, constructed, and reconstructed.

At times it is the simplicity of asking the patient to explain literally exactly what he is afraid of, to explain in as simple and specific a way as possible what is the danger from which he is protecting himself. When this cannot be done in the present tense at a certain moment, the potential of inquiry expands from unconscious assumption set in a past context to a greater range of thought, feeling, sensation, and current perception. That is, to address what it is for both patient and analyst to be fully engaged with each other in the present moment, and to engage the assumptions and fears that deflect the patient's capacity to experience fully this moment.

The patient and analyst become coauthors of a new story, creating a current meaning that allows a growing distinctness of the interwoven new and old stories. The set of experiences, language, symbols, shared memories, and particular collaborative reconstructions of the past are unique to the analytic pair. One patient remarked at how strikingly different her own experience of her mother had become during this, her second analysis. In listening to her characterization and in reflecting on our shared understanding, I commented, "You had a different mother in your first analysis than in this one." She laughed her agreement.

The analyst is both interpreter and codeterminer of events. The intersubjective framework considers that each person has unique organizing principles that consciously and unconsciously shape the analysis, adding another dimension to the question of what is curative in psychoanalysis. Both the patient and the analyst bring an emotional history and organizing principles to the analytic exchange, and both sets of experiences are important in order to fully understand the exchange. What we inquire about, what we interpret, and what we leave alone are all products of what we bring.

The emotional bond that develops as a result of the interaction of the patient and analyst constitutes the central curative determinant of psychoanalysis. The patient and the analyst mutually create an interaction, the therapeutic relationship, and the result. The analyst is experienced as a provider of necessary functions as the patient activates unmet needs, rekindles traumatic experiences, and examines antecedent conflictual relationships.

Corresponding to the patient's use of symptoms that foreclose growth may be the analyst's alliance to ideology, theory, and adherence to a particular position that loses aliveness and uniqueness. Insight and understanding are no more magical than couch and theory. It is the relationship that cures, the shared moments of new implicit learning, creating new procedural memory and explicit meaning. The process of the work cannot be technical, habitual, routine, or rote, not the voice of silence or sterile interpretation, but uniquely the voice of this pair at this moment. The analyst must speak with his own voice, not a borrowed voice from prepackaged theory of formulaic thought and dead language. The freedom to create one's own voice from an internal point of reference, enhanced yet unencumbered by history of how the voice developed, is prerequisite to a creative and collaborative process of constructing a new analytic story with the patient. A part of the process of our own professional development is to take everything we have learned, the plurality of theories and approaches, to inform rather than to direct, to create rather than to conform, to not do analysis like anyone else, or as a mosaic of those who are meaningful to us, but to metabolize it as our own, just as we help patients to internalize their own experiences and to become their own authority. In short, to have our own voice as we work analytically. Then we are able, free, to help our patients create their own story as unique autobiography, and for every analysis to have its own rhythm, personality, and plot.

Foreground, Background

It is useful to consider whether defensive/past experience/repetitive (object specific transferential) dimensions of a patient's experience are predominantly in the foreground, or whether developmental needs/reparative (self-object transferential) efforts are more salient and more immediate in the patient's experience and engagement. The patient's mind is never operating in isolation, but is always engaged at some level with the analyst, a dialectic internally, externally, and together, though not necessarily in conscious representation. Multiple self states are involved for both, finding a fit to engage in the most meaningful way for the patient's understanding and evolution.

We are always teaching others how to respond to us. A patient is always teaching the analyst what it is like to be him or her, creating an in vivo demonstration of what is needed to be known, so that the analyst can teach it back to him or her, out loud. We must be ever open to that learning, and not let teaching the patient *our* theories get in the way. The patient is telling secrets out loud, though some of the assumptions, past and present, are as yet unknown. We inevitably listen within the context of our own system of meaning and knowing, but continuously bridge to the experience and system of meaning of the patient.

Analogous to the empathic caregiver respecting and allowing the potential space that the child needs, the analytic space facilitates the true self to fully emerge and flourish rather than the development of a false self to accommodate the assumptions and theories of parent/analyst. "Analytic space can be thought of as the space between patient and analyst in which analytic experience (including transference illusion) is generated and in which personal meanings can be created and played with. It is a potential space, the existence of which can by no means be taken for granted" (Ogden, 1985).

What our patients want from us as analysts (not dissimilar from what we as children wanted from our parents) is this: unselfconscious participation in serious work and sometimes in play; total acceptance of praise without having to deflect it or feel the need to reflect it totally back to the giver; full immersion in (yet not full reaction to) their passionate feelings from loving to hating; never losing sight of their internal perspective and best interest. To hope that we will see the self obscured from view by the symptom, that the symptom is an answer to a question its creator has not consciously dared to ask. To hope that we will not mistakenly clothe a symptom (such as bulimia or paranoia) with the essence of personality, as the protagonist of a story of fear and pathology, rather than as a sentinel in a story of hope and desire (to focus on the developmental *intent* rather than the pathological *result*). To not pejoratively give nicknames to clusters of secrets hiding in the open (symptoms) and obfuscate the person and the valiant attempt to splint the missing link to the self.

Sometimes, for certain patients at times it is helpful to share a picture, a story, or read something together, sometimes what they have written, or at times perhaps to read together something that the analyst has written. Likewise, for a patient having difficulty sustaining an internal representation of the analytic process, or object constancy of the analyst, taking something from the analyst's office may sustain the continuity of contact, and represent the mutual collaborative work during an interruption such as a weekend or vacation. Not saying something "analytic" may at certain times sustain rather than disrupt the necessary connection of two real people engaged in working together. Sometimes just the embodiment of togetherness, just to breathe together, to laugh or cry together can be quite therapeutic. Throughout, for the analyst to not be awkward, to not be self-conscious, to not do anything that would detract or distract from the patient's need for total absorption of self. To know that an experience can create its own reasons. Rather than attempting to remove a symptom that may be a patient's best friend of predictable comfort, relief, and loyalty such as food, smoking, or the idea of death, and instead to understand the self-object need and relationship with the symptom, while creating another, different, shared intimacy. As analysts, we must empathically resonate with and convey understanding of the comfort and investment in their symptom, of its immediacy and power of tension reduction, of the difficulty and anxiety in relinquishing its power and effectiveness to change the way they feel, of the addiction to the symptom itself, of its organizing function in identity. Such symptoms cannot be abandoned as a prerequisite to analysis, but they may diminish in intensity and utility over time and with understanding. Empathic listening and analytic collaboration may reveal the use and motivation of the symptom and its change throughout the course of analysis.

All of this is necessary, throughout, for the patient to not have to trade freedom for safety, or aliveness for certainty, to be human in a fuller sense than previously allowed or dared. At times just to say, as Ben (chapter 11) said to his 4-week-old son who was crying when having a shot, "I know." As he said to his wife, who did not seem as attuned to his son as he, "Keep talking to the baby, even when you can't know exactly what it feels like to be him, just keep talking, because it's important for him to hear your soothing voice." Ben knew from previous silence how the music of talking is at times necessary to convey a message and connection in which the words disappear.

Experiences in the clinical exchange are at times of reclaiming early developmental needs derailed or muted in nonresponse and non-affirmation, and establishing ownership of one's body. The patient quoted in the Introduction reflected on the first year of a very meaningful analytic engagement, unique in her mind from 20 years of multiple therapies and two unsuccessful analytic attempts, to say that most memorable from our first year of work was that we laughed together. Our laughing together gave oxygen to dormant hope, of having new, different, good bodily experiences of relief and release, of letting go in a way that she was not quite able to do with her family of origin, having to practice restraint and vigilance. Protection had been practiced internally by dissociation when she could not get away externally from the physical and verbal onslaughts of a father and a brother (passing on his abuse by the father to her). We would later come to know the selves partitioned in fear and hiding, but first we had to know together the safety, the bond, the connection allowing her, finally, to exhale, to breath freely and laugh readily, and join in that experience of laughing together. She emphasized how important it was to her during those initial months that I did not try to analyze our laughter, that we both knew it was necessary, that we would, in due time, come to understand it. The architecture of trust was silently forming while we talked about other things.

At one point she spoke of her concern for me and for my feelings after an outburst about an office mate's behavior to her in the shared waiting room. I knew by now that there was no one else she could trust with her anger, that she needed to bring it all to me. After her cathartic rage, as she began to show concern about giving me her full fury, I indicated that she would not have to worry about me or take care of me, assuring her (I thought) so she could stay immersed in her feelings. She became more infuriated at me, and told me that these were also her feelings: her concern, compassion, and care for me needed to be recognized and accepted. She added that she needed to be able to comfort me, and it was important that I allow it. My words, "You don't have to take care of me," said to her that I did not recognize in her the ability to be caretaking, attuned, merciful, in a reciprocal way. To have it rejected in our exchange disregarded one of the core issues that brought her to me: that so much of who she really was had been disregarded, not seen by anyone in her life. In addition to the safety in expressing danger, she needed to see me seeing her be more decidedly human and capable than she had previously dared. She needed to know that someone knew her, believed in her, and recognized those growing capacities within her. When I finally got it, I assured her that I would never underestimate the amount or the power of her ability and affection, nor the totality of who she was. I was speechless at certain moments with her, not because there was nothing to say, but because there was too much to say.

This woman was experiencing within the analytic process the analogue to what, for another patient, would be a transference neurosis: Her
organization, rather than around a neurotic, Oedipal configuration was
constructed at a more fundamental, core level previously dissociated and
unintegrated. By immersion within the trust of the analytic relationship,
she experienced simultaneously the empathic attunement and involvement, allowing the full expression of previously unspoken, unknown,
preverbal and nonverbal experiences. This experiencing from her central
core of being present in an unaltered state was an initial step in awareness of previously unintegrated, even nonperceived aspects of somatic
and self awareness.

Winnicott (1945) once suggested that the very process of breathing
both personalizes and solidifies our sense of self as well as connecting us
to the world in a fluid and very mysterious way. Freud taught us how
important it is to wear negative attributions; Kohut taught us how important it is to wear positive ones as well.

We listen carefully, simply, literally; deepest truths are clothed in the
simplest of garments. Believing what is said the first time, before other
words get in the way: the slip of tongue like the adolescent sneaking out
of an upstairs window late at night yearning to be caught and contained;
the twinkle of an eye from the little girl hiding deeply within the woman
before us; the rumbling stomach shouting swallowed pain; the second
"no" that always means "yes" (or once would have been sufficient). Listening from inside another, that most uncommon of bonds, because the
more we learn, the more simply we can speak. Sometimes words are not
important enough, yet for many things, they are sufficient. We enter a
domain of closeness into which the patient has never before allowed anyone else, even and especially themselves.

So often our patients need to discover their core organizing assumptions, to know that the failures to have their developmental needs met in
childhood were not their fault, and not the fault of their needs, and certainly not of their badness and defectiveness. They, and we, learn that
their parents may have been inaccurate mirrors, such as a funhouse mirror giving back a distorted image, or a mirror with certain portions blackened out. Their conclusions of badness or defectiveness were natural and
understandable unconscious assumptions based on not having had developmental needs met, or of having toxic insertions. To know that these
unconscious conclusions of defect, malignancy, or magnetism for misery
were ways of creating hope, of believing that if they were better, per-
forming or doing more, that then these needs would be met, and they
could feel satisfied with being "good enough." Even in current time they
may have difficulty in staying with a good feeling due to the anxiety of its

newness. To reconstructively understand rather than blame parents allows the patient to not blame himself or herself.

More essential to our patients than training, theoretical positions, and all the variables of experience and reputation, is the fundamental question: How usable are we to our patients? This depends in part on how aware we are of our own and our patients' experiences of both mind and body, that we do not delete, disregard, or omit any of our or their experiences. We traffic in enigmas such as communicating back to the patient experiences for which there may be no usable words or language. The patient should never have to guess if we are "here," fully and totally immersed in the analytic experience. We may get it wrong, we may misperceive, we may not have an explanation or an understanding, but we must be fully immersed, inside our own skin, and inhabiting the mutual and shared space created together so patients can be inside their skin and experience themselves as fully as possible. This passion, this presence, should never be a question.

Bromberg (1996) has emphasized the importance of standing with the patient in the spaces of the patient's different experiences from all the aspects of the self. Every experience that we have as analysts, every thought, sensation, and feeling is uniquely specific and important in the context of the clinical exchange with this patient at this moment, a nonpareil intersubjective coconstruction. Both patient and analyst may share the same experience: I have never been here before, yet I feel I have returned. For patients to become their own authority, to not have their lives ghostwritten by inflexible predetermination or invisible presupposition, analysts must be their own authority, have their own voice.

We must immerse ourselves in all the sensory experiences of our patient, in the form and texture of their experience, in their passions, to make the daring leap (through the microprocess of successive approximations) to the center of their own experience from the center of ours. Self states must be understood and traversed by sensory bridges, constructed from the detail of self and somatic attunement. We must be willing, as the child patient of Dr. Looker (1998) stated to her to, "Stop thinking and talking so much. Pay attention to how the moment feels. Why don't you put your feet on the ground?"

We can't reenter an old story with a patient and write a better ending as a way of getting into the present any more than the patient has been able in their repetitions: all the better endings later still re-creates the process of the old story. Invention has been sabotaged and creativity imprisoned by remaining in the old story, repeating the same storylines. We have to be in the present moment and develop a new story together with our patients. Then we both can see the difference between the present and past, true self from false self.

The analyst listens and responds more literally as well as more meta-phorically/symbolically for the patient to listen and experience more fully. The story of one's life, like working with a dream, can be heard at different levels. A dream as a simple story, yet restated in its most elemental ways may take on a profound meaning; the dream's components as symbols collectively speak the nighttime language of the unconscious; the dream as "self-state" speaks of the current context and issues of the individual, each of the animate and inanimate inhabitants of the dream articulates a component of the dreamer's self.

Dreams meaningfully elaborate basic life narratives at both conscious and unconscious levels, as well as conflicts left over from the day dripping back into the limbic system's emotional memory. Wishes and fears dance together in the moonlight of the dreamscape, revealing and concealing simultaneously. Over the course of analytic treatment, dreams change as certainly as life's narrative story does, as both emanate from the same source. Just as there are recurrent themes in the stories of our lives, there are recurrent themes in the stories of our dreams, and these evolve and change over time in parallel ways.

An unconscious organizing position may be that one's life has already been organized, predesigned (meaning preconstrained), thus one is continually trying to break free of those constraints, which, of course, continue to engage the restriction. We always come back to what we run away from, sometimes simply by creating its reverse image. One's life story, not just neurosis, then becomes a closed system, a self-fulfilling prophecy, as if one is living out an assignation. Assumptions are our individual ways of stopping time. An invisible aspect of self-fulfilling prophesies is that they both include and explain everything that validates them, as well as invalidating everything that may disprove them.

Psychoanalysis is the study of the ways in which we deceive ourselves. One's own model or system is not a belief, but just the way things are. In psychoanalysis, despite dedicated empathy, we invariably have an error of parallax: that difference between looking at the speedometer from the passenger's side and the driver who reads it dead-on. We can approximate the patient's subjective experience and reality, but we can never *be* that individual.

The process is analogous to impressionistic painting, in which each experience is like a dab of paint on a pointillist canvas. Only when you step back and view the entire picture do you recognize that the points form a portrait of a particular segment of our lives, and that the segments have a unity.

What we find when we keep studying psychopathology is psychopathology. When someone does not have oxygen, the focus is always on oxygen; however, when it is present and sufficient, focus can transcend survival to an aliveness more vibrant, creative, and full of color. We help the patient move beyond a search for psychopathology, to what is healthy, to be built on, for the creative and interactive things two people do in a partnership to address the developmental needs of one of them. While we fear precisely, yet dream vaguely, we help the patient to focus more specifically on what to look *for* and *toward*.

One is always loyal to the central theme, the plot, of one's life, always returning to it. Any departure from it creates trepidation and uncertainty, a temporary slippage from the known, central organizing principles, conscious and unconscious. The developmental needs that are unmet become organizing themes as unconscious assumptions.

The search for psychopathology has evolved to focus on what is healthy, to be built on, to the creative and interactive things two people do in this powerful and delicate healing partnership to address the developmental needs of one of them. What we look for and toward with our patients is evolving.

Of the many possibilities for guides in theory and in practice, the most abiding and most central may be that of lived experience in the present moment, with all its fluidity and multidimensionality. Both patient and analyst are engaged, the analyst leading the way, tracking in each clinical exchange the affective–cognitive, intrapsychic, and intersubjective dimensions (Lichtenberg, 1998).

Creating New Procedural Memory

While Freud emphasized the exploration of specific childhood memories in psychoanalysis, it is probably more an immersion in the affective experience of "this moment" that constitutes the healing and transforming power of psychoanalysis. The explicit memory of specific events or facts may be much less important than the process created for which implicit memory is the record. This implicit memory of process and procedure is of the dynamic experience of how we do something, such as engage in a relationship. A new experience has to be repeated and grooved in repetition in order to be etched as a procedural memory that can ultimately be taken for granted. Creating a process, and thereby implicit memory, changes both biology and psychology.

There are times, for some patients, that the remembrance of old, forgotten feelings and experiences is illuminating, as Freud initially indicated in his first attempts at understanding neurosis by abreaction, a purging of the trauma, expunging the abscess in order for healing to occur. Even in these instances, the healing is in doing it together, a mutual immersion in the experience, here and now. This remembering and experiencing together, a two-person process, in itself creates a further cleavage of the present and past. This transformation of implicit, procedural experience recodifies the sense of self.

The interchange between patient and analyst takes place at many levels. Throughout most of the 20th century, many levels of meaning and conceptualization allowed more windows through which to view the experience of the patient and of patient-analyst. Some of these views allow a more microscopic focus on what was previously indiscernible to the naked eye, and some creative and more macroscopic views conceptualize at a level previously impossible. An analogy is our understanding and having access to multidimensional readings of the earth to understand the particular layering and zones. When an oil well is dug to pierce through the various layers, the oil that flows may be from two, three, or more zones simultaneously, and we cannot know in which zone the final wellhead flow of oil originated. The analyst, appearing on the surface to be responding to one dimension of experience, may really be responding, both consciously and unconsciously, at multiple levels.

Many intrapsychic and intersubjective processes occur simultaneously: affective, cognitive, internalized object relations, systems, drive and conflict, the self, and ego state. Motivational systems span all of these and inform at another level. The lived experiences of the past, intersecting and often amalgamated with those of the present, are mutually influenced by the analyst and patient pair.

These two fundamental elements of the activation and information processing (establishing the meaning of representations) are the fundamental focus of our analytic work. The patient's state of mind determines which set of internal representations become cued, how information is accessed, and how information is processed. Out of an infinite sea of possibilities, we determine what we perceive based on our own personal and emotional values, and once perceived, how we attribute meaning and significance. The state of mind of the individual determines the access to the particular software program for each processing. Self-regulation is the mastery to determine the state of mind with its software package that is most adaptive and advantageous for a particular circumstance.

If a patient has current activation beyond a window of tolerance, emotional flooding creates a particular state of mind, eclipsing higher reflective and cognitive functions. In this state, meanings, symbolism, unconscious process, or any other form of interpretive intervention will likely not be useful. Any interpretive focus on the patient's state of mind may be perceived as critical or condescending. Rather, focus may be on building an empathic bridge to the patient's central, core experience in which relaxation-regulation allows greatest synthetic and integrative potential, a prerequisite to reflection. After the self-regulation, moving to a calming centerdness brings an understanding of the particular affective or symbolic trigger for a specific defense will be important, as well as the meanings and interactions internally. Through this process, the patient can continuously approximate a unity of thought and feeling, mind and body.

This internal recovery process to diminish the disorganizing effects of a particular instance of emotional arousal may be generated in the analytic context by empathic resonance with the internal scenario activated by the external trigger. Then the patient can engage collaboratively to become more centered in her own experience, more empathically attuned to her own feeling state of mind, and ultimately to self-regulation. Each individual will find her own way to modulate intensity of arousal in the recovery process. For some, grounding techniques may be helpful. For some, internalizing the model experienced within the analytic session may be sufficient. For any one person, it may also vary from state to state. Emotions are central, the most important single factor in self-regulation, and in ultimate mastery of defensive obfuscation and state changes.

For the analyst to enter the patient's story, and for the patient to be able to reflect on the story, the specific affect has to be identified. In certain affectively charged states of mind, such as affect states of elation, rage, depression, the self-reflective ability (even at times the sense of self), is lost. The patient must be empathically joined for mutual regulation of the affective state to move to a more central, integrative state that allows self reflection. Then the affect triggering the state change can be reconstructed and understood, perhaps reentered to be experienced as feeling free of defensive masking.

The tracking of even trace amounts of affect gives more dimensions to the experience in focus, to disembodied intimacies, and to the evolution developmentally from action to symbolic action, ultimately to true symbols and the mastery of words.

Affects manifest in three ways. Discrete subjectively experienced *feelings*, such as sadness, anger, or affection, are our best allies in the clinical exchange to provide entry into a state of mind, as they are most on the surface, most recognizable somatically and psychologically. Identifying the affect initiating the experience is important, yet what the patient is seeking (the motivation) must also be discerned. We are never without motivation and experience. The sense of self develops as a sometimes independent, sometimes interdependent center of initiation, organization, and integration of motivation and experience. *Moods* are more analogous to the climate in an area than the prevailing weather at a moment in time, such as irritability, loneliness, or crankiness. *Affect states* are distinct psychophysiological states of mind ranging from relaxed with full reflective access to extremes of rage, vigilance, or somnolence; in certain affective states an individual's sense of self may be lost in the intensity of the state.

For an individual who has been severely traumatized and has post-traumatic stress reaction, it may be necessary initially to totally avoid particular situations and stimuli that evoke the strongest emotional reactions. A lived experience, such as deadness-nothingness or of actual terrorizing trauma, cannot be replaced by a theory, but has to be replaced by a new and different lived experience, so that the person can compare and contrast the two, to distinguish the present from the past, as a way of coming to the end of the past. Inhabiting a new experience confronts one with what was missed, and crystallizes the mourning of what was, what never was, and what should never have been.

In addition to bonding, relating, and communicating with others, is the need of a fully developed individual to respect and preserve the need for solitude. Winnicott also speculates that the fear of psychoanalysis, and the loathing expressed to its theories, may be in part due to its penetration into the human personality and its understanding; the defense against the threat to the individual; incessant, demand that there not be a continued demand for free association, and instead the analyst should resonate with the silence as its own voice. This respect by the analyst may be expressed by not probing every silent, personal, internal space.

The analytic dialogue is unique in its focus and text of having the entirety of one individual the subject of scrutiny by each and by both together. It is also unique in that the analyst and patient create a context in which there are no limits to what the patient can think, feel, experience, express, and imagine, and for everything to remain totally confidential, no matter what. I explain that this is in order for the patient to be able to bring in all of himself or herself for a lifetime, to experience and to express in ways that have not been dared, and that nothing needs to be left out, even that which the patient does not yet know at a conscious level. It is unique in another way, in that feelings, fantasies, and experiences can be fully and freely expressed, but without coupling any of these to action, which, for certain action-prone patients, is unique.

Rather than authoritatively insisting or admonishing the patient to say everything that comes to mind, I would simply invite the patient to do so. We mutually create this context as a place to bring and experience all of himself or herself, though I acknowledge how foreign that may feel, especially at the beginning, and how antithetical it may be to some very basic assumptions.

It is up to the analyst to come to know and appreciate, through collaboration with the patient, when silence is to be respected as a necessary component of contemplation, an unintruded space of reflection or integration of a new experience. These silences are distinguishable from those times when silence is the product of resistance, of not seeing or actively obfuscating something that needs to enter mutual focus.

In this mutually constructed space of the work, we come to see the activation of fears creating constriction of expression or blocking of internal awareness of feeling. We see not only the reining-in of feelings and passions, but also the deflecting of full capacities and their potential application, curtailing of ambition, failure to fully define and focus on ideals and goals, and even disallowing the continuity of feeling good. One of the most baffling experiences for the patient is to recognize that as they have become accustomed to feeling bad, even seeing it as an identity, they stop themselves regularly if they feel good for very long. The excursion into new territory of feeling good may be unaccustomed, without familiar landmarks and beyond where they have been before in their own growth and development. To dare to experience and express their best feeling may be their greatest risk and vulnerability.

A life is retold, as described by Schafer (1992) not simply by telling it again, but in creating a new story by recasting the past and the present, of laying new experiences internally and intersubjectively alongside the old experiences and the assumptions inherent in them, to create a new context and a new sense of identity. Past and present are both current constructions. This new narrative has the purpose of making sense of the past as well as of the present in a coherent, unlimited way, allowing full potential and capacity to come to life. Missed developmental experiences, even though forgotten or disregarded, remain until they can be mourned rather than repeated. This retelling and creation of the narrative, a new plot for one's life, activates unconscious assumptions, and allows scrutiny regarding which ones work and which ones do not. The ones that work don't need fixing, and the ones that don't work are seen in the full and vivid focus of their limitations presently, and of their adaptation in a prior context.

One patient spoke during the last sessions of the termination process of our analytic work, remembering his fantasy of finding the perfect woman, and of his perpetual search for that woman throughout his life. His hope had concretized of finding answers, of filling emptiness, of listening to a clarion call of ancient needs always disappointingly found lacking as soon as he had gotten to know a particular new and enchanting woman.

In earlier aspects of our analytic work, he sought the same perfection in idealizing me. His reminiscences in this mourning were crystallized by our discussion of the "curtain call" of the end of the analytic work in which all of the issues in analysis, as well as all of the internal characters of his life story were reappearing in the termination process.

He recalled vividly his sadness and disappointment, as well as the liberation of "saying goodbye to the spell of that illusion." He added that the curtain call also broke the spell, the trance-like experience of being inside the play, merged with the characters, to be able to see with different eyes the entire process. We likened it more to viewing the real body at a funeral, as a catalyst of mourning, to see that, indeed, there is change, to feel it by being inside a new experience. Change is not a theory.

In the consultation room, we do not make sense of life in prepackaged forms, in bold recognitions of clarity, and there are few "ah-ha" moments. Rather, we deconstruct nuances, details, murmurs, vapors of derivatives of experience, and reconstruct it into meaningful patterns that may fit with a current motivation in a current context, rather than long-ago, ever-so-subtle patterns of attempted adaptation, of accommodation for distant needs and archaic hungers. We reassemble nuances and strivings into meaningful patterns of relatedness for a continuity of internal and external, of past with present.

How can we, in a treatment setting, eavesdrop on the internal life and experience of a patient who has no ready words, nor even a language for those experiences? How can we collaboratively conceptualize unformulated experiences, even thoughts and feelings that do not as yet have a shape, a form, or a container of syntax to transfer to another? How can an analyst and a patient reconstruct unlived experiences? How can we not lose scent of the trail of affect while somehow bridging the gulf of no-man's land between soma and concept, between experience and its registry in a recognizable form? We must listen with a sense of privilege rather than of knowing, of questioning without preformed context or concept, for experiences ghost-written from a realm of development long since forgotten.

Pattern recognition, the uncovering of the unconscious, as well as insight and understanding are not enough. They may result in an analyzed but not necessarily changed or happy individual. The matching, the fit, of analyst and patient is quintessential. I can generally tell soon within the first meeting with someone if he or she is a person in whom I can believe. Believing in someone, at least for me as a psychoanalyst, is the most essential and fundamental quality that I can find in a patient. A similar sense must exist in the patient, embodying their hope of not only ending their suffering, but of finding someone who can believe in them until they can believe in themselves. Because I consider so essential believing in someone until they can believe in themselves, I will not work with someone in whom I don't believe. This does not mean that they are unacceptable as a person or as a patient, or that they are untreatable. The caveat of both suitability for treatment and treatability should be followed by the question, "By whom?"

This belief in someone is suffused throughout analytic discussions, forms the backdrop of conversations, and illuminates the various theories employed by the analyst. It is the foundation on which the structure can be built.

There is a corollary to believing in the patient that was pointed out to me by a patient. The analyst must be the kind of person in whom the patient can believe. The interaction and internalization of the analyst as a person occurs, in my view, in the process of the analytic exchange. The patient has to believe in the analyst to respond, to guide, and to teach in a way that she needs to grow, teaching the analyst along the way. She added, "I'm shaping you in the ways I need to grow, too." And we both knew she would persist until we created together what she needed.

Knowing, from the patient's point of view, that someone believes in her, gives her in this ultimate quest an essential hope in telling the most intimate, embarrassing, and shameful aspects of herself, previously unknown even within herself. Anonymity, being a blank screen on which the patient projects, is a stifling illusion. A great deal is known about the analyst over time: not necessarily factual information to distract the patient, but the person of the analyst is revealed as certainly as the person of the patient is revealed. Our style emotionally and cognitively, our own humanness, our sense of humor, our taste in surroundings, and the daily reading of us as a person are all so definingly known that it is almost beyond words. The subject and focus of the collaborative work is on the internal experience of the patient.

Both patient and analyst evolve as distinct people in the developmental course of analysis. Beginning as a self-object in which we are the echo and resonance of the patient, the part of him that he cannot do or be himself, such as a mirroring, affirming, idealizing, or twinship experience, we eventually become more separate, more distinct in the patient's mind, often discovering our separateness as psychoanalysts in a parallel way that the patient discovers distinctness as an individual. Often at these times, there are aspects of my office that a patient may suddenly discover; he or she may see a painting for the first time, recognize that I have pre-Columbian pieces in my office, that I am partial to sports and business metaphors and love literary quotes.

My relative anonymity is not to be aloof, less real or human, but to facilitate and not contaminate the patient's evolving internal point of reference, to know him- or herself more clearly and fully, rather than to know me per se, or to shape any of his or her experience in order to be seen more fully on my radar screen. I am not silent for long periods of time, as earlier analysts might have been in order to see only the broad brush strokes and themes of the unconscious, but more interactive, often interrupting, clarifying, or asking for details. I want to be inside each moment and incident with a patient, fully experiencing as much as I can, asking for more detail if any aspect of the full experience is omitted, or if I don't sense it fully or clearly.

This bond, this psychoanalytic experience, this immersion and understanding within the present moment, may be the most powerful and the most change-making experience that the patient has ever experienced. Because of this, he may never have to have anything like this again.

Psychoanalysis is a subspecialty of helping individuals change their minds. We must also remember, always, that psychoanalysis and psychotherapy have no franchise on change. There are many experiences and relationships that serve as catalysts for change.

I remain inevitably curious about how my patients' narratives continue to be written after we end analysis. As we end, their life is a mutual uncertainty, and I wonder if the current consideration by some analysts, including myself, that follow-up sessions at periodic intervals of every year or so to review, and to mutually witness and reflect on continued growth and development might be facilitative and mutually informative. I believe that psychoanalysis as a developmental process continuing in its influence throughout life, may include beneficial witnessing (booster shots?) and collaborative developmental integration at incremental points in a continuing journey. I have indicated to some patients that I believe that it would be useful to continue to integrate and synthesize developmental progress and evolution at specific points, always to be determined by them, in the future to meet periodically, perhaps on a yearly basis. Unlike our beginning, something does not have to be the matter for them to come back to review and to reflect. I indicate that I am interested, and that I care. I wonder if this will be a burden to them, if they feel they must do this for me, or if they would be benefited by having some future reference point to look to in order to look back.

What we do with each patient is not about being right, having pristine theory and technique, or idealizing insight and understanding, but the bottom line is: *Does it work?*

References

Ackerman, D. (1991). *A natural history of the senses.* New York: Vintage.

Ackerman, D. (1999). *Deep play.* New York: Vintage.

Alexander, F. (1950). *Psychosomatic medicine.* New York: Norton.

Allen, J., Console, D., & Lewis, L. (1999). Dissociative detachment and memory impairment: Reversible amnesia or encoding failure? *Comprehensive Psychiatry, 40,* 160–171.

American Psychiatric Association. (1994). *Diagnostic and statistical manual of mental disorders* (4th ed.). Washington, DC: Author.

Anderson, F. (1998). Psychic elaboration of musculoskeletal back pain. In L. Aron & F. Anderson (Eds), *Relational perspectives on the body* (pp. 287–322). Hillsdale, NJ: Analytic.

Anzieu, D. (1990). *Psychic envelopes.* London: Karnac.

Armstrong, J. G., & Loewenstein, R. J. (1990). Characteristics of patients with multiple personality and dissociative disorders on psychological testing. *Journal of Nervous and Mental Disorders, 178,* 448–454

Aron, L. (1995). The internalized primal scene. *Psychoanalytic Dialogues, 5,* 237–244.

Aron, L. (1998). The clinical body and the reflexive mind. In L. Aron & F. Anderson (Eds), *Relational perspectives on the body* (pp. 3–38). Hillsdale, NJ: Analytic.

Arvanitakis, K., Jodoin, R.-M., Lester, E. P., Lussier, A., & Robertson, B. (1993). Early sexual abuse and nightmares in the analysis of adults. *Psychoanalytic Quarterly, 62,* 572–587.

Attias, R., & Goodwin, J. (1999). Body image and distortion and childhood sexual abuse. In J. Goodwin & R. Attias (Eds), *Splintered reflections: Images of the body in trauma* (pp. 155–166). New York: Basic.

Atwood, G., & Stolorow, R. (1984). *Structures of subjectivity: Explorations in psychoanalytic phenomenology.* Hillsdale, NJ: Analytic.

Aubarch, J., & Blatt, S. (1996). Self representation in severe psychopathology:

The role of reflexive self-awareness. *Psychoanalytic Psychology, 13,* 297–341.

Baddelly, A., & Hitch, G. (1974) Working memory. In G. Bower (Ed), *The psychology of learning and motivation: Advances in research and theory* (pp. 71–78). New York: Academic Press.

Barth, F. (1998). Speaking of feelings: Affects, language and psychoanalysis. *Psychoanalytic Dialogues, 8,* 685–705.

Bass, A. (1997). The problem of concreteness. *Psychoanalytic Quarterly, 66,* 642–682.

Battegay, R. (1991). *Hunger diseases.* Lewiston, NY: Hogrefe & Huber.

Bauman, S. (1981). Physical aspects of the self. *Psychiatric Clinics North America, 4,* 455–469.

Beebe, B. (1999, November). *Forms of intersubjectivity in infant research and adult development: Toward a theory of interaction for psychoanalysis.* Paper presented at the International Conference of Self Psychology, Chicago.

Benjamin, J. (1995). *Lights, subjects, love objects.* New Haven, CT: Yale University Press.

Bernstein, D. (1993). *Female identity conflict in clinical practice.* In Freedman & B. Distler (Eds.). Northvale, NJ: Aronson.

Blatt, S. (1974). Levels of object representation in analytic and introjective depression. *The Psychoanalytic Study of the Child, 29,* 107–157.

Blum, H. (1973). The concept of erotized transference. *Journal American Psychoanalytic Association, 21,* 61–76.

Bollas, C. (1987). *The shadow of the object.* New York: Columbia University Press.

Bollas, C. (1989). *Forces of destiny.* London: Free Association Books.

Boris, H. (1986). Bion revisited. *Contemporary Psychoanalysis, 22,* 159–184.

Bowlby, J. (1973). *Attachment and Loss,* Vols. 1, 2. New York: Basic Books.

Brenner, I. (1994). The dissociative character: A reconsideration of "multiple personality." *Journal of the American Psychoanalytic Association, 42,* 819–846.

Breuer, J., & Freud, S. (1955). Studies on hysteria. In J. Strachey (Trans. & Ed.), *The standard edition of the comple psychological works of Sigmund Freud* (Vol. 2). London: Hogarth Press. (Original work published 1893–1895)

Bromberg, P. (1994). Speak! That I may see you": Some reflections on dissociation, reality, and psychoanalytic listening. *Psychoanalytic Dialogues, 4,* 517–548

Bromberg, P. (1996). Standing in the spaces: The multiplicity of self and the psychoanalytic relationship. *Contemporary Psychoanalysis, 32,* 509–535.

Brothers, D. (1994). Dr. Kohut and Mr. Z. Is this a case of alter ego countertransference? In A. Goldberg (Ed.), *Progress in self psychology, Vol. 10. A decade of progress* (pp. 99–114). Hillsdale, NJ: Analytic.

Brothers, D. (1998). Exploring the "bi" ways of self experience: Dissociation, alter ego self object experience and gender. In A. Goldberg (Ed.), *Progress in self psychology, Vol. 14. A decade of progress* (pp. 233–253). Hillsdale, NJ: Analytic.

Butler, J. (1995). Melancholy gendered—Refused identification. *Psychoanalytic Dialogue, 5*, 165–180.

Button, E., Fransella, F., & Slade, P. (1977). A reappraisal of body perception disturbances in anorexia nervosa. *Psychological Medicine, 7*, 235–243.

Cohen, B., & Mills, A. (1999). Skin/paper/bark: Body image, trauma and the diagnostic drawing series. In J. Goodwin & R. Attias (Eds.), *Splintered reflections: Images of the body in trauma* (pp. xx–xx). New York: Basic.

Coltart, N. (1992). *Slouching towards Bethlehem*. London: Free Association.

Damasio, A. (1994). *Descartes' error*. New York: Scribner's.

Davies, J. (1996). Linking the "pre-analytic" with the post classical: Integration, dissociation, and a multiplicity of unconscious processes. *Contemporary Psychoanalysis, 32*, 553–578.

Davies, J. (1999). Getting cold feet, defining "safe enough" borders: Dissociation, multiplicity and integration in the analyst's experience. *Psychoanalytic Quarterly, 66*, 184–208.

Davies, J., & Frawley, M. (1994). *Treating the adult survivor of childhood sexual abuse: A psychoanalytic perspective*. New York: Basic.

de Groot, J. (1994). Eating disorders and developmental disorders. In M. Winkler & L. Cole (Eds.), *The good body* (pp. 127–155). New Haven, CT: Yale Universities Press.

Demos, V. (1985, October). *Affect and the development of the self: A new frontier*. Paper presented at teh International Self Psychology Conference, New York.

Dimen, M. (1991). Deconstructing difference: Gender, splitting, and transitional space. *Psychoanalytic Dialogue, 1*, 335–352.

Dimen, M. (1998). Polyglot body: Thinking through the relational. In L. Aron & F. Anderson (Eds.), *Relational perspectives on the body* (pp. 65–96). Hillsdale, NJ: Analytic.

Dimen, M. (2000). The body as Rorschach. *Studies in Gender and Sexuality, 9*, 39–47.

Doctors, S (1999). Further thoughts on "self-cutting": The intersubjective context of self-experience and the vulnerability to self loss. *Psychoanalytic Review, 86*, 733–744.

Donatti, D., Thibodeaux, C., Krueger, D., & Strupp, K. (1990, May). *Sensory integrative processes in eating disorder patients*. Paper presented at The American Occupational Therapy Association National Meeting, New York.

Dowling, S. (1977). Seven infants with esophageal atresia: A developmental study. *Psychoanalytic Study of the Child, 32*, 215–256.

Ebert, T., Panther, C., Wienbruch, C., Hokem, Rockstromb, and Taub, E. (1995). Increased use of the left hand in string players asssociated with increased cortical representation of the fingers. *Science, 264*, 221–224.

Eckman, M. (1999, November). *"I feel, therefore I am."* Paper presented at the International Conference on the Psychology of the Self, Chicago.

Edelman, G. (1992). *Bright air, brilliant fire*. New York: Basic.

Eich, E., Reeves, J., Jaeger, B., & Graff-Radford, S. (1985). Memory for pain: Relation between past and present pain intensity. *Pain, 23*, 375–379.

Eissley, L. (1971). *The night country*. Lincoln, NE: University of Nebraska Press.

Elise, D. (1997). Primary femininity, bisexuality, and the female ego ideal: A reexamination of female developmental theory. *Psychoanalytic Quarterly, 66,* 489–517.

Emde, R. (1983). The prerepresentational self. *The Psychoanalytic Study of the Child, 38,* 165–192.

Eshel, O. (1998). "Black Holes," deadness and existing analytically. *International Journal of Psychoanalysis, 79,* 1115–1130.

Faber, M. (1985). *Objectivity and human perception.* Alberta, Canada: University of Alberta Press.

Farber, S. (1997). Self medication, traumatic enactment, and somatic expression in bulimic and self-mutilating behavior. *Clinical Social Work Journal, 25,* 87–106.

Farber, S. (2000). *When the body is the target: Self-harm, pain, and traumatic attachments.* Northvale, NJ: Aronson.

Fenster, S. (1999). Body as autistic and illusory object in somatic states and the creation of the psychic skin. In S. Alhanati (Ed.), *Primitive mental states* (Vol. 2). London: Karnac.

Fenster, S. (2000, Spring). *Reinventing echo's body through voice and skin of the analyst.* Presented at the Spring meeting of Division 39, the Division of Psychoanalysis of the American Psychological Association, San Francisco.

Ferenczi, S. (1980). Transitory symptom-constructions during the analysis. In M. Balint (Ed.), *The first contributions to psychoanalysis* (pp. 193–212). London: Karnac. (Original work published 1912)

Ferenczi, S. (1988). *The clinical diary of Sandor Ferenczi* (J. Dupont, M. Balint, & N. Jacks, Eds.). Cambridge, MA: Harvard University Press. (Original work published 1932)

Finn, S. Hartman, M., Leon, G., & Lawson, L. (1986). Eating disorders and sexual abuse: Lack of confirmation for a clinical hypothesis. *International Journal of Eating Disorders, 5,* 1051–1060.

Fisher, S. (1970). *Body experience in fantasy and behavior.* New York: Appleton-Century-Crofts.

Fisher, S. (1989). *Sexual images of the self: The psychology of erotic sensations in illusions.* Hillsdale, NJ: Erlbaum.

Fitzpatrick, K. (1999). Terms of endearment in clinical analysis. *Psychoanalytic Quarterly, 68,* 119–125.

Flax, J. (1990). *Thinking fragments: Psychoanalysis, feminism, and post modernism in the contemporary west.* Berkeley: University of California Press.

Fonagy, P. (1998). Moments of change in psychoanalytic theory: Discussion of a new theory of psychic change. *Infant Mental Health Journal, 19,* 346–353.

Fonagy, P. (1999). Points of contact and divergence between psychoanalytic and attachment theories: Is psychoanalytic theory truly different? *Psychoanalytic Inquiry, 19,* 448–480.

Fonagy, P., & Target, M. (1995). Understanding the violent patient: The use of the body and the role of the father. *International Journal of Psycho-Analysis, 76,* 487–501.

Fonagy, P., & Target, M. (1996). Playing with reality: I. Theory of mind and the normal development of psychic reality. *International Journal of Psycho-Analysis, 77,* 217–333.

Fonagy, P., & Target, M. (1998). Mentalization and changing aims in child psychoanalysis. *Psychoanalytic Dialogue, 8,* 87–114.

Fonagy, P., & Target, M. (1997). Attachment and reflective function: Their role in self-organization. *Development and Psychopathology, 9,* 679–700.

Fosshage, J. (1995). An expansion of motivational theory: Lichtenberg's maturational systems model. *Psychoanalytic Inquiry, 15,* 421–436.

Freeman, W. (1994). *Societies of brains.* Hillsdale, NJ: Erlbaum.

Freud, S. (1961). Beyond the pleasure principle. In J. Strachey (Ed. & Trans.), *The standard edition of the complete psychological works of Sigmund Freud* (Vol. 18, pp. 1–64). London: Hogarth Press. (Original work published 1920)

Freud, S. (1958a). The dynamics of transference. In J. Strachey (Ed. & Trans.), *The standard edition of the complete psychological works of Sigmund Freud* (Vol. 12, pp. 97–108). London: Hogarth Press. (Original work published 1912)

Freud, S. (1958b). Remembering, repeating, and working through (Further recommendations on the technique of psycho-Analysis). In J. Strachey (Ed. & Trans.), *The standard edition of the complete psychological works of Sigmund Freud* (Vol. 12, pp. 145–156). London: Hogarth Press. (Original work published 1914)

Freud, S. (1961). Inhibitions, symptoms and anxiety. In J. Strachey (Ed. & Trans.), *The standard edition of the complete psychological works of Sigmund Freud* (Vol. 20, pp. 75–172). London: Hogarth Press. (Original work published 1926)

Freud, S. (1951). The Ego and the Id. In J. Strachey (Ed. & Trans.), *The standard edition of the complete psychological works of Sigmund Freud* (Vol. 19, pp. 1–59). London: Hogarth Press. (Original work published 1923)

Freud, S. (1964). *New introductory lectures on psycho-analysis,* In J. Strachey (Ed. & Trans.), *The standard edition of the complete psychological works of Sigmund Freud* (Vol. 21, pp. 1–182). London: Hogarth Press. (Original work published 1933)

Freud, S. (19xx). Papers on metapsychology. In J. Strachey (Ed. & Trans.), *The standard edition of the complete psychological works of Sigmund Freud* (Vol. 14, pp. 105–332). London: Hogarth Press. (Original work published 1915)

Furst, S. (1986). Psychic trauma and its reconstruction with particular reference to post childhood trauma. In A. Rothstein (Ed.), *The reconstruction of trauma. Its significance in clinical work* (pp. 137–148). Madison, CT: International Universities Press.

Fuster, J. (1997). The prefrontal cortex. In *Anatomy, physiology and neurophysiology of the frontal lobe* (4rd ed.). Philadelphia: Lippincott-Raven.

Galenson, E., & Roiphe, H. (1974). The emergence of genital awareness during the second year of life. In R. Friedman, R. Richart, & R. Van de Wides (Eds.), *Sex differences in febavior* (pp. 134–146). New York: Wiley.

Garner, D., & Garfinkel, P. (1981). Body image in anorexia nervosa: Measurement, theory and clinical implications. *International Journal of Psychiatric Medicine, 11,* 263–284.

Goldberg, P. (1995). The physiology of psychoanalysis: Is psychoanalysis a treatment of the body? *Modern Psychoanalysis, 20,* 207–212.

Goldberg, P. (1995). "Successful" dissociation, pseudovitality, in inauthentic use of the senses. *Psychoanalytic Dialogue, 5,* 493–510.

Good, M. (1998). Screen reconstruction: Traumatic memory, conviction, and the problem of verification. *Journal of American Psychoanalytic Association, 46,* 149–183.

Goodwin, J., & Attias, R. (1999). *Splintered reflections: Images of the body in trauma.* New York: Basic.

Green, A. (1993). The dead mother. In *On private madness* (pp. 142–173). Madison, CT: International Universities Press.

Grotstein, J. (1990). Nothingness, meaninglessness, chaos, and the "Black Hole." Part I & II. *Contemporary Psychoanalysis, 26,* 257–290, 337–467.

Grotstein, J. (1997). Mens sane in corpore sano?: The mind and body as an "odd couple" and as an oddly coupled unity. *Psychoanalytic Inquiry, 17,* 204–222.

Gunsberg, L., & Tylim, I. (1998). The body-mind: Psychopathology of its ownership. In L. Aron & F. Anderson (Eds), *Relational perspectives on the body* (pp. 117–138). Hillsdale, NJ: Analytic.

Hansell, J. (1998). Gender identity, gender melancholia, gender perversion. *Psychoanalytic Dialogue, 8,* 337–351.

Harris, A. (1996). Animated conversations: Embodying and gendering. *Gender and Psychoanalysis, 1,* 361–383.

Harris, A. (1998). Psychic envelopes and sonorous baths. In L. Aron & F. Anderson (Eds.), *Relational perspectives on the body* (pp. 39–64). Hillsdale, NJ: Analytic.

Hawking, S. (1993). *Black holes and baby universes, and other essays.* New York: Bantam.

Hegel, G. (1977). *Phenomenology of spirit.* A. V. Miller (Trans.). London: Oxford University Press. (Original work published 1807)

Heindel, W., & Salloway, S. (1999). Memory systems in the human brain. *Psychiatric Times, June,* 19–21.

Hopper. (1991). Encapsulation as a defense against the fear of annihilation. *International Journal of Psycho-Analysis, 72,* 607–624.

Jacob, T. (1994). Nonverbal communications: Some reflections on their role in the psychoanalytic education. *Journal of American Psychoanalytic Association, 41,* 741–762.

Jones, E. (1953). *The life and work of Sigmond Freud* (Vol. 1). New York: Basic Books.

Kandel, E. (1999). Biology and the future of psychoanalysis: An: intellectual framework for psychiatry revisited. *American Journal of Psychiatry, 156,* 505–524.

Kaplan, L. (1996). Transformations of desire and the logic of life narratives: An essay review. *Gender and Psychoanalysis, 1,* 499–508.

Kearney-Cooke, A. (1988). Group treatment of sexual abuse among women with eating disorders. *Women and Therapy, 7,* 5–22.

Kernberg, O. (1975). *Borderline conditions and pathological narcissism.* New York: Aronson.

Kestenberg, J. (1975). *Children and parents: Studies in development.* New York: Aronson.

Kestenberg, J. (1985, October). *The use of creative arts as prevention of emotional disorders in infants and children.* Paper presented at the National Coalition of Arts Therapy Association, New York.

Kiersky, S. (1998, October). *Perilous crossings: Tales of gender, identification, and exiled desires.* Paper presented at the 21st Annual International Conference on the Psychology of the Self, San Diego.

Kiersky, S., & Bebe, B. (1994). The reconstruction of early nonverbal relatedness in the treatment of difficult patients: A special form of empathy. *Psychoanalytic Dialogue, 4,* 389–408.

Kirshner, L. (1998). Problems in falling in love. *Psychoanalytic Quarterly, 67,* 407–425.

Kluft, R. (1992). Discussion: A specialist's perspective on multiple personality disorder. *Psychoanalytic Inquiry, 12,* 139–171.

Kluft, R. (2000). The psychoanalytic psychotherapy of dissociative identity disorder in the context of trauma therapy. *Psychoanalytic Inquiry, 20,* 259–286.

Knoblauch, S. (1996). The play and interplay of passionate experience: Multiple organizations of desire. *Gender and Psychoanalysis, 1,* 323–344.

Knoblauch, S. (1997). Beyond the word in psychoanalysis: The unspoken dialogue. *Psychoanalytic Dialogues, 7,* 491–516.

Kohut, H. (1971). *The analysis of the self.* New York: International Universities Press.

Kohut, H. (1977). *The restoration of the self.* New York: International Universities Press.

Kohut, H. (1985). On courage. In C. Strozier (Ed), *Self psychology and the humanities* (pp. 5–50). New York: Norton.

Kolan, R. (1999). *States of mind.* New York: Wiley.

Kramer, S. (1990). Residues of incest. In H. Levine (Ed.), *Adult analysis and childhood sexual abuse.* Hillsdale, NJ: Analytic.

Kramer-Richards, A. (1996). Ladies of fashion: Pleasure, perversion, or paraphilia. *International Journal of Psycho-Analysis, 77,* 337–351.

Krueger, D. (1978). Unilateral ptosis as a conversion reaction. *Journal of Clinical Psychiatry, 39,* 351–356.

Krueger, D. (1983). Diagnosis and management of gender dysphoria. In W. Fann, I. Karacan, A. Pokorny, & R. Williams (Eds.), *Phenomenology and treatment of psychosexual disorders* (pp. 128–137). New York: SP Medical and Scientific.

Krueger, D. (1986). *The last taboo: Money as symbol and reality in psychotherapy and psychoanalysis.* New York: Brunner/Mazel.

Krueger, D. (1988a). Body Self, psychological self, and bulimia: developmental and clinical considerations. In H. Schwartz (Ed.), *Bulimia: Psychoanalytic treatment and theory* (pp. 55–73). New York: International Universities Press.

Krueger, D. (1988b). On compulsive spending and shopping: A psychodynamic inquiry. *American Journal of Psychotherapy, 42,* 574–584.

Krueger, D. (1989a). *Body self and psychological self: Developmental and clinical Integration in disorders of the self.* New York: Brunner/Mazel.

Krueger, D. (1989b). The "parent loss" of empathic failures and the model symbolic restitution of eating disorders. In D. Dietrich & P. Shabab (Eds.), *The problems of loss and mourning: New psychoanalytic perspectives* (pp. 213–224). New York: International universities Press.

Krueger, D. (1990). Developmental and psychodynamic perspectives in body-image changes. In T. Cash & T. Pruz (Eds.), *Body images: Development, deviance, and change* (pp. 225–271). New York: Guilford.

Krueger, D. (1992). *Emotional business: The meanings of work, money, and success.* San Mateo, CA: Slawson.

Krueger, D. (1997). Food as selfobject in eating disorder patients. *Psychoanalytic Review, 84,* 617–630.

Krueger, D. (1998, November). *The good old days: Nostaligia and selfobject transferences.* Presented at the 21st International Psychology of the Self, San Diego.

Krueger, D. (2000). The use of money as an action symptom: A psychoanalytic view. In A. Benson (Ed.), *I shop, therefore I am: Compulsive buying and the search for self* (pp. 288–310). Northvale, NJ: Aronson.

Krystal, H. (1988). *Integration and self-healing: Affect, trauma, alexithymia.* Hillsdale, NJ: Analytic.

Krystal, H. (1997). Desomatization and the consequences of infantile psychic trauma. *Psychoanalytic Inquiry, 17,* 126–150.

Kuchenhoff, J. (1998). The body and ego boundaries: A case study on psychoanalytic therapy with psychosomatic patients. *Psychoanalytic Inquiry, 18,* 368–382.

Kuhn, T. S. (1970). *The structure of scientific revolutions* (2nd ed.). Chicago: University of Chicago Press

Lacan, J. (1977). The function and field of speech and language in psychoanalysis. In *Ecritis* (pp. 30–113). New York: Norton.

Lacan, J. (1988). *The seminars of a Jacques Lacan* (Book 1). Cambridge: Cambridge University Press. (Original work published 1953–1954)

Lang, J. (1984). Notes toward a psychology of the feminine self. In P. Stepansky & A. Goldberg (Eds.), *Kohut's legacy: Contributions to self psychology* (pp. 51–70). Hillsdale, NJ: Analytic.

Laub, D., & Auerhahn, N. (1993). Knowing and not knowing massive psychic trauma: Forms of traumatic memory. *International Journal of Psycho-Analysis, 74,* 287–302.

LeDoux, J. (1996). *The emotional brain: The mysterious underpinnings of emotional life.* New York: Simon & Schuster.

Lenche, E. (1998). The development of the body image in the first three years of life. *Psychoanalytic and Contemporary Thought, 21,* 155–275.

Levy, K., & Blatt, S. (1999). Attachment theory and psychoanalysis: Further differentiation within secure attachment patterns. *Psychoanalytic Inquiry, 19,* 541–575.

Lewis, M., & Brooks-Gunn, J. (1979). *Social cognition and the acquisition of self*. New York: Plenum.

Lichtenberg, J. (1978). The testing of reality from the standpoint of the body self. *Journal American Psychoanalytic Association, 26*, 357–385.

Lichtenberg, J. (1985). *Psychoanalysis and infant research*. Hillsdale, NJ: Analytic.

Lichtenberg, J. (1989). *Motivation and psychoanalysis*. Hillsdale, NJ: Analytic.

Lichtenberg, J. (1998). Experience as guide to psychoanalytic theory and practice. *Journal American Psychoanalytic Association, 46*, 19–36.

Lichtenburg, J., Lachmann, F., & Fosshage, J. (1992). *Self and motivational systems*. Hillsdale, NJ: Analytic.

Loewald, H.W. (1980). On the therapeutic action of psychoanalysis. In *Papers on psychoanalysis* (pp. 221–256). New Haven, CT: Yale University Press. (Original work published 1960)

Looker, T. (1998). Mama, why don't your feet touch the ground?: Staying with the body and healing moment in psychoanalysis. In L. Aron & F. Anderson (Eds), *Relational perspectives on the body* (pp. 237–23?). Hillsdale: NJ: Analytic.

Looker, T. (1996, May). *Impinging anxiety and bodily experience. A treatment enactment*. Paper presented at annual meeting, Division of Psychoanalysis (39), American Psychological Association, New York City.

Mahler, M., Pine, R., & Bergman, A. (1975). *The psychological book of the human infant*. New York: Basic.

Mahler, M., & Furer, M. (1968). *On human symbiosis and the vicissitudes of individuation*. New York: International Universities Press.

Main, M. (1995). Attachment: Overview, with implications for clinical work. In A. Goldberg, R. Mair, & J. Kerr (Eds), *Attachment theory: Social, developmental, and clinical perspectives* (pp. 407–474). Hillsdale, NJ: Analytic.

Main, M., & Solomon, J. (1991). Procedures for Identifying infants as disorganized/disoriented during the Ainsworth Strange Situation. In M. Greenberg, D. Cicchetti, & E. Cummings (Eds.), *Attachment in pre-school years: Theory, research, and intervention* (pp. 121–160). Chicago: University of Chicago Press.

Mayer, E. (1995). The phallic castration complex and primary femininity: Paired developmental lines to a female gender identity. *Journal of the American Psychoanalytic Association, 43*, 17–38.

McDougall, J. (1989). *Theatres of the body. A psychoanalytic approach to psychosomatic illness*. New York: Norton.

Meissner, W. (1997a). The self and the body. I. The body self and the body image. *Psychoanalysis and Contemporary Thought, 20*, 419–448.

Meissner, W. (1997b). The self and the body. II. The embodied self versus nonself. *Psychoanalysis and Contemporary Thought, 21*, 85–111.

Meissner, W. (1998a). The self and the body: III. The body image in clinical perspective. *Psychoanalysis and Contemporary Thought, 21*, 113–146.

Meissner, W. (1998b). The self and the body: IV. The body on the couch. *Psychoanalysis and Contemporary Thought, 21*, 277–300.

Mondaressi, T., & Kinney, T. (1977). Children's response to their true and distorted mirror images. *Child Psychiatry and Human Development, 8*(2), 94–101.

Morris, J. (1991). Traveling writer. In J. Sternberg (Ed.), *The writer and her work* (Vol. 2, pp. 72–76). New York: Norton.

Muecke, L., & Krueger, D. W. (1981). Physical findings in a psychiatric outpatient clinic. *American Journal of Psychiatry, 138,* 1241–1242.

Ogden, T. (1985). On potential space. *International Journal of Psycho-Analysis, 66,* 129–142.

Ogden, T. (1994). *Subjects of analysis.* Northvale, NJ: Aronson.

Ogden, T. (1997). *Reverie and interpretation: Sensing something kuman.* Northvale, NJ: Aronson.

Oppenheimer, R., Howells, K., Palmer, L., & Chaloner, D. (1985). Adverse sexual experiences in childhood and clinical eating disorders: A preliminary description. *Journal of Psychiatric Research, 129,* 157–161.

Orange, B., Atwood, G., & Stolorow, R. (1997). *Working intersubjectively: Contextualism in psychoanalytic practice.* Hillsdale, NJ: Analytics.

Ornstein, A. (1991). The dread to repeat: Comments on the working-through process in psychoanalysis. *Journal of the American Psychoanalytic Association, 39,* 377–398.

Palef, S. (1999, October). *A self psychological perspective on multiple personality disorder.* Paper presented at the International Conference On the Psychology of the Self, San Diego.

Pangrel, S. (1996). Self psychology: A famous re-visiting. In A. Goldberg (Ed.), *Basic ideas reconsidered: Progress in self psychology: Vol. 12* (pp. 285–298). Hillsdale, NJ: Analytic.

Papousek, H., & Papousek, M. (1975). Cognitive aspects of preverbal social interaction between human infants and adults. *Chicago Foundation Symposium, Parent-Infant Interaction.* New York: Associated Scientific Publishers.

Perry, B., Pollard, R., Blakley, T., Baker, W., & Vigilante, D. (1995). Childhood trauma, the neurobiology of adaptation and use-dependent development of the brain: How states become traits. *Infant Mental Health Journal, 16*(4), 271–291.

Peto, A. (1959). Body image and archaic thinking. *International Journal of Psycho-Analysis, 40,* 223–231.

Phillips, A. (1998). *The best in the nursery.* New York: Pantheon Books.

Piaget, J. (1945). *Play, dream and imagination of childhood.* New York: Norton.

Piaget, J. (1959). *Judgment and reasoning in the child.* Ottowa, Canada: Littfield, Adams.

Pines, D. (1994). *A woman's unconscious use of her body.* New Haven, CT: Yale University Press.

Plassman, R. (1998). Organ worlds: outline of an analytical psychology of the body. *Psychoanalytic Inquiry, 18,* 344–367.

Putnam, F. (1992). Discussion: Are alter personalities fragments or figments? *Psychoanalytic Inquiry, 12,* 95–111.

Rangell, L. (1996). The "analytic" in psychoanalytic treatment: How analysis works. *Psychoanalytic Inquiry, 16,* 140–166.

Raphael-Leff, J. (1989). Where the wild things are. *International Journal of Pre- and Perinatal Studies, 1,* 78–89.

Raphel-Leff, J. (1994). Imaginative bodies of childbearing: Visions and revisions. In A. Erskine & D. Judd (Eds), *The imaginative body* (pp. 13–42). Northvale, NJ: Aronson.

Reiser, M. (1999). Memory, empathy, and interactive dimensions of a psychoanalytic process. *Journal of American Psychoanalytic Association, 47,* 45–501

Rizzuto, A., Peterson, M., & Reed, M. (1981). The pathological sense of self in anorexia nervosa. *Psychiatric Clinics of North America, 4,* 471–487.

Rose, G. (1980). *The power of form.* New York: International Universities Press.

Ross, C. (1991). The epidemiology of multiple personality disorder and dissociation. *Psychiatric Clinics of North America, 14,* 503–517.

Rothstein, A. (1985). *Models of the mind.* New York: International Universities Press.

Rothstein, A. (Ed.) (1986). *The reconstruction of trauma. Its significance in clinical work.* Madison, CT: International Universities Press.

Russell, D. (1986). *The secret trauma.* New York: Basic.

Sacks, O. (1998). Origins of genius: Freud's early years. *Doubletake, 4,* 119–126.

Sander, L. (1980). Investigation of the infant and its caregiving environment as a biological system. In S. E. Greenspan & G. Pollack (Eds.), *The course of life* (Vol. 1, pp. 117–202). Rockville, MD: Natural Institute of Mental Health.

Sander, L. (1997). Paradox and resolution: From the beginning. In J. Noshpitz (Ed.), *Handbook of child and adolescent development* (pp. 153–159). New York: Wiley.

Sandler, J. (1994). Fantasy, defense, and the representational world. *Infant Mental Health Journal, 15,* 26–35.

Sandler, J., & Fonagy, P. (Eds), (1997). *Recovered memories of abuse: True or false?* London: Karnac.

Sands, S. (1997). Protein or foreign body? Reply to commentaries. *Psychoanalytic Dialogues, 7,* 691–706.

Schilder, P. (1956). *The image and appearance of the human body.* New York International Universities Press. (original work published 1925)

Schafer, R. (1992). *Retelling a life.* New York: Basic.

Schecter, (1996). *Searching for memory: The brain, the mind, and the past.* New York: Basic.

Schore, A. (1994). *Affect regulation and the origin of the self.* Hillsdale, NJ: Erlbaum.

Schore, A. (1998). Localizing the unconscious: Look in right brain. *Clinical Psychiatry News, December,* 14–15.

Schwaber, E. (1998). The nonverbal dimension in psychoanalysis: "State" and its clinical vicissitudes. *International Journal of Psycho-Analysis, 79,* 667–679.

Segal, H. (1978). On symbolism. *International Journal of Psycho-Analysis, 59,* 315–319.

Seligman, S. (1998). Child psychoanalysis, adult psychoanalysis and developmental psychology: Introduction to symposium on child analysis, Part II. *Psychoanalytic Dialogue, 8,* 79–86.

Sharp, E. (1937). *Dream analysis.* London: Hogarth Press.

Shevrin, H., & Toussieng, P. (1965). Vicissitudes of the need for tactile stimulation in instinctual development. *Psychoanalytic Study of the Child, 20,* 310–339.

Shimanura, A. (1995). Memory and frontal lobe function. In M. Gazzaniga (Ed.), *The cognitive neurosciences* (pp. 803–813). Cambridge, MA: MIT Press.

Siegel, D. (1999). *The developing mind: Toward a neurobiology of interpersonal experience.* New York: Guilford.

Siegel, E. (1996). *Transformations.* Hillsdale, NJ: Analytic.

Simon, B. (1991). Is the Oedipus complex still the cornerstone of psychoanalysis? Three obstacles to answering the question. *Journal of American Psychoanalytic Association, 39,* 641–668.

Spiegel, D. (1991). Dissociation in trauma. In A. Tasman & S. Goldfinger (Eds.), *American Psychiatric Press Annual Review of Psychiatry* (Vol. 10, pp. 261–275). Washington, DC: American Psychiatric Press.

Spiegel, D. (1994). *Dissociation: Culture, mind and body.* Washington, DC: American Psychiatric Press.

Spitz, R. (1957). *No and yes.* New York: International Universities Press.

Spitz, R. (1965). *The first year of life.* New York: International Universities Press.

Sroufe, L (1997). Psychopathology as an outcome of development. *Development and Psychopathology, 9,* 251–268.

Stechler, G., (1987). Clinical applications of a psychoanalytic systems model of assertion and Aggression. *Psychoanalytic Inquiry, 1,* 348–363.

Stein, M. (1986). A reconsideration of specificity in psychosomatic medicine: Olfaction to the lymphocyte. *Psychosomatic Medicine, 48,* 3–22.

Stephanos, S. (1980). Analytical psychosomatic in internal medicine. *Annual Review Psychoanalysis, 7,* 219–232.

Stern, D. (1985). *The interpersonal world of the infant.* New York: Basic.

Stern, D. (1990). *Diary of a baby.* New York: Basic Books.

Stern, D. (1998). The process of therapeutic change involving implicit knowledge: Some implications of developmental observations of adult psychotherapy. *Infant Immunity Health Journal, 19,* 300–308.

Stern, D., Sander, L., Nahum, J., Harrison, A., Lyons-Ruth, K., Morgan, A., Vruschweiler-Stern, N., & Tronick, E. (1998). Non-interpretive mechanisms in psychoanalytic therapy. *International Journal of Psychoanalysis, 79,* 903–921.

Stern, Donnel (1997). *Unformulated experience: From dissociation to imagination in psychoanalysis.* Hillsdale, NJ: Analytic.

Sternberg, E. (1999). Emotions and disease: A balance of molecules. In R. Conlan (Ed.), *States of mind* (pp. 23–34). New York: Wiley.

Stoller, R. (1975). *Perversion: The erotic form of hatred.* New York: Pantheon.

Stoller, R. (1976). Primary femininity. *Journal of the American Psychoanalytic Association, 24*(Suppl.), 59–78.

Stolorow, R. (1999). The phenomenology of trauma and the absolutisms of everyday life. *Psychoanalytic Psychology, 16,* 464–468.

Stolorow, R. (1995). Intersubjective view of self psychology. *Psychoanalytic Dialogue, 5,* 393–399.

Stolorow, R., & Atwood, G. (1992). *Contexts of being: The intersubjective foundations of psychological life* (pp. 41–50). Hillsdale, NJ: Analytic.

Stolorow, R., & Branchaft, B. (Eds.). (1994). *The Intersubjective Perspective.* Northvale, NJ: Jason Aronson.

Stolorow, R., Brandchaft, B., & Atwood, G. (1987). *Psychoanalytic treatment: An intersubjective approach.* Hillsdale, NJ: Analytic.

Summers, F. (2000, Spring). *Ownership of the body: A contemporary psychoanalytic view.* Paper presented at the Division 39, American Psychological Association, San Francisco, CA.

Sweetnam, A. (1996). Baby boomer bisexuality. Presented at the meeting of the *American Psychological Association* Division 39. New York.

Sweetman, A. (1999). Sexual sensations and gender experience: A psychological positions and the erotic third. *Psychoanalytic Dialogue, 9*(3), 327–348.

Thomkins, S. (1962). *Affect/imagery/consciousness* (Vol. 1). New York: Springer

Totten, N. (1999). *The water in the glass: Mind and body in psychoanalysis.* New York: Other Press.

Tronick, E (1989). Emotions and emotional communications in infants. *American Psychologist, 44,* 112–119

Tuch, R. (1999). The construction, reconstruction, and deconstruction of memory in the light of social cognition. *Journal American Psychoanalytic Association, 47,* 153–186.

Tulving, E. (1983). *Elements of episodic memory.* New York: Oxford University Press.

Tustin, F. (1986). *Autistic barriers in neurotic patients.* London: Karnac.

Ulman, R., & Brothers, D. (1988). *The shattered self: A psychoanalytic study of trauma.* Hillsdale, NJ: Analytic.

van der Kolk, B. (1986). *Psychological trauma.* Washington, DC: American Psychiatric Press.

van der Kolk, B. (1994). The body keeps the score: Memory and the evolving psychobiology of post-traumatic stress. *Harvard Review Psychiatry, 1,* 252–265.

van der Kolk, B. (1996). The body keeps the score: Approaches to the psychobiology of post traumatic stress disorder: In B. van der Kolk, B., McFarlane, A., & Weisaeth, L. (Eds.), *Traumatic stress* (pp. 214–241). New York: Guilford.

van der Kolk, B. (1998, October). Self psychology integrating and evolving: Trauma and dissociation. Paper presented at the International Self Psychology Conference, San Diego.

van der Kolk, B., Pelcovitz, D., Roth, S., Mandel, F., McFarland, A., & Herman, J. (1996). Dissociation, somatization, and affect dysregulation: The complexity of adaptation to trauma. *Amererican Journal of Psychiatry, 153*(Suppl.), 83–93.

Vanderlinden, J. & Vandereyecken, W. (1999). *Trauma, dissociation, and impulse dyscontrol in eating disorders.* Bristol, PA: Brunner/Mazel.

Van der Velde, C. (1985). Body images of one's self and of others: Developmental and clinical significance. *American Journal of Psychiatry, 142,* 527–537.

Vaughan, S. (1997). *The talking cure: The science behind psychotherapy.* New York: Henry Holt.

Waugaman, R. (2000). Multiple personality disorder and one analyst's paradigm shift. *Psychoanalytic Inquiry, 20,* 207–226.

Wayne, D. (1999). The male analyst on the maternal erotic playground. *Gender and Psychoanalysis, 4,* 23–24.

Welles, J. (1993, Spring). Counterfeit analyses: Maintaining the illusion of knowing. Paper presented at the Division 39 meeting of the American Psychological Association, New York.

Wells, J., & Wrye, H. (1991). The maternal erotic countertransference. *International Journal of Psychoanalysis, 72,* 93–106.

West, L. J. (1967). The dissociative reactions. In A. M. Freeman & H. I. Kaplan (Eds.), *Comprehensive textbook of psychiatry* (pp. 885–898). Baltimore: Williams & Wilkins.

Weston, D., & Gabbard, G. (in press, a). Developments in cognitive neuroscience I: Implications for theories of conflict and compromise. *Journal of American Psychoanalytic Association.*

Weston, D., & Gabbard, G. (in press, b). Developments in cognitive neuroscience II: Implications for theories of transference. *Journal of American Psychoanalytic Association.*

Weston, D., & Gabbard, G. (in press, c). Developments in cognitive neuroscience, III: Implications for theories of therapeutic action. *Journal of American Psychoanalytic Association.*

White, R. (1959). Motivation reconsidered: The concept of competence. *Psychological Review, 66,* 297–333.

Williams, J. (1962). Autobiographical memory and emotional disorders. In S. Christianson (Ed.), *The handbook of emotion and memory: Research and theory* (pp. 451–477). Hillsdale, NJ: Erlbaum.

Winnicott, D. (1965). *Communicating and not communicating leading to a study of certain opposites.* In *The maturatioal processes and the facilitating environment* (pp. 179–192). New York: International Universities Press. (Original work published 1963)

Winnicott, D. (1957). Primitive emotional development. In *Through pediatrics to psychoanalysis.* London: Hogarth. (Original work published 1945)

Winnicott, D. (1960). The theory of the parent–infant relationship. In *Maturational processes and the facilitating environment* (pp. 37–55). New York: International Universities Press.

Winnicott, D. (1965). *The maturational processes and the facilitating environment.* New York: International Universities Press.

Winnicott, D. (1966). Psychosomatic illness in its positive and negative aspects. *International Journal of Psycho-Analysis, 47,* 510–516.

Winnicott, D. (1971). *Playing and reality.* London: Tavistock

Winnicott, D. (1986). Fear of breakdown. In G. Kohon (Ed.), *British School of Psychoanalysis* (pp. 173–182). New Haven: Yale University Press.

Wolff, P. (1960). The developmental psychologies of Jean Piaget and psychoanalysis. *Psychological Issues*, Monog. 5. New York: International Universities Press.

Wrye, H (1996). Bodily states of mind: Dialects of psyche and soma of psychoanalysis. *Gender and Psychoanalysis, 1,* 283–296.

Wrye, H. (1999). Embranglements on the maternal erotic playground. *Gender and Psychoanalysis, 4,* 3–22.

Wrye, H. (1998). The embodiment of desire: Relinking the mindbody within the analytic dyad. In L. Aron & F. Anderson (Eds.), *Relational perspectives on the body* (pp. 97–116). Hillsdale, NJ: Analytic.

Wrye, H., & Welles, J. (1994). The *narration of desire: Erotic transferences and countertransferences.* Hillsdale, NJ: Analytic.

Wyman-McGinty, W. (1998). The body in analysis: Authentic movement and witnessing in analytic practice. *Journal Psychoanalytic Psychology, 43,* 239–260.

Yorke, C. (1985). Fantasy and the body-mind problem: Some preliminary observations. *The Psychoanalytic Study of the Child, 40,* 319–328. New Haven, CT: Yale University Press.

Young, L. (1992). Sexual abuse and the problem of embodiment. *Child Abuse and Neglect,16,* 89–100.

Yovell, Y. (2000). Affect theory and the neurobiology of affect dysregulation. *Journal of the American Academy of Psychoanalysis, 28,* 467–481.

Index